CISTERCIAN STUDIES SERIES:
NUMBER SEVENTY-SEVEN

ATHIRST FOR GOD

CISTERCIAN STUDIES SERIES: NUMBER SEVENTY-SEVEN

Athirst for God

Spiritual Desire
in Bernard of Clairvaux's
Sermons on the
Song of Songs

Michael Casey
Monk of Tarrawarra

CISTERCIAN PUBLICATIONS
KALAMAZOO
1988

Cum permissu superiorum

Available in Britain and Europe from
A. R. Mowbray & Co. Ltd.
St Thomas House Becket Street
Oxford OX1 1 SJ

Available elsewhere (including Canada) from the publisher

Cistercian Publications, Inc.
WMU Station
Kalamazoo, Michigan 49008

The work of Cistercian Publications is made possible in part
by support from Western Michigan University to the Institute
of Cistercian Studies.

Library of Congress Cataloging-in-Publication Data

Casey, Michael, monk of Tarrawarra.
  Athirst for God.

  (Cistercian studies series; no. 77)
  Includes bibliographies and indexes.
  1. Bernard, of Clairvaux, Saint, 1090 or 91–1153. Sermones
super Cantica Canticorum. 2. Bible. O.T. Song of
Solomon — Sermons. 3. Desire for God — History of doc-
trines — Middle Ages, 600–1500. I. Title. II. Series.
BS1485.C36 1987   223'.906   87–13217
ISBN 0-87907-877-4

Typeset by Solaris Press
Printed in the United States of America.

IN MEMORY OF MY PARENTS

RICHARD AND MARY CASEY

FOREWORD

THIS BOOK is a reworking of a thesis presented to the Melbourne College of Divinity in 1979. Although substantially the same as that former work, there has been both expansion and contraction of material to suit the requirements of a wider readership; some corrections have been made and some new evidence introduced.

My intention in writing has been to present the monastic doctrine of Bernard of Clairvaux in a medium which reflects, as far as possible, his own priorities. This means that there have been some technical and historical questions that I have deliberately excluded from my presentation, partly because they are already adequately covered and partly because I wished to do nothing which would interfere with the primarily spiritual focus of this work.

In some ways I would hope that this book might serve as an introduction to the reading of Bernard's *Sermons on*

The Song of Songs rather than as a handbook of certified bernardine doctrine. Some sections have been deliberately written to facilitate this, treating the texts in sequence so that the reader might follow the flow of the teaching in his own text as he reads the commentary.

The conclusions offered are as objectively sound as I can make them and generally reflect the mainstream of current bernardine scholarship. I have made no effort, however, to present them dispassionately, but have consistently attempted to discuss them in a way which would invite a contemporary reader to relate what Bernard said to his own experience. If the intention in writing were merely historical, then the charge of anachronism could, no doubt, be made occasionally. In point of fact, however, my primary purpose here is the writing of spirituality and the presentation of Bernard as a master of spiritual living for today. This not only permits but demands that some such fusion of horizons be attempted.

There is a problem with exclusive language in Bernard which I have softened in my translations in order to reduce abrasiveness to modern sensibilities. Thus *ecclesia* and *anima* are both feminine words in Latin and are serviced by feminine pronouns and qualifiers. In both cases I have used an inclusive 'it'.

The appearance of this work has been made possible only through the kindness and interest of a number of confrères and friends who have supported me and it through many difficulties and reversals of fortune. I am particularly grateful to them and to others who made available to me their insights and resources. My hope is that the end result might prove to be proportionate to their generosity.

18 March 1983

TABLE OF CONTENTS

CHAPTER ONE

HISTORICAL BACKDROP

B ERNARD OF FONTAINES (1090–1153) was arguably the most influential figure in European affairs during his own lifetime. Although he was only the abbot of the new monastery of Clairvaux, in Champagne, he became the confidant of princes and prelates and travelled the length and breadth of Europe generating support for the policies he espoused. He was a man with many powerful friends; and there were few among the ruling classes who dared to run the risk of having the Abbot of Clairvaux as an adversary.[1]

One fact, however, must be kept in mind if the

1. Bernard's status as an historical actor is indicated, for instance, by the choice of the Abbot of Clairvaux as 'the man of the century' in the series *Le Mémorial des Siècles,* where he is placed alongside such figures as St Paul, Attila the Hun, Napoleon, and Lenin. Cf. Zoé Oldenbourg, *Saint Bernard,* (Paris: Éditions Albin Michel, 1970).

specific features both of Bernard and of the period in which he lived are not to be missed. A surprising quality of Bernard's ascendancy among the councils of the great was his own lack of interest in gaining direct political power. Bernard remained a spiritual man. He was not one of history's many worldly churchmen, using ecclesiastical status as a means of dominating secular authorities. He remained a monk all his life, both in habit and in fact, resisting even ecclesiastical advancement. The leadership he exercised and enjoyed exercising rested on foundations which were primarily personal. He won a following because of the sort of man that he was; to many he appeared as the embodiment of the noblest aspirations of those times.

To understand the 'chimerical' existence of Bernard[2] and the paradox of his impact on secular affairs, it is necessary to appreciate the spiritual and religious frame of reference within which he operated. The key to unlocking the riddle of Bernard's life and influence is the recognition of the primacy of the spiritual in all that he did. He was a man passionately dedicated to spiritual values and to the search for close union with God. His zeal for the Church, which led to his public life, was an extension of this basic concern. His life can be understood visually as a number of concentric circles, each denoting a wider circle of influence. The values which he tried to live he imparted also to members of his family, then to the monks of Clairvaux and, progressively, to the whole monastic world. From here he became involved in the affairs of the Church and, finally, became a figure of influence throughout Europe. His audience grew but his basic philosophy remained the same; to all alike he preached one fundamental theme: the absolute primacy

2. The expression is Bernard's own; cf. Ep 250.4; SBO 8:147,2.

of the divine in all human affairs. To misunderstand this is to lose sight of the one unifying principle in a lifetime filled with varied and sometimes contradictory events.

This is to say that Bernard's spiritual teaching is an essential part of the data to be examined in assessing his role as an historical actor. To view his involvement in such controversial incidents as the preaching of the Second Crusade, the condemnation of Abelard, or his intrusion into the York election without reference to the fundamental values which animated his entire career, is to run the risk of never confronting the real paradox. To ignore the broader context of Bernard's activities is to render such interventions not only unacceptable, but also beyond comprehension.

Conversely, it is impossible to grasp the full sense of Bernard's spiritual doctrine without a knowledge of his career and a feeling for the society of which he was a part. Bernard was a man of his own era. He drew his inspiration from the times in which he lived, striving to impress upon them the character which gave form to his own life. To appreciate the timelessness of his literary work it is necessary, first of all, to perceive that Bernard was a twelfth-century man whose message was directed to and shaped by his own contemporaries.[3]

A BIOGRAPHICAL OUTLINE

Bernard's life is well chronicled. Although there are gaps in our information and ambiguities which will,

---

3. Cf. Friedrich Heer, 'Saint Bernard au tournant du siècle', in *Homme d'Église*, pp. 15–22. Adalbert de Vogüé responds to this in 'Bernard, homme du xiie siècle', *ibid.*, pp. 23–34. Of considerable value in locating Bernard within the flow of his contemporary world is Wolfram von den Steinen, *Der Kosmos des Mittelalters: Von Karl dem Grossen zu Bernhard von Clairvaux*, (Bern: Franke Verlag, 2nd edn 1967).

perhaps, never be resolved, it is possible to arrive at a fairly clear understanding of the interplay of people, places and events which together constitute the life and times of the Abbot of Clairvaux.

A basic source of information is the series of biographical accounts written by his contemporaries, of which the *Vita Prima*, initiated by his close friend and collaborator, William of St Thierry is the most significant.[4] Like most medieval hagiographies, these accounts cannot be regarded as critical historiography.[5] Used carefully, however, interpreted according to the rules of their *genre* and related to other sources, these Lives provide us with a factual framework upon which a critical biography can be built.

Bernard was a man of sufficient prominence to ensure the publicity of the least of his actions. It is not surprising therefore, that he figures in the chronicles of the period and is mentioned in the writings of many of his contemporaries. The fact that not all such references are complimentary —some, such as those in Berengar's *Apologeticus,* are openly hostile—gives us a clue to certain aspects of Bernard's character and behaviour which were not emphasised by his admirers.

There is also information to be culled from Bernard's own writings, particularly his letters. Bernard's

4. Mabillon's edition of these lives is in PL 185:225–550. I use the edition published in *Sancti Bernardi abbatis Clarae-Vallensis Opera Omnia* (abbreviated *Opera Omnia*) (Paris: Gaume, 1839). Excerpts in translation can be found in Geoffrey Webb and Adrian Walker, *St. Bernard of Clairvaux* (London: A. R. Mowbray & Co., 1960).

5. Cf. Adriaan H. Bredero, 'Études sur la "Vita Prima" de S. Bernard", ASOC 17 (1961), 3–72, 215–260; 18 (1962) 3–59. *Id.,* 'St. Bernard and the Historians', *Canonization Studies*, pp. 63–100. *Id.,* 'San Bernardo di Chiaravalle: Correlazione tra fenomeno cultico e storico', *Studi*, pp.23–48. J. Leclercq, 'Le premier biographe de saint Bernard', *Nouveau Visage*, pp. 11–34.

public life was chronicled by a vast correspondence. Five hundred forty-seven letters are extant, although some of them have clearly been modified in the process of transmission to render them suitable for different situations.[6] Such a body of writing enables us not only to form an idea of the occupations in which Bernard was engaged, but also to penetrate the external events to make contact with the personality of the man himself.[7]

Although the secondary literature on Bernard and his writings is vast,[8] there is currently no authoritative biography of him available. The work of Elphège Vacandard, which first appeared in 1894, is still quoted with respect, but it is severely outdated.[9] Watkin Williams' 1935 volume is probably the most scholarly attempt at a biography in English, but its value is reduced both by its age and by the fact that it is a very difficult book to

6. Cf. J. Leclercq, 'Nouveaux Temoins de la survie de saint Bernard'. *Homenaje a Fray Justo Perez de Urbel O. S. B.* vol. 2 (Silos, 1977) 83–109.

7. Bernard's letters are found in volumes 7–8 of *Sancti Bernardi Opera.* The best English translation of these is currently that by Bruno Scott James, *The Letters of Saint Bernard of Clairvaux* (London: Burns Oates, 1953). It is to be regretted that the translator has adopted his own system of numbering the letters. The same author demonstrates to what an extent the letters may be used in confecting a biography in his *Saint Bernard of Clairvaux: An Essay in Biography* (London: Hodder and Stoughton, 1957).

8. This is indicated by the three comprehensive bibliographies presently available. L. Janauschek, *Bibliographia Bernardina* (Vienna: A. Hoelder, 1891); Jean de la Croix Bouton, *Bibliographie Bernardine 1891–1957,* (Paris: Lethielleux, 1958); and Eugène Manning, *Bibliographie Bernardine 1957–1970,* Documentation Cistercienne, (Rochfort, 1972). Pending the appearance of a projected cumulative listing, supplements to these may be found in the *Bulletin of Monastic Spirituality* published regularly in CSt and in COCR.

9. Elphège Vacandard, *Vie de saint Bernard, abbé de Clarivaux,* (2 vols) (Paris: J. Gabalda, 4th edn 1927).

read.[10] Much has been clarified, in recent decades, by the
articles written for the centenaries of his death in 1953
and of his canonisation in 1974 and by the work of Jean
Leclercq and others.[11] No synthesis of these advances,
however, has yet been attempted.

The main lines of Bernard's life are straightforward.
He was born to the ranks of the lower aristocracy, probably in the summer of the year 1090. His father,
Tescelin the Red, was a military man with a small castle
less than four kilometers from Dijon, the newly-
established capital of the duchy of Burgundy.[12] His
mother was Aleth, the daughter of Bernard of Montbard, with connections to many of the aristocratic
families throughout France.[13] After giving birth to six

10. Watkin Williams, *Saint Bernard of Clairvaux* (Historical Series
No. LXIX) (Manchester: University Press, 1935).

11. Cf. J. Leclercq, *Saint Bernard Mystique*, (Paris: Desclée de
Brouwer, 1948): *Id.*, *Bernard of Clairvaux and the Cistercian Spirit*, CS
16 (Kalamazoo: Cistercian Publications, 1976); *Id.*, *Nouveau visage de
Bernard de Clairvaux: Approches psycho-historiques* (Paris: Cerf,
1976). The various collections of articles which have appeared on the occasion of the centenaries are listed in the bibliography.

12. Tescelin had the nickname *Sorus* (*le Sor* or *le Saur*) because of his
reddish-blond hair. Cf. Geoffroy of Auxerre, *Fragmenta ex tertia vita* in
Opera Omnia t. 2: col. 2475A. Cf. M. Chaume, 'Les origines familiales
de saint Bernard', in *Son Temps 1*, pp. 75–112. J. Richard, 'Le milieu
familiale', in *Commission d'histoire*, pp. 3–16. There are charts of
Tescelin's family on pp. 558–559 of this volume. R. Fossier, 'La fonda-
tion de Clairvaux et la famille de saint Bernard', in *Mélanges*, pp.
19–27. On what remians of the residence of Bernard's family, see l'abbé
Chomton, *La chambre natale de saint Bernard: notes historiques et ar-
chéologiques* (Dijon: Union typographique, Imprimerie de l'évêché,
1891). This pamphlet is a digest of a larger work by the author, *Saint
Bernard et la Château de Fontaines-lès-Dijon*, which I have not had the
opportunity to consult.

13. Cf. J. Laurent, 'A propos de l'ascendance maternelle de saint
Bernard: Seigneurs de Montbard et Seigneurs de Ricey', in *Mélanges*,
pp. 9–18. There are genealogical tables in *Commission d'histoire*, pp.
560–563.

sons and one daughter, Aleth died in 1103 or 1104, as Bernard, her third son, passed into adolescence.[14] Tescelin lived until he was about 70, spending his last years as a monk of Clairvaux.[15]

Bernard's education was entrusted to the canons of St Vorles at Châtillon-sur-Seine, some eighty kilometres north of Dijon, where the family maintained a residence.[16] Bernard's elders appear to have been more literate than most, and so he was exempted from the para-military training customary for his rank and permitted to complete his education. It is clear from the standard of his later literary output that the canons were excellent teachers. Apart from a comment about his *ingenium naturale*,[17] the only information we have on Bernard's schooldays is the charge later made (and withdrawn under advisement) by Berengar that the boy was the author of a number of ribald rhymes.[18]

Several likenesses of Bernard as abbot of Clairvaux have come down to us, including one which grandly proclaims itself the *vera effigies*. It seems likely, however, that these are of little value in forming a picture of what Bernard looked like.[19] More reliable is a word-picture

14. There is a note on the death of Aleth in *Commission d'histoire*, p. 26, note 63. Bernard's brothers were Guy, Gerard, Andrew, Bartholemew, and Nivard; his sister was Humbelina. All eventually entered monastic life. Aleth is buried with her sons at Clairvaux.

15. The primary sources for this assertion are listed in Anselme Dimier, *Saint Bernard: 'Pêcheur de Dieu'* (Paris: Letouzey & Ané, 1953) p. 193.

16. Cf. Jean Marillier, 'Les premières années: les études à Châtillon', in *Commission d'histoire*, pp. 17–27.

17. *Vita Prima* 1.3, (col 2093C).

18. *Liber Apologeticus*, PL 178: 1857. Leclercq doubts the seriousness of the assertion: *Monks and Love*, pp. 17–20.

19. Cf. H. Beuer-Szlechter, 'Contribution à l'iconographie de saint Bernard', CN 26 (1975) 241–254. P. Quarré, 'L'iconographie de saint Bernard à Clairvaux et les origines de la *Vera effigies*', in

from the pen of Geoffroy of Auxerre, his secretary and travelling-companion for over a decade.[20]

Bernard is represented to us as being of average height, although he may have seemed taller to some observers because he was very thin. He appears to have inherited the germanic features of his father: fair skin, blue eyes, blond hair and a reddish beard.[21] An examination of his relics reveals that he had a long head and a high forehead.[22] According to William of St Thierry, his face was pleasant and his whole bearing was attractive, even elegant.[23]

Such a good-looking young man was, if we are to believe his biographers, eagerly sought after by women. There are several stories which convey this suggestion. It may be, however, that the emphasis on Bernard's sex-appeal is nothing more than a conventional compliment offered by admiring narrators to highlight the heroism of his chastity. The 'temptations' of Bernard are more

---

Mélanges, pp. 342–349. J. Leclerq, 'Pour l'iconographie de saint Bernard', in *Études*, pp. 40–45, with an addendum on pp. 226–228.

20. Geoffroy, a disciple of Abelard, was 'converted' by Bernard in 1140 and became a monk of Clairvaux. From 1145 he acted as Bernard's secretary and travelling companion. Primary sources for his life are listed in Dimier, *Pêcheur de Dieu*, p. 182. See also, J. Leclercq, 'Les écrits de Geoffroy d'Auxerre', in *Recueil 1*, pp. 27–46; *Id.*, 'Le témoinage de Geoffroy d'Auxerre sur la vie cistercienne', in *Analecta 2*, pp. 174–201; *Id.* 'Les souvenirs inédits de Geoffroy d'Auxerre sur S. Bernard', in *Études*, pp. 151–170. F. Gastadelli, 'Regola, spiritualità e crisi dell' ordine cisterciense in tre sermoni di Gofredo di Auxerre su San Benedetto', CN 31 (1980) 193–225.

21. *Vita Prima* 3.3.1, (col 2189–2190).

22. Cf. *Commission d'histoire*, p. 25, note 60.

23. *Vita Prima* 1.3.6, (col 2096A): . . . *eleganti corpore, grata facie praeeminens, suavissimis ornatus moribus* . . .

literary than historical, and perhaps reveal more about the writers than they do about Bernard himself.

In point of fact, Bernard seems never to have been a very physical person. He took no part in the jousting so loved by his contemporaries, he was indifferent to his personal comfort and never much interested in food and drink. In fact, he was inclined to go to extremes to avoid any semblance of pandering to the flesh, although one may suspect that such detachment was easier for him than for many. Some explanation for his attitude may be found in the amount of sickness he experienced. Even as a youth his health seems to have been delicate; in later years he was often beset by prolonged illness, especially of the digestive tract. These have been diagnosed by Jean Leclercq as 'chronic gastritis developing into a pyloric ulcer, accompanied by neuralgia, stomach spasms and cramps, intestinal difficulties and asthenia'.[24]

That Bernard was able to live such an energetic life despite such debilitation indicates something of his inner drive. From the accounts we have of him he appears as an intense, passionate, and decisive man, of quick intellect and good memory, who drove himself hard and lived off his nerves. He seems to have compensated for his lack of physical prowess by more interior aptitudes and attainments. In his writings he manifests a high aesthetic sensitivity as well as literary craftsmanship. He was an artist with words. His elegant prose often approaches poetry in its power to touch and move, and in his *apparently* effortless command of the nuances of rhythm and assonance. Although he gives vent in the *Apologia* to a reformist diatribe against the preciosity of some contemporary endeavours, yet his role in the building of Fontenay and

24. *Spirit*, p. 17

other examples of romanesque perfection and his contribution to the reform of Cistercian chant indicate that he was a
man of fine sensibility to beauty. What disturbed him was
not art *per se*, but unprincipled extravagance, especially in
the case of monks, whom he presumed should have known
better.[25]

There is no doubt that Bernard's was a commanding
personality. The darker side of his character was his tendency to ambition and domination.[26] Not his the uncertainties
and hestitations projected onto him by William of St
Thierry.[27] On the contrary, Bernard was forthright and
decisive. He had a strong and resourceful mentality which
was adept in seeing beyond immediate issues and capable of
great deviousness, if he thought the situation warranted it.
He was courageous in following his principles, even when it
meant overcoming indifference or opposition. So deft was
he in dealing with difficult situations that occasionally he
overreached himself and fell. This was probably good for
him as, generally, he was a little too sure of himself. The

25. Cf. Henry-Bernard de Warren, 'Bernard et les premiers Cistercians face au probleme de l'Art', in *Commission d'histoire*, pp.
487–534. A Dempf, 'Die geistige Stellung Bernhards von Clairvaux
gegen die Cluniazenische Kunst', in *Die Chimaere*, pp. 29–53. A
summary of this appears in *Mélanges*, pp. 220–221. A. Dimier,
'Saint Bernard et l'art', in *Sint Bernardus*. A. Fracheboud, 'S. Bernard est-il seul dans son attitude face aux oevres d'art?' COCR 15
(1953) 113–129. See also Apo 28–29 and our notes thereto in CF 1,
pp. 63–67. On Bernard's role in the reform of the chant, see
Chrysogonus Waddell, 'A Plea for the *Institutio Sancti Bernardi
quomodo cantare et psallere debeamus*', in *Canonization Studies*,
pp. 180–208; *Id.*, Introduction to Bernard's *Prologue to the An-
tiphonary* in CF 1, pp. 153–164. On architecture, see P. Dalloz,
'L'architecture de S. Bernard', COCR 42 (1980) 36–51.

26. Cf. J. Leclercq, 'Littérature et spontanéité', in *Nouveau
Visage*, pp. 35–60; *Id.*, 'Aggressiveness or Repression in St. Bernard
and in his Monks', in *Monks and Love*, pp. 86–108.

27. Cf. J. Leclercq, *Nouveau Visage*, pp. 27–30.

curious thing about such a commanding personality is that, although his strong views and manipulativeness gained him a few enemies, he won many more friends, and it was mainly for his charm that he was remembered by his contemporaries. He was a pleasant man who treated persons of all ranks with an easy forthrightness and, on occasion, with great kindness and friendliness. The simplest way of summarising this aspect of his personality is to say that he was a born leader and that for much of his life he was happiest whan he had a following.

In many of the controversies in which he was involved, Bernard sided with the sterner pary, a fact which can give the impression that he was a harsh, unyielding figure, relentlessly opposed to any concessions to human frailty and devoid of any appreciation of what might be called the 'liberal agenda'. Certainly, he was a conservative man with a zeal for discipline and reform and a suspicion of frivolous innovation. He was not, however, dull or pompous. He had a great capacity for friendship and, on occasion, great tenderness in dealing with those in trouble. Even on important occasions he could be lighthearted,[28] as he was when his seal was stolen, and he averred that the humorous tone of a letter would be sufficient to authenticate it.[29] Bernard was a very complex personality; he was both charming and personable in the way he dealt with others and uncompromising and even narrow in his assessment of issues. Both facets of his personality need to be taken into consideration if an accurate picture of his disposition is to be achieved.

In his early twenties, this promising young man turned his back on his prospects and entered the insignificant

28. Cf. J. Leclercq, 'The Theme of Jesting in St Bernard and his Contemporaries', CSt 9 (1974) 97–142.

29. Ep 402; SBO 8:382, 9–10: *Maneries locutionis pro sigillo sit, quia ad manum non erat, nam neque Gaufredus vester.*

'New Monastery' at Cîteaux. This was probably in 1113, when this radical new form of Benedictinism was just beginning to flourish.[30] With him, according to the ancient accounts, he brought a crowd of relatives and associates including some of those who had used their best efforts to dissuade him from his choice. All his brothers eventually became monks, as did his father and many other of his kin.

Within three years Bernard was nominated as abbot of Cîteaux's third foundation. This was situated some hundred kilometres from the motherhouse and was given the name Clairvaux. There were many difficulties involved in the selection of the site and in the erection of the requisite buildings, but eventually the monastery was established. It is not possible to determine the extent ot Bernard's personal involvement with the practicalities of setting up the new monastery and seeing to its economic stability. His health was a source of concern and at one point he seems to have been on the point of collapse and was obliged to go away for a time.

Bernard's first ten years as abbot were occupied mainly with the establishment of his community and with monastic business. Seventy-seven of his letters date from this time, although only forty-four of these have survived.[31] Around 1125 his literary career began with the writing of the *Apologia*, a work aimed at easing the controversies raging between Black Monks and Cistercians

---

30. 'L'anticipation de la date d'entrée dans certains mss est une falsification volontaire, qui avait pour but de mettre le développement de l'ordre cistercien entièrement à l'actif de saint Bernard, et de détruire ainsi l'objection de La Ferté qui se savait fondée dès avant l'entrée de saint Bernard à Cîteaux.' A. Bredero, 'Etudes sur la 'Vita Prima' de Saint Bernard (I)', ASOC 17 (1961) 62, note 2.

31. Cf. Damien van den Eynde, 'Les premiers écrits de saint Bernard', in J. Leclercq, *Recueil 3*, pp. 343–422.

on monastic values and observances. At about the same time he published his treatise *On the Steps of Humility and Pride* and his celebrated book *On the Necessity of Loving God.* In the years which followed he published a mature theological essay *On Grace and Free Will* and a devotional manual for the use of the Knights Templar.

From about 1130, as his fame increased, Bernard began to become more involved in the affairs of the Church and to move about outside his monastery. He was successful in championing the claims of the reformist Innocent II against those of the anti-Pope, Anacletus. Until the matter was finally resolved by the Second Lateran Council in 1139, the Abbot of Clairvaux was constantly on the road, soliciting new supporters and bolstering those who had begun to waver. His letters numbered 124–140 are largely concerned with this issue and testify to his zeal in promoting a cause, once he had become convinced of it.

In 1135 Bernard began his most accomplished literary scheme, a series of sermons *On the Song of Songs,* a project which occupied him for the remaining eighteen years of his life and was unfinished at his death. These eighty-six sermons offer a panoramic presentation of the life of the soul with God, drawing their inspiration from the text of the Song of Songs and from his own experience. In them Bernard demonstrated his brilliance and verve, combining practical and pastoral wisdom with lyric composition and mystical fervour to produce a unique and beautiful synthesis of christian spiritual tradition.

Yet strangely enough, it was while he was thus engaged that Bernard allowed himself to become involved in a number of politico-religious issues which cast a less creditable light upon him. The decade beginning with 1140 saw him at the height of his power and prestige. In 1139 he was offered the archbishopric of Rheims, and in

1145, one of his former monks became Pope Eugene III. It seemed that his ascendancy was complete.

1140 saw Bernard's zeal for conservative orthodoxy triumph over the original and innovative theology of Peter Abelard. This battle between the two giants of the age was uneven, since Bernard took steps to ensure that it was fought in the political rather than in the intellectual arena. Abelard was unfairly crushed by Bernard's superior lobbying-power.[32] This 'success' was followed by Bernard's reprehensible interference in the election of a new Archbishop of York, imposing his own reform-minded candidate against the will of both English King and cathedral Chapter.[33] His attempts, at the same period, to effect a reconciliation between King Louis VII of France and the Pope pleased neither party. In 1145, Bernard began preaching against the incipient movement of Catharism, then gaining ground in Languedoc.

32. A select bibliography on Abelard up to 1967 is given by Eligius Buytaert in his General Introduction to *Petri Abaelardi Opera Theologica*, Corpus Christianorum: Continuatio Mediaeualis XI (Turnhout: Brepols, 1969) pp. xxix–xxxviii. Abelard's *Apologia contra Bernardum* is in the same volume, pp. 341–368. See further, J.-C. Didier, "Un scruple identique de saint Bernard à l'egard d'Abélard et de Gilbert de la Porrée," in *Mélanges*, pp. 95–99. Sister Edmée, "Bernard and Abelard," in *Influence*, pp. 89–134. E. Little, "Relations between St Bernard and Abelard before 1139," in *Canonization Studies*, pp. 155–168: Id., "Bernard and Abelard at the Council of Sens, 1140," in *Leclercq Studies*, pp. 55–72; Id., "The Source of the *Capitula* of Sens in 1140," in *History 2*, pp. 87–91. N. d'Olwer, "Sur quelques lettres de saint Bernard. Avant ou après le concile de Sens?" in *Mélanges*, pp. 100–108. T. Renna, "Abelard versus Bernard: An event in monastic history," CN 27 (1976), pp. 189–202. R. Klibansky, "Peter Abailard and Bernard of Clairvaux. A letter by Abailard," *Mediaeval and Renaissance Studies* 5 (1961), pp. 1–27. P. Zerbi, "San Bernardo e il Concilio di Sens," in *Studi*, pp. 49–74.

33. Cf. Derek Baker, "San Bernardo e l'elezione di York," in *Studi*, pp. 75–92.

The following year saw his most important commission, the preaching of the Second Crusade. Bernard's empassioned oratory won a great following for the cause and his name seems to have been on everyone's lips. He had reached the apogee of his personal power.[34]

As the decade drew to a close, Bernard's fortunes declined. He was blamed for the failure of the Crusade; once the armies left behind them the unifying influence of the great preacher and gave themselves more practically to warfare, the high moral tone of the participants was eroded; factions developed and alternative goals became paramount. The remnant that was left to confront the infidel was easily and totally overcome.

Bernard quitted his public life. Much of the superficial ambition and the need to dominate which had hitherto distorted the candour of his personality had burnt down, leaving him a chastened and holier man. The last of his sermons *On the Song of Songs,* and the handbook which he wrote for Pope Eugene III, *On Consideration,* present a much more tranquil and mellow perception of spiritual reality than he had ever before shown. His external activities diminished and he stayed at home more. His lifelong infirmities began to get the

34. For a background to Bernard's activities see the articles of Bernard Hamilton collected under the title *Monastic Reform, Catharism and the Crusades,* Variorum Reprints, London, 1979. In reviewing Bernard's dealings with the dualist movement, it is important to remember that it existed in different forms and under various names from the tenth century onwards. There is no question here of a single easily isolable heresy. Among the numerous studies of the issues associated with Bernard's role in the Second Crusade, the attempt to comprehend his underlying motivations has been made in E. Delaruelle, 'L'idée de croisade chez S. Bernard', in *Mélagnes,* pp. 53–67. B. Flood, 'St Bernard's View of Crusade', in CS 9 (1974) 22–35. J. Leclercq, 'Saint Bernard's Attitude toward War', in *History 2,* pp. 1–40.

upper hand. Finally, at 9.00 AM, on 20 August 1153, Bernard died.

Bernard was, without doubt, the most famous man of his time. Although a sequestered monk by profession, he was one of the most travelled men in twelfth-century Europe. His various campaigns led him to cut a swathe through Europe from Italy to the English Channel, touching on Spain and penetrating deep into Germany.[35] He was well known to all the great personages of his time.[36] At least partly through his efforts, the Cistercian Order and the line of Clairvaux flourished. At his death Clairvaux had spawned over one hundred sixty filiations, some of them with populations numbered in

35. The most complete catalogue of Bernard's peregrinations to date is to be found in A. Dimier, 'Sur le pas de saint Bernard', CN 25 (1974) 223–248. Cf. also W. Williams, *St Bernard*, Appendix VIII, 'Itineraria', pp. 397–398; this includes a small illustrative map. On Bernard's presence in specific localities, see V. Boucard, 'Les deux venues de saint Bernard à Nantes', in *Mélanges*, pp. 218–219. Abbé Carlet, 'Saint Bernard à Pralon: Culte et souvenirs', in *Son Temps 2*, pp. 57–65. J.-M. Canivez, 'Les voyages et fondations monastiques en Belique', in *Son Temps 1*, pp. 29–40. E. Chartraire, 'Le sèjour de saint Bernard à Sens, en 1140', in *Son Temps 2*, pp. 66–69. H. Dacremont, 'Saint Bernard: Orval, Arlon', in *Son Temps 2*, pp. 70–77. K. Lutz, 'Saint Bernard dans la Cathédrale de Spire', in *Mélanges*, pp. 120–125. E. Mâle, 'Souvenir des voyages de saint Bernard à Rome dans l'art romain', in *Son Temps 1*, pp. 216–223. Chanoine Marcel, 'Les séjours de saint Bernard à Langres', in *Son Temps 1*, pp. 224–233. R. Mathieu, 'Saint Bernard et Montmartre', in *Son Temps 2*, pp. 125–128. M. Reymond, 'L'oeuvre de saint Bernard dans les diocèses de Lausanne et Genève', in *Son Temps 1*, pp. 262–291.

36. Cf. N. Häring, 'Saint Bernard and the *literati* of his day', in CN (1974) 199–222. B. Golding, 'St Bernard and St Gilbert (of Sempringham),' in *Influence*, pp. 41–52. Anselme Le Bail, 'L'influence de saint Bernard sur les auteurs spirituels de son temps', in *Son Temps 1*, pp. 205–215. W. Paulsell, 'Saint Bernard on the Duties of the Christian Prince', in *History 2*, pp. 63–74.

the hundreds.[37] These houses could be found from Ireland to Italy and from Sweden to Portugal. No wonder that Bernard's friend and disciple, Peter of Celle, was to write in his regard some thirty years afterwards: 'It was through him that God has caused the Order of Cîteaux to spread even as far as the sea and beyond.[38]

Yet for all his worldly *éclat*, it was as a writer and teacher that Bernard's importance lay.[39] It was his power in wielding the written word which first caught the attention of his contemporaries; he was a leader in mind and spirit through his writing. And it is this aspect of his career which we must now briefly review.

BERNARD THE WRITER

Bernard's influence over his contemporaries was less the effect of political ambition than the outcome of his spiritual and intellectual vitality. He led by the power of his mind. If others followed him it was because he was able to communicate to them something of the commanding vision

37. A. Dimier in 'Le monde claravallien à la mort de saint Bernard', *Mélanges*, pp. 248–253, gives the number at 167. J. Leclercq in *Spirit*, p. 16, gives 164. Here he is, presumably following *Commission d'histoire*, p. 614; at this time the whole Cistercian Order had 345 monasteries. See also, A. Dimier, 'S. Bernard et ses abbayes-filles', ASOC 25 (1969) 245–268; *Id.*, 'S. Bernard, fondateur des monastères', COCR 15 (1953) 45–60, 130–138; 16 (1954) 122–127, 192–203. Dom Alexis, 'La filiation de Clairvaux et l'influence de S. Bernard au XIIe siècle', in *Son Temps 1*, pp. 9–12.

38. Ep 174 (PL 202:632d).

39. Cf. J. Leclercq, 'Saint Bernard, docteur', COCR 16 (1954) 284–286; also in *Recueil 2*, pp. 387–390. On the difficulty of arriving at a sound appreciation of Bernard's role as an historical actor see A. Bredero, 'The Conflicting Interpretations of the Relevance of Bernard of Clairvaux to the History of his own Time', CN 21 (1980) 53–81.

that guided his own steps.

The wide contemporary acceptance of Bernard evidenced by the number of extant manuscripts of his works dating from his lifetime can be explained by reference to three principal points.

In the first place, Bernard, as a writer, was deeply attuned to the sensitivities of his age. He manifested a unique talent for articulating some of the most profound values and ideals of his times. His writings won acceptance, therefore, because they expressed coherently what his readers were themselves feeling in a confused and unformulated way. This is not to say that Bernard was merely the mouthpiece for acceptable platitudes. On the contrary, he often ignored what was in the forefront of popular consciousness in order to penetrate to a deeper level of experience and awareness. Thus he countered the popularity of Ovid's *Ars amatoria* not by fiery denunciation but by developing an alternative and more chaste appreciation of the role of love in human life which appealed to and satisfied deeper aspirations than those titillated by Ovid's scabrous treatise. The force of Bernard's writing was supplemented by the strength of the subliminal; he had the knack of mobilising the forces of the unconscious.

In a similar way, he tempered the enthusiasm of young knights for war by drawing many of his own class into spiritual warfare in the monasteries, thus proposing a more wholesome outlet for their energies. Those who remained warriors he sought to re-motivate, seeing their service in terms of a holy war fought according to spiritual principles. The teaching he offered to the Knights Templar and to the Crusaders may have been militarily impractible, but it was, at least, an attempt to bring into subjection to christian morality the untrammelled violence of war.

Bernard was in touch with contemporary social movements, but was never bemused by them. He understood his own role as an agent of conscience, bound to confront the mindless flow of events with the firm teaching of Christ. His it was to teach and to explain, to coax where necessary and, if all these failed, vociferously to condemn. He was never an utterer of tired irrelevancies, but a beacon of conscience to which all Europe looked, one respected as a man of God and feared because he could not be bought.

The second reason for Bernard's widespread acceptance is paradoxical. He won a following for reasons exactly opposite to those which made Peter Abelard popular. Abelard was a startingly innovative thinker, whose speculative methods and cavalier attitude to the past caused alarm to the established generation. Bernard, on the other hand, although sparkling and original in his presentation, was scrupulous in avoiding any suggestion of novelty. Bernard won acceptance because his outlook and values were traditional. He had the weight of precedent on his side and, as a result, his writings were less threatening to the generality of his contemporaries than they would have been if he had been proposing something new. Bernard had, furthermore, the knack of making old values come alive, expressing traditional positions in original, personable and stimulating forms. He was never stodgy.

In addition Bernard, as one of the keenest reformers of the twelfth century, rode the crest of the wave which had formed under Gregory VII and had since washed over the greater part of Europe. Everyone was concerned, at least in a distant way, with the reform of the Church and, in this way, Bernard was able to exploit a momentum which already existed. Rallying to the cause of reform in the first half of the twelfth century inevitably brought one into line with the views of the Abbot of Clairvaux.[40]

The third reason which contributed to the spread of Bernard's influence and to his success as a writer is simple. He wrote well. He was a skilled craftsman with words who not only had a natural flair for language and the acquired ability to use it, but also worked very hard in the process of composition and in the subsequent correction and revision of his manuscripts. Whatever natural talent he had was enhanced by his care and cunning in ensuring that the final version said exactly what he wanted.

Bernard wrote beautiful and distinctive Latin. Not only do the words flow with a near-musical lilt but, simultaneously, they stimulate the reader with their cleverness and verve. Everywhere one meets the unexpected turn of phrase, the sudden reversal of normal thought-progression, the familiar quotation combined with new elements to effect a surprising conclusion, the constant involvement of the reader's sub-consious mind through the skilful use of assonance, reminiscence, and suggestive imagery. R. W. Southern attributes the vigour of Bernard's prose to two main elements: his mastery of biblical undertones, and his openness to influence from the French vernacular, 'which let in new words and new construction and gave the old language a

40. Cf. A. Fliche, 'L'influence de Grégoire VII et des idées grégoriennes sur la pensée de saint Bernard', in *Son Temps 1*, pp. 137–150. Bede Lackner, *The Eleventh Century Background of Citeaux*, CS 8 (Washington: Cistercian Publications, 1972). John R. Sommerfeldt, 'Charismatic and Gregorian Leadership in the Thought of Bernard of Clairvaux', in *Leclercq Studies*, pp. 73–90. P. Villaret, 'Les principes de l'activité de saint Bernard', in *Commission d'histoire*, pp. 185–191. On different aspects of the career and influence of Gregory VII, see the seven volumes published by the Abbey of St Paul-outside-the-Walls under the title, *Studi Gregoriani: Per la Storia di Gregorio VII e della Riforma Gregoriana* (1947–1961).

fresh fluency and vivacity'.[41]

So successful was Bernard as a writer that he is almost impossible to translate: so much of his message is indissolubly married to the medium. And whereas the logical content of his words is certainly valuable and significant for comprehending his role in history, the full human content of his writing can be appreciated fully only in the radiance of his own characteristic style. Bernard the man is as fascinating again as the tidings he proclaimed. Bernard's life and his writings cannot be separated. His teaching on desire for God, for instance, was fuelled simultaneously by his own temperament as a *vir desideriorum*,[42] by his personal spiritual experiences, by his pastoral perception of the needs of his readers, by the demands of the texts and circumstances which occasioned his comments as well as by the accepted tradition of teaching on this theme. Nearly all his writings manifest this clear interplay of personalilty, situation, and tradition. It was the successful combination of these elements which gave such contemporary relevance and appeal to the writings of the Abbot of Clairvaux. It is this same rich and complex dialectic which makes the task of the modern interpreter so difficult.

It is easy enough to become so dazzled by the brilliance

41. R. W. Southern, *The Making of the Middle Ages* (London: Hutchinson, 1967) 205. See also, J. Leclercq, 'Saint Bernard, écrivain', in *Recueil 1*, pp. 321–351. C. Mohrmann, 'Le style de saint Bernard', in *Études sur le latin des Chrétiens* (Rome: Edizioni di Storia e Letteratura, 1961) Vol. 2: pp. 347–367; *Id.*, 'Observations sur la langue et le style de saint Bernard', in SBO 2 (Introduction) pp. ix–xxxiii. Dorette Sabersky-Bascho, *Studien zur Paronomasie bei Bernhard von Clairvaux* (Fribourg [Switzerland]: Universitätsverlag, 1979).

42. The description of Daniel in Dan 9:23 as a *vir desideriorum* appealed to Bernard. Cf. SC 32.2 (SBO 1:227,7) and Div 9.3 (SBO 6a:119,20).

of Bernard's writing that one forgets the serious import of his words. Bernard's 'poetic amusements' are not merely an exercise in linguistic virtuosity on the part of a talented and professional writer.[43] They are not contrived flourishes, but part of his personal style of communication. Bernard was the sort of man who could not speak or write without being conscious of the quality of his language. Any study of bernardine texts must, therefore, take account of the passion that was their genesis.

To understand the man, to undertand his situation, to understand his writings: these three distinct and irreducible tasks are yet, somehow, one.

BERNARD THE READER

Although the *Vita Prima* quotes Bernard as light-heartedly claiming the oaks and the beeches as his only instructors, it is clear that he remained a reader and a listener to readings throughout his life.[44] He had a retentive memory and a reflective disposition and, as a result, texts stayed with him for years after he first encountered them. They would re-appear spontaneously as he developed a theme, mingling unselfconsciously with the outpourings of his fervid spirit, adapting themselves to the flow of discourse and the mentality of its recipients.

43. Cf. A Dimier, 'Les amusements poétiques de S. Bernard', COCR 12 (1950) 52–55.

44. Cf. *Vita Prima* 4.23 (*Omnia Opera*, 6.2109b). Attempting to confute the 'legend of a Bernard who never studied', Gilson writes, 'It is already known that he was filled with the theology of the Greek Fathers, especially perhaps Gregory of Nyssa, and it will be seen more and more that the core of his work is the creation of a necessary synthesis of Greek and Latin theology', (Translated from E. Gilson, 'La cité de Dieu de saint Bernard', in *Homme d'Église*, pp. 101–105, at p. 102.) Not all bernardine specialists would accept this proposition.

Bernard not only read and assimilated. To use his own unlovely image, he also belched forth from his own inner fullness the texts and ideas he had garnered over the years.[45]

We must presume that it was the canons of St Vorles who gave him his basic grounding in classical literature. Quotations and reminiscences from the classics are relatively frequent in his writings. This is especially true of the discourse *De conversione* addressed to students at Paris about the year 1139. Such quotations are often introduced playfully: they rarely concern the substance of Bernard's message as much as its apt and literate presentation.[46] Perhaps universalising his own experience, Bernard came to believe that the study of letters was not altogether appropriate for monks; he seems to take for granted that it was complete before their entry into monastic life. A generation later, Gilbert of Swineshead, gives frequent evidence of pastoral concern at monks wasting their time reading pagan authors. By this time the divorce between monastery and school had become irreversible.

The monk's book was the Bible. This was Bernard's

---

45. Cf. Mohrmann, *Le style*, p. 353.

46. Cf. J. M. Déchanet, 'Aux sources de la pensée philosophique de saint Bernard', in *Théologien*, pp. 56–77. R. S. Gelsomino, 'S. Bernardo di Chiaravalle e il "De Amicitia" di Cicerone', in *Analecta 5*. B. Jacqueline, 'Repertoire des citations d'auteurs profanes dans les oeuvres de saint Bernard', in *Commission d'histoire*, Appendix IV, pp. 549–554; this listing needs to be augmented. T. Renna, 'St. Bernard and the Pagan Classics', in *Chimaera*, pp. 122–131. See also, in part, W. Williams, *St Bernard*, Appendix I: Literaria, pp. 363–373. The relationship between Bernard and the burgeoning of courtly literature remains unclear on many points, although Leclercq reflects what seems to be a growing consensus when he writes, 'Bernard was quite definitely acquainted with the secular love literature of his times' (*Monks and Love*, p. 121).

principal source and main inspiration. The Scriptures saturated his whole subjectivity, not only with their teaching, but also with images and languages and associations. So fully had Bernard made the Bible his own that it is often very difficult to decide where the Bible ends and where Bernard begins. Denis Farkasfalvy has, for example, estimated that in the sermons *On the Song of Songs* there is one scriptural quotation for every two lines of text.[47] Bernard's facility in bringing forth a creative analogue at a time when there was no universal system of chapter and verse division rivals that of Augustine. Both had an extensive knowledge of the whole Bible which served as the primary determinant not only of the content but also of the form of their preaching.

---

47. Denis Farkasfalvy, 'The Role of the Bible in St Bernard's Spirituality', ASOC 25 (1969) 3–13. The author counts a total of 5526 'biblical quotations' in the sermons *On the Song of Songs*. See also, *Id.*, 'L'inspiration de l'Écriture sainte dans la théologie de saint Bernard', StA 53 (Rome: Herder, 1964). Claude Bodard, 'La Bible, expression d'une expérience religieuse chez S. Bernard', in *Théologien*, pp. 24–45. P. Dumontier, 'Saint Bernard et la Bible', (Paris: Desclée de Brouwer, 1953). G. Frischmuth, *Die paulinische Konzeption in der Frömmigkeit Bernhards von Clairvaux* (Gutersloh: Bertelsmann, 1934). J. Leclercq, 'Saint Bernard et l'Ecriture sainte', in *Saint Bernard Mystique* (Paris: Desclée de Brouwer, 1948) pp. 483–489. The same author has also contributed a number of dictionary entries on this subject. *Id.*, 'Saint Bernard et la tradition biblique d'après les sermons sur le Cantique', in *Recueil 1*, pp. 298–319; *Id.*, (with J. Figuet), 'La Bible dans les homélies de saint Bernard sur "Missus est"', in *Recueil 3*, pp. 213–248. H. de Lubac, *Exégèse Mediévale: Les quatre sens de l'Ecriture*, Vol 1.2 (Paris: Aubier, 1959) pp. 586–620 and *passim* throughout the four volumes. Luigi Negri, 'Posizione dello "stile biblico" di san Bernardo', *Studium* 12 (1954) 3–8. E. Stiegman, *The Language of Asceticism in St. Bernard of Clairvaux's 'Sermons super Cantica Canticorum* (Ph. D. dissertation, Fordham University, 1973), pp. 51–56.

It is important that one recognise that Bernard's command of the biblical text was not the result of sustained solitary scrutiny as much as prolonged exposure to the liturgy and to the writings of the Fathers of the Church. It is clear from his choice of texts and the versions he quoted that his use of the Bible was profoundly influenced by the cycle of liturgical texts. The several hours spent daily by the Cistercian monk in the celebration of the *Opus Dei* provided a constant contact with the Word of God that could not but be formative of his sprituality.

It is not, however, to be thought that Bernard was a preacher who merely inserted bald blocks of biblical text into his discourses. His relationship with the inspired text was rather more subtle and organic. The Scriptures inspired nearly everything he wrote, at least distantly; often his words take for granted that the recipient was as familiar with the Bible as Bernard himself, and hence able to catch the fine allusions he had scattered throughout his text. Furthermore, it was not only the written Bible that Bernard used, but also the auditory Bible, that heard day by day in the liturgy and elsewhere, which triggered associations as much by its sound as by its content. Bernard was not a biblical fanatic, quoting the sacred text rigidly, almost as if it were magical, and interpreting it in a narrow, fundamentalist mode. He used the Bible easily and naturally as one of God's greater gifts; he marvelled at the mysteries it enshrined but did not hesitate to incarnate its meaning into his own human discourse.

Beyond and around the text of the Bible stands the whole monastic tradition according to which Bernard had been formed in spritual discipline and whose principles guided his thought and action throughout his life. Bernard can be appreciated only within the context of

this unwieldy whole which is partly the transmission of
rules and texts and teaching and partly the living communication of life and experience from one generation to
its succedant. It is a difficult area to explore not only
because of the fact that it covers eight centuries and has
generated an enormous volume of material, but also
because pedigrees have become obscured through
generations of cross-breeding. An author may quote
Augustine, for example, but we have no means of knowing quickly whether he had ever read his source either in
whole or in part. Perhaps his quotation may have been
borrowed from another author or picked up from the
liturgy, perhaps it came from a collection of *auctoritates*
or by word of mouth from a friend who had himself
found it somewhere. One can never be more than
moderately sure of direct dependence without knowing
something of an author's reading habits.

With regard to Bernard we are fortunate in having
at least a partial catalogue of the contents of the library at
Clairvaux during his abbacy. From these known volumes
we can ascertain not only what books were available for
his perusal, but also which works he himself regarded as
being worth copying.[48] Although founded without
books, the *armarium* at Clairvaux boasted a collection of
several hundred twelfth-century manuscripts by 1472, of

48. The information in this paragraph comes from an article of
André Wilmart, 'L'ancienne bibliothèque de Clairvaux', COCR 11
(1949) 100–127 and 301–319. The original and longer version of
this may be found in the 1917 issue of *Mémoires de la Société
Academique*, pp. 125–190. Cf. A. Vernet, 'Note sur la bibliothèque
de Clairvaux', in *Commission d'histoire*, Appendix V, pp. 555–556.
F. Gastadelli, 'Proposed Inventory for the Greek Fathers in the
Library of Clairvaux', in *One Yet Two*, pp. 401–404. The most recent work can be found in André Vernet, *La Bibliothèque de l'abbaye de Clairvaux du XIIe au XVIIIe siècle* (Paris: Editions du
C.N.R.S., 1979).

which three hundred-forty are extant, most of them copied in Clairvaux's own *scriptorium*. This collection included many works of Augustine, all of Gregory the Great, and much of Origen, Basil, and Gregory of Nyssa as well as a representative selection of the major works of both eastern and western traditions. There was, as well, an important collection of eleventh and twelfth-century authors, many texts of the Bible, both partial and complete, and several profane texts. All in all we get the impression that Bernard's choice of reading inclined to mainline western tradition with the emphasis on biblical commentaries and on spiritual and monastic treatises. Canon law, dogmatics, and polemic do not seem to have been given a high priority.

Texts which we can be certain that Bernard knew are those which were included in the readings of the Office of Vigils. Here the emphasis is strongly on Leo, Augustine, Gregory, Ambrose, and Jerome. These authors were heard year by year in the liturgical cycle and have had a demonstrable impact on the shaping of Bernard's own thought.

A partial list of sources and paralells has been drawn up by Jean Leclercq for the sermons *On the Song of Songs*. Over one hundred fifty reminiscences and *rapprochements* are noted there from a wide range of potential provenances.[49] Later volumes of the critical edition of *Sancti Bernardi Opera* regularly identify similarities, where this is possible, but it is clear that the major work of tracking down the sources of Bernard's thought remains to be done.

Nevertheless the general lines of influence are clear enough, even if the precise means of transmission cannot always be fully established.

49. J. Leclercq, 'Aux sources des sermons sur les Cantiques', in *Recueil 1*, pp. 275–319.

An important source which is often underestimated is the *Rule* of St Benedict.[50] Apart from overt references to Benedict and his *Rule* whenever Bernard dealt with monastic matters, there is often a clear kinship with the text of Benedict's *Rule* elsewhere. This is not surprising, since a section of the *Rule* was read daily in Chapter and it is unlikely that the document which was the mainstream of the Cistercian reform would ever be far from consciousness of one of its most dedicated proponents. After a penetrating analysis of this matter, Jean Leclercq concludes thus: 'It is to the Rule of St Benedict, taken as a whole, and above all in its spiritual doctrine, that Bernard owes the balance and harmony of his monastic teaching.'[51]

Like every other thinker and writer in the christian West, Bernard is clearly indebted to the genius of Augustine of Hippo. Here again it is almost impossible to gauge the extent of his personal reading; certainly he knew the *Confessions*, he was familiar with many of the great sermons used in the liturgy, and he knew the famous phrases which had passed into general usage. It is possible that direct influence is weaker than one would anticipate and that Bernard draws rather upon a diffuse, generalized 'Augustinianism' than on the works of the

50. J. Leclercq, 'St Bernard and the Rule of the St Benedict', in M. Basil Pennington (ed.), *Rule and Life* CS 12 (Spencer: Cistercian Publications, 1971) 151–167. E. Gilson, *The Mystical Theology of Saint Bernard* (London: Sheed and Ward, 1940) 13–16. D. Farkasfalvy, 'St. Bernard's Spirituality and the Benedictine Rule in the *Steps of Humility*', ASOC 36 (1980) 248–262. In the two volume *Fichier saint Bernard* privately circulated from Chambarand by Robert Thomas in 1958, seventy specific references to parts of the *Rule* of Benedict are located in the bernardine writings (pp. 566–587). There is also a list of honorifics applied by Bernard to Benedict (pp. 65–67). Both catalogues could be considerably augmented.

51. J. Leclercq, 'St Bernard and the Rule of St Benedict', p. 167.

Master himself.[52] At the same time there are substantial similarities in the themes treated, in the terminology employed, and in the strength of their personalities. Their situations were different and their pre-occupations distinct, but both were holy men who worked with style and conviction to communicate a renewed appreciation of mainline western Christianity. Whatever lines the pedigree may eventually be proved to follow, the fact remains that one of the best ways of coming to an appreciation of Bernard's originality and traditionality is through the reading of the sermons of Augustine.[53]

More direct links can be established between Bernard and Gregory the Great. Gregory had great prestige in the West as a successful and holy pope. Among monks he was particularly well regarded because he himself had been a monk and remained devoted to monastic values throughout his life. He was also the author of an account of Benedict's life and was generally presumed to have been a disciple of the Patriarch, even though he was born only a few years before Benedict's death.[54] His sermons

52. Cf. André Fracheboud, 'L'influence de saint Augustin sur le cistercien Isaac de l'Etoile', COCR 11 (1949) 1–17 (note especially p. 2), 264–278, and 12 (1950) 5–16. Some of the complexities of the question can be gleaned from a study on Bernard's associate, William of St Thierry: J. Déchanet, *Guillaume de Saint-Thierry: Aux sources d'une pensée* (Paris: Beauchesne, 1978). The relationship between Bernard and Augustine is, in general, territory unexplored beyond the obvious. For general indications see Gilson, *Mystical Theology*, pp. 220–221, note 24.

53. Notwithstanding its methodological deficiencies and its general defensiveness, there remains much of merit in Cuthbert Butler's compilation, *Western Mysticism: The Teaching of SS. Augustine, Gregory and Bernard on Contemplation and the Contemplative Life* (London: Constable, 2nd edn rp., 1951). A balanced re-assessment of the value of Butler's work is given by Benedetto Calati, 'Western Mysticism', *Downside Review* 98 (1980) 201–213.

54. Cf. Jeffery Richards, *Consul of God: The Life and Times of Gregory the Great* (London: Routledge and Kegan Paul, 1980). K.

were read at Vigils and his scriptural commentaries, particularly his *Moralia in Iob* were widely available and often read. Bernard is similar to Gregory in vocabulary, style, and content, though he is less wooden in his presentation. What he particularly owes to Gregory is his method of biblical exposition, especially his emphasis on the spiritual and practical meanings of the text.[55]

Bernard certainly read the latin version of Origen and seems to have followed Origen's Commentary *On the Song of Songs* whilst writing his own *semones*.[56] This is not surprising, since Origen enjoyed something of a renaissance in the twelfth century and among the first Cistercians.[57] At the same time, Bernard was suspicious of and heartily condemned on several occasions the error of Origenism,[58] and in one sermon he clarified the meaning of a text from Origen which had been read the previous day.[59] The position with regard to other Eastern Fathers is less straightforward. Bernard was less influenced

---

Hallinger, 'Papst Gregor der Grosse und der hl. Benedikt', in B. Steidle (ed.), *Commentationes in Regulam S. Benedicti*, StA 42 (Rome: Herder, 1957) 231–319. The possibility of some contact between John Cassian and Gregory is potentially a worthwhile line of inquiry.

55. On this see especially H. de Lubac, *Exégèse Mediévale*, Vol 1/2: pp. 586–620.

56. Gustave Bardy, 'Saint Bernard et Origène', RMAL 1 (1945) 420–421. Eugène Manning, 'S. Bernard et Origène', COCR 25 (1963) 385–386; this is a summary of a thesis written, under the same title, by J. Deroy. The similarities between the early sermons *On the Song of Songs* and the commentary of Origen are detailed in the listing of J. Leclercq already referred to, *Recueil 1:* 281–283. The treatments of Gregory the Great and Gregory of Nyssa show a similar awareness of Origen's work.

57. J. Leclercq, 'Origène au XIIe siècle', *Irenikon* 24 (1951) 425–439.

58. For instance, SC 54.3 (SBO 2:104,27) but cf. Jerome's Ep 96.10. Other texts are noted in Thomas' *Fichier*, pp. 479–480.

59. Div 34 (SBO 6a.228–233).

by Gregory of Nyssa than was his friend, William of St Thierry,[60] his connections with Maximus through Erigena are tenuous enough,[61] and it has been shown that Pseudo-Dionysius had scarcely any impact at all.[62] Bernard's favoured points of contact with the christian past were predominantly western.

Bernard's own style and presentation, especially when compared with the works of scholasticism, led to his being called 'the last of the Fathers'. He was constantly guided by their teaching, especially with regard to speculative points, where he was uncharacteristcially cautious in trusting his own insights.[63] He stated that he was reluctant to give an answer to any theological problem until he had found

60. One must treat with reserve the article of J. Daniélou, 'Saint Bernard et les Pères grecs', in *Théolgien*, pp. 46–55. See also Bede Lackner, 'Early Cîteaux and the East', in *One Yet Two*, pp. 373–400. Aelred Squire, 'The Cistercians and the Eastern Fathers', in *One Yet Two*, pp. 168–182. Even with regard to William of St Thierry, whose works breathe a more eastern atmosphere than Bernard's, there have been severe reservations about some of the facile links between William and the Eastern Fathers which have followed the research of J. Déchanet. To date, the evidence is not sufficient. Cf. John D. Anderson, 'The Use of Greek Sources by William of St Thierry: Especially in the *Enigma Fidei*', in *One Yet Two*, pp. 242–253. *Id.*, 'Sources of the *Enigma of Faith*', in the Introduction to his translation of that work published by Cistercian Publications, CF 9, (Washington, 1974). E. Rozanne Elder, 'William of St Thierry and the Greek Fathers: Evidence from Christology', in *One Yet Two*, pp. 254–266. Most trenchantly, David N. Bell, 'The Alleged Greek Sources of William of St Thierry', in *Noble Piety*, pp. 109–122.

61. Despite E. Gilson, 'Maxime, Erigène et saint Bernard: à propos du *De Diligendo Deo*', *Revue d'histoire ecclésiatique* 31 (1935) 188–195.

62. Cf. E. Boissard, 'Saint Bernard et le Pseudo-Aréopagite', RTAM 26 (1959) 214–263. B. McGinn, 'Pseudo-Dionysius and the Early Cistercians', in *One Yet Two*, pp. 200–243.

63. Ep 77 (= Bapt), *praefatium* (SBO 7:185, 18–19).

one in their writings,[64] and was concerned when he discovered that he had proposed an opinion which lacked their support.[65] Beyond this overt and conscious linkage of Bernard and his predecessors is a much stronger current of influence deriving from the fact that in many ways he inhabited the same world as they, spoke the same language, shared the same values and concerns and operated within similar parameters. To appreciate Bernard's links with the past, and many other things besides, it is necessary to have some understanding of the immediate context in which his theology was generated.

'MONASTIC THEOLOGY'

Jean Leclercq has done a great service in isolating a particular body of literature in pre-scholastic and early scholastic times and categorising it as 'monastic theology'. In fact the literature emanating from the medieval cloisters was quite distinct from that being produced in the schools and centres of learning. It was a humane and devotional literature more concerned with penetrating the inner heart of existing theology than with extending the theological frontiers into the unknown. Understanding this theological ambience is absolutely vital in coming to a perception of Bernard's writings.[66]

64. SC 5.7 (SBO 1:24,22) Ep 98.1 (SBO 7:248, 16–18).
65. Hum *Retractatio* (SBO 3:15,14).
66. Cf. J. Leclercq, 'S. Bernard et la théologie monastique du XIIe siècle', *Théologien*, pp. 7–23; *Id.*, *The Love of Learning and the Desire for God* (New York: Fordham, 1962), Ch. 9 'Monastic Theology': *Id.*, 'Théologie et Prière', in *Chances*, pp. 179–224. A. Hallier, *The Monastic Theology of Aelred of Rievaulx*, CS 2 (Spencer: Cistercian Publications, 1969) especially pp. 85–112. Odo Brooke, 'Monastic Theology and St Aelred' and 'Towards an Integral Theology' in *Studies in Monastic Theology*, CS 37 (Kalamazoo: Cistercian Publications, 1980) pp. 219–225 and 226–231. J. Morson, 'Symbolic Theology: The Cistercian Fathers, Heirs to a Tradition', in *Ideals*, pp. 245–261.

'Monastic theology' was a form of reflection and discourse on revealed truth which was closer to art than to science. It did not deal with sacred mysteries as though they were specimens lined up for objective analysis and description. The mystery of God and the economy of salvation were clearly grasped as being beyond human scrutiny. As far as the monks were concerned, theology was a discipline by which the mind and heart were schooled so that they might venture reverently and humbly further into faith. Its end object was not so much the discovery of new corollaries or the solution of old problems as the personal growth of its participants. It was a subjective discipline, intended to aid the monk's appropriation of his faith and thus facilitate its translation into behaviour.

This is not to say that monastic theology was ignorant, mindless, or obscurantist. It involved different skills from those being employed in the schools. It required an ability to appreciate literature and to be moved by the rhythms of rhetoric and the subtleties of fine language. The texts which purveyed such theology worked as much through stimulating the sub-conscious as through providing data for conscious processing. It was a poetic and symbolic theology, deeply traditional in its content but often original and elegant in its form. It was not less interesting because it was not innovative; it stimulated the mind not by advancing new conclusions but by the style and fervour with which accepted beliefs were re-expressed.

Monastic theology was not a professional specialisation which could be pursued in isolated objectivity. It was necessarily bound up with the quality of the theologian's life. This was because it flowed from his own experience and had a role to play in helping him to live with greater fidelity. In modern terminology it might be called 'existential' rather than 'essential' or it might easily be discussed in terms of 'orthopraxy'. It had a goal which was distinct from that pursued by scholastic theology; it was not inferior to it because it failed to conform to the model followed in the Schools; it simply belonged to another species.[67]

The privileged locale of monastic theology was the monastery and within the monastery it was especially the liturgy which sustained and nourished it. Here the Word of God was heard in daily, weekly, seasonal, and yearly cycles, the same texts recurring, fixing themselves in the memory, blending with a variety of other elements and interacting among themselves. Here the Fathers were read, adding their interpretations and developments to the scriptural texts, beginning a process of meditation and rumination which would continue not only throughout the day but throughout life. It was in the liturgy that the chief factors of the monastic sub-culture were most precisely mirrored and continually made present to the monk in a way that could not fail to influence his manner of thinking and his own style of expression.

The monk's daily practice of *lectio divina* served to reinforce and personalise both the content and the style of the liturgy. The books that he read were the same or

67. It is possible to detect in the works of Gilson, as in the famous articles written by Standaert in the 1940s, a defensiveness as to Bernard's theological status. As one who had been eagerly claimed by many as a pious author and who certainly did not conform to the standard Scholastic usage then considered normative, Bernard could easily be dismissed as something less than a 'real theologian'. The wealth of theological studies emanating from the 1953 centenary, particularly the volume *Saint Bernard Théologien* settled the question once and for all. Now, in the 1980s, Bernard is perhaps regarded as a more impressive and 'relevant' theologian than most of the scholastic authors. Cf. my article, ' "Emotionally Hollow, Esthetically Meaningless and Spiritually Empty": An Inquiry into Theological Discourse', *Colloquium* 14 (1981) 54–61.

spoke the same language as the liturgy itself, and the two sources of contact with the faith of the Church easily mingled. If abbots spoke to their communities in the same way as Peter of Celle, Bernard, Guerric of Igny, or Isaac of Stella, then a further channel of formation in monastic theology would have existed alongside the others.

There was, moreover, a communitarian dimension to this mode of theologising. It was not an individual endeavour to ascertain truth as much as the result of the creation of a climate of corporate meaning . This was the philosophy of life embodied not only in the lives of those famous proponents whose names we associate with its transmission, but also in the humbler careers of the silent and unknown majority. At least part of the reason for this is the emphasis placed in monastic theology on love over knowledge. The Gregorian axiom *amor ipse notitia est* recurs frequently in this ambience.[68] Love is also a source of understanding in so far as it binds subject and object together; knowledge, with its concern for objectivity, can be divisive both of subject and object and also of brothers living together. With love paramont, understanding has a greater potential for being shared around.

To appreciate the work of the Abbot of Clairvaux, it is necessary to perceive that he operated in this context. His theology was the result of a life of personal dedication and prayer and, in large measure, it was written for the edification and instruction of those living a similar way of life. It was not classroom theology, nor is it particularly systematic. Even his most technical work, *On Grace and Free Will*, contains much to nourish devotion and to guide behaviour. He is content to raise questions and evoke reverent admiration for the mysteries of God's dealing with human beings; the few essays at solution that the

68. Gregory the Great, *In Evangelium homilia* 27.4 (PL 76:1207a). This text was familiar to both Bernard and William of St Thierry.

treatise contains are less the work of a speculative mind than the application of experience to the question at issue. Bernard could, perhaps, have become a substantial theologian in the scholastic mould if it had been his desire, but years of monastic living had made him appreciate a more excellent way.

Often in his sermons, Bernard shows that he was aware of the trends growing in the theological schools of his time. That the adversary of Abelard, Gilbert of Poitiers, and Berengar was unenthusiastic about them can come as no surprise. In his periodic forays into polemic, his special barbs were reserved for heretics and philosophers, between whom he scarecely bothered to make any distinction. He proposed an 'interior philosophy' which was to know Jesus and him crucified.[69] He pointed out that Peter 'was not drawn from the school of rhetoricians and philosophers',[70] nor did he teach his followers after the manner of the schools.[71] Bernard's objection was not to learning as such;[72] he was happy enough to receive students such as Geoffroy of Auxerre into Clairvaux and to make use of their talents. What he particularly inveighed against was the 'wind' and the sterility of those who made a cult of words and minute distinctions and became involved in the intricacies of Aristotelian syllogisms.[73] Not that there was anything wrong with such pursuits per se; the danger was that their practitioners

69. Cf. SC 43.4 (SBO 2:43,21). See also J. Leclercq, 'Philosophia', in Études sur le vocabularie du moyen âge, St A 48 (Rome: Herder, 1961) pp. 39–79. B. Baur, 'The Philosophical Life according to Adam of Perseigne', COCR 24 (1962) 225–242, 25 (1963) 31–43.

70. SC 36.1 (SBO 2:4,4–5).

71. Cf. PP 1.3 (SBO 5:189,28–190, 2).

72. Cf. SC 36.2 (SBO 2:4,14–17), SC 37.2 (SBO 2:9, 23–24).

73. Cf. SC 41.1 (SBO 2:29, 8–9), SC 58.7 (SBO 2:131,26), SC 79.4 (SBO 2:274,21).

would become so absorbed in them that they would become forgetful of themselves and of ultimate priorities. Bernard saw such men as mental wanderers, never attaining the solidity and certainty of truth, but always moving on, 'always learning and never coming to an understanding of the truth'.[74] This undesirable outcome he sought to prevent by argument rather than through the use of force,[75] since he recognised that, in such cases, faith has to appeal to reason rather than impose itself from without.[76] Such principles did not stop him from pursuing the ringleaders of the New Wave; it was their popularity and their success in generating a following that particularly motivated his actions. What Bernard did in his whole involvement in such controversies was to signal to us that he himself operated out of different pre-suppositions. He was not an academic, he was a monk; he read the Scriptures not as an exegete but 'more wondering than examining'.[77]

Bernard was a product of monastic theology as well as its most accomplished practioner. Nowhere is his skill more in evidence than in his eighty-six sermons *On the Song of Songs*. To appreciate the soul of this man of affairs it is necessary to give measured consideration to this, his most finished work. These sermons are, perhaps, the supreme example of monastic theology and, as such, are the most satisfactory embodiment of his life and work.

74. SC 33.8 (SBO 1:239,19–22); the phrasing in this passage is clearly modelled on RB 1.11.
75. SC 64.8 (SBO 2:170,13).
76. SC 66.12 (SBO 2:187,13).
77. SC 62.4 (SBO 2:158,3).

CHAPTER TWO

THE SERMONS ON THE
SONG OF SONGS

SOMEONE WHO IS AWARE of the continuing acclaim accorded to Bernard's *Sermones super Cantica canticorum* over the centuries, is often disappointed by initial contact with the work, especially if this is made through the medium of a translation. Although there are passages of easily accessible brilliance scattered throughout the eighty-six sermons, the direction of ideas is not evident without a great deal of study. It is not unusual for someone reading the sermons for a fourth or fifth time to feel diffident about claiming that he really understands the construction and scope of this great literary production.

Jean Leclercq has published a text which demonstrates that even Bernard's coevals did not always find the sermons easy reading.[1] For the modern reader, the need

1. 'Difficulté des sermons de saint Bernard', in *Recueil 1*, pp. 191–192.

for preparation and industry is even more important. It is not only that he has to work at clearing away the detritus of obscurity and misunderstanding which has accumulated in the intervening centuries. He also has to labour to come to grips with a work which substantially and by the deliberate choice of its author escapes classification. The *Sermones super Cantica canticorum* constitute an *opus sui generis,* a unique literary masterpiece which demands of its readers a response quite unlike that given to any other work.

Bernard's text was composed over a period of eighteen years which included the most tempestuous decade of his life. The different portions of his work, which were circulated in blocs as they were finished, reflect different stages of his development and must often be read in the context of contemporary concerns or with reference to other works which date from the same period. Thus sermons 32–39 are tinged with the acrimony typical of his controversy with Abelard, whereas the deeply reflective tone of the final sermons is echoed in the mellow wisdom of *De consideratione.* This means that the ambience of the sermons changes, highlighting different facets of the complex personality and career of their author. To some extent, the reader must be prepared to anticipate this variation.[2]

2. Cf. J. Leclercq, 'The Making of a Masterpiece', introduction to Bernard of Clairvaux, *On the Song of Songs IV,* CF 40 (Kalamazoo, Cistercian Publications, 1980) pp. ix–xxv. The usual dating proposed for the sermons on the basis of the scant internal and external information available to us is as follows.

I Sermons 1–24		1135–1136	
II Sermons 24 bis–49		1138–(1145)	
Sermon 26	1138		
Sermon 33	1139		
III Sermons 50–83		(1145)–(1152)	
Sermons 65–66	after 1144		
Sermon 80	after 1148		
IV Sermons 84–86		(1152)–1153	
Sermon 86	1153		

An enlightened appreciation of the total context of Bernard's work is indispensable if one is to arrive at a precise understanding of his spiritual doctrine. This includes, in a special way, a knowledge of the specific literary characteristics of this remarkable composition. Without acquaintance with such fundamental resources, it is unrealistic to hope that the sermons will yield the substance of what they contain.

LITERARY PRECEDENTS

The fact that the Song of Songs, although included in the biblical canon, manifests no overt religious message, has been traditionally regarded as an invitation to search diligently for hidden meanings. It was not thought that the Holy Spirit should have inspired a book whose content, although exotically and beautifully presented, was limited to a simple retelling of the fluctuations inherent in any love-story. And so it happened that commentators began to see the Song as an intimation of higher realities, interpreting it as an allegory of the relation of God and his people or, later, between God and the individual soul.[3]

---

3. The history of the interpretation of the Song of Songs is covered by a number of overlapping studies. F. Cavallera, art. 'Cantique: Histoire de l'interprétation spirituelle', DSp 2/1: cols 93–101. Roland E. Murphy, 'Patristic and Medieval Exegesis—Help or Hindrance', *Catholic Biblical Quarterly* 43/4 (1981) 505–516. Friedrich Ohly, *Hohelied-Studien: Grundzüge einer Geschicthe der Hoheliedsauslegung des Abendlandes bis um 1200*, (Wiesbaden: Franz Steiner Verlag GMBH, 1958). W. Reidel, *Die Auslegung des Hohenliedes in der jüdischen Gemeinde und der griechischen Kirche*, (Leipzig, 1898). Helmut Riedlinger, *Die Makellosigkeit der Kirche in den lateinischen Hoheliedkommentaren des Mittelalters* (Münster, Aschendorffsche Verlagsbuchhandlung, 1958). Emero S.

Although not the most ancient christian treatment of the Song of Songs, the commentaries of Origen were instrumental in delineating the agenda of subsequent exposition.[4] In fact, Origen seems to have had a life-long passion for this biblical book which gave him the opportunity of expatiating on so many of his favourite themes. Unfortunately not all that he wrote is extant. There is a fragment preserved in the *Philokalia* which appears to be part of a more substantial work undertaken in his youth. This is reprinted in Migne.[5] Then there are two homilies on Song 1:1–2:14, which have come down to us in a version by St Jerome.[6] These were probably written

---

Stiegmann, Jr., *The Language of Asceticism in St. Bernard of Clairvaux's 'Sermones super Cantica Canticorum'*, unpublished dissertation, Fordham University, 1973) pp. 56–71. More generally, cf. A. Robert *et al.*, *Le Cantique des Cantiques: Traduction et Commentaire* (Paris: Gabalda, 1963) pp. 43–55, Histoire de l'interprétation.

4. Cf. F. Cavallera, 'Cantique', cols 95–96. J. Daniélou, *Origène* (Paris: La Table Ronde, 1948) 297–301. O. Rousseau, introduction to Origène, *Homélies sur le cantique des cantique*, SChr 37 (Paris: Cerf, 1953) pp. 7–57. A. Ceresa-Gastaldo, 'L'esegesi origeniana del "Cantico dei Cantici"', in H. Crouzel (ed.), *Origeniana Secunda* (Rome: Edizioni dell' ateneo, 1980) pp. 245–252. M. Wiles, 'Origen as a Biblical Scholar', in P. Ackroyd and C. F. Evans (edd.), *The Cambridge History of the Bible* (Cambridge University Press, 1978) vol 2:454–489. Bertrand de Margerie, *Introduction à l'histoire de l'exégèse* (Paris: Cerf., 1980) vol. 1: 113–136. The far-reaching lines of Origen's influence on subsequent exposition of the Song of Songs is well illustrated in the comparative commentary of J. de Monleon, *Le Cantique des Cantiques: Commentarie mystique d'après les Pères de l'Eglise* (Paris: Nouvelles Editions Latines, 1969). For general information on Origen, see H. Crouzel, *Bibliographie Critique d'Origène*, Instrumenta Patristica 8 (Steenbrugge, 1971). Supplementary notices can be found in *Id.*, art. 'Origène' DSp 9 (1982) cols 933–961.

5. PG 13:35–36.

6. O. Rousseau, SChr 37, gives a critical edition and a French translation.

around 244, four years after Origen had begun his major commentary, and are intended as a simpler version for the less advanced, even including the catechumens.[7] Origen's principal exposition of the Song of Songs was begun when he was in his mid-50s. It comprised ten books, the first five written while the author was at Athens, the latter half completed at Caesarea. Of the original Greek text only the fragments preserved by Procopius remain. Rufinus left a loose and unfinished translation of the first four books, which enables us to appreciate the scope of the endeavour, believed to have run to 20,000 lines of text in its entirety.[8]

Origen used the commentary on the Song of Songs as a medium for his mystical teaching, yet he was disciplined in the manner of his exposition. In line with his habitual distinction of the various levels of meaning to be found in the Scriptures,[9] he begins by recalling the historical sense of the text and then proceeds to its spiritual and allegorical meanings and its mystical and moral applications. The interpretations Origen proposed were not merely fanciful irrevelvancies designed to avoid the intricacies of an obscure text. He genuinely believed that he had attained the deeper meanings intended by the Holy Spirit. He felt that the details of material realities and events given in the sacred text could be explained only by viewing them as symbols or images of less overt truths. The applications were not selected arbitrarily but in the context of personal reflection on the tradition of experience and teaching within the Church.

7. *Homilae in canticum canticorem* 2.7 (SChr 37:92) p. 34.

8. PG 13:62–198. The excerpts of Procopius follow in cols 198–216.

9. On this, see Henri de Lubac, *Exégèse Médiévale: Les quartre sens de l'Ecriture* (Paris: Aubier, 1959–1964). See especially vol. 1/2: 586–599.

Origen was using the text of the inspired canticle as a means of giving instruction about life; it was not mere exegesis but a more integral teaching that he intended. He could easily have said what Bernard later affirmed: *Hodie legimus in libro experientiae* — Today we read in the book of experience.[10]

Furthermore his teaching was preserved from whimsy by being bound together around a central theme, the relationship of the Word and the Church. This interpretation, already found in Hippolytus and Tertullian, understands the Song as a description of the continuing drama of the love of Christ, the heavenly bridegroom, for his bride, the Church.[11] Origen innovates in this respect, understanding the bride of Christ not only as the whole body of Christians which constitute the *Ecclesia,*

---

10. SC 3.1 (SBO 1:14,7). On the similarities between Bernard and Origen, cf. Riedlinger *Die Makellosigkeit,* pp. 156–157. L. Brésard, 'Bernard et Origène commentent le Cantique', COCR 44 (1982) 111–130, 192–209, 293–308.

11. References are given in Rousseau, SChr 37: p. 16. While affirming the interchangeability of the Church with the individual believing soul as the bride of the Word, both Origen and Bernard manifest a practical preference for speaking at the level of the individual. This results in both commentaries having a spiritual rather than a theological tone. The equivalence of *ecclesia* and *anima* in this respect is noted in Origen's prologue, PG 13:62d–63a: *Adamavit enim eum [Deum] sive anima quae ad imaginem eius facta est sive Ecclesia.* Bernard indicates the same dual interpretation in SC 29.7 (SBO 1:207,21), SC 29.9 (SBO 1:209,9–10), SC 58.3 (SBO 2:128,21–22), SC 58.4 (SBO 2:129,20), SC 61.2 (SBO 2:149, 15–17) and elsewhere. Preference for the individual seems to be manifested in Origen's statement in Book I, *Simili autem expositione utimur, etiamsi ad unamquamquam animam in amore et desiderio Verbi Dei positam transferatur hic sermo . . .* (PG 13:92c). Bernard habitually identifies the bride as *anima sitiens Deum* (SC 7.2; SBO 1:31, 18) or something equivalent (e.g. SC 68.1; SBO 2:196, 21–22).

but also, in a derivative sense, as the individual, believing *Anima*. The Song of Songs is capable of giving formation both to the corporate life of the Church and to the spiritual strivings of the individual within the Church.

The lyric recital of the vicissitudes of love provided Origen with an occasion to offer a phenomenology of spiritual experience and its development. He did this, predictably, by making use of categories and themes developed elsewhere in his writings; he speaks of the distinction of the different degrees of spiritual life: ethic, physic, and theoric, of the ascent from carnal to spiritual, and from *psyche* to *nous*. He delineates his understanding of the role of the Holy Spirit in spiritual living and propounds his theories on the workings and influence of angels and demons. He re-affirms his views on purification and asceticism, on self-knowledge, on *gnosis*, and describes the contemplative experiences which result from the divine visitation of the soul. And above all, he returns to the theme of the centrality of Christ in the spiritual endeavour; it is Christ's love that is the motive force of all spiritual advancement.

What Origen offered was far more than a verbal explanation of the inspired text. He brought to the text not merely an analytical mind and a prodigious power of association. He read and explained the Song of Songs, mindful of the whole economy of salvation and with a heart willing to recognise and respond to divine love universally present. Origen's *Books on the Song of Songs* are more a compendium of christian theology than a commentary on the text; and it is not only a theology of the mind, it is also a theology of the heart.

It is an undoubted fact that Bernard of Clairvaux knew this commentary of Origen. He had read it and was influenced by it not only with regard to content, but also concerning the *spirit* in which he wrote his own reflections on the book.

The examination of the catalogued contents of the library at Clairvaux reveals that among the titles possessed in the twelfth century was Origen's *Explanatio super cantica canticorum ab exordio usque 'capite nobis vulpes'*.[12] It is obvious that Bernard repeatedly refers to this, especially in the opening sermons, until he passes the place where Origen's exposition petered out (2:15).[13] It is possible that the immediate provenance for the phrase *super cantica canticorum* with the plural reading, which Bernard includes in his title, is to be found in the inscription of this manuscript — notwithstanding Origen's own insistence that the singular *canticum* was the correct reading.[14]

Allowance being made for the differences in style and situation, the general tone of Bernard's writing is not

12. André Wilmart, 'L'ancienne bibliothéque de Clairvaux', COCR 11 (1949) 117. A. Vernet, *La Bibliothèque*, pp. 122–123.

13. This is clear from the traces uncovered by Jean Leclercq and listed in *Recueil 1:* 281–295. The fact that Bernard used Origen's work is not to say that he followed it slavishly. A good example of how he moulds his source to suit his own message is found in SC 1.2 (SBO 1:3, 16–20). The passage is so elliptic that it is difficult to understand without reference to its forebears. Bernard changes Origen's traditional order of reading the biblical books, to give Proverbs a higher rating than Ecclesiastes, thus signalling his greater concern for positive behavioural change over mere negative attitudes to temporal realities. This was notwithstanding the fact that Origen's position was entrenched in monastic tradition. Cf. Origen *In Canticum prologus* (PG 13:73ab), John Cassian, *Conferences* 3.6 (SChr 42:146), Gregory of Nyssa, *In Cantica* I (PG 44:766d), Gregory the Great, *In Cantica proemium* 9 (PL 79:477ab), Jerome, *Commentarius in Ecclesiastem* (PL 23:1063–1064).

14. Origen *In Canticum prologus* (PG 13:82bc). The title could equally have been borrowed from the work of Gregory the Great, *Expositio super Cantica Canticorum*.

dissimilar from that found in Origen's commentaries. Partly this may be explained by the fervent and lyrical pitch demanded by the subject-matter and the text itself. Partly the similarity may be traced to a common purpose of exploiting the Song of Songs as a quarry of practical spiritual teaching for those who are somewhat advanced. It is not, however, entirely out of the question that Bernard is substantially indebted to Origen and to the line of commentators which followed him. It seems likely that Bernard has been a willing inheritor of this tradition, has internalised it and brilliantly transformed it to suit himself. The *Sermones super Cantica canticorum* are not less original because they draw their inspiration from previous spiritual tradition; they are entirely bernardine compositions. Appreciating Bernard's utilisation of Origen is, in fact, a means of recognising more finely in what Bernard's sparkling originality consisted.

To what extent was Bernard familiar with other patristic commentaries on the Song of Songs either at first hand or at one or several removes?

It is generally agreed that Bernard seems to have had no contact with the fifteen homilies of Gregory of Nyssa on the Song of Songs, a conclusion confirmed by a comparative reading of the two treatments. The few similarities which exist are readily explained in terms of their utilisation of a common source, Origen.[15]

The random remarks of St Ambrose on the Song of Songs were also inspired by the work of Origen as well as by the earliest christian commentary on the text, that of Hippolytus, now preserved only in fragments. Ambrose's *obiter dicta*, drawn from the whole range of his writings, but particularly from those addressed to virgins, were collected and by the eleventh century were formed into

15. Thus Ohly, *Hohenlied-Studien*, p. 141, expressing the consensus.

something approaching a sequential commentary. William of St Thierry composed a similar anthology for his own use around 1130–1135, perhaps as a preparation for his own original exposition which would occupy him from 1138 until his death ten years later. There is a theoretical possibility that Bernard may have had some contact with this stream of thought either through his friendship with William or by his own reading, but there is no evidence sufficient to impose a positive conclusion.

The influence of Augustine on the thought of Bernard was, as has been already noted, vast and diffuse. Augustine left no systematic explanation of the Song of Songs, which he regarded as a most difficult book,[16] and would probably have agreed with Jerome's suggestion that it be left till last in the reading of the Bible.[17] Augustine's attitude to the book, like that of his fellow-Africans Cyprian and Tertullian, was theological or ecclesiological, strongly shaped by the specific requirement of polemic. Apart from the occasional foray, Augustine's expositions were not principally mystical. He was not, furthermore, at home with the Logos-mysticism typical of Alexandria and its dependents, so that the intimacies described in the Song of Songs seemed to him as defective in solid theological content. Nevertheless he has had some influence on the compilation of Bernard's sermons, but it has been chiefly as a restraint on the unbridled use of sponsal imagery. Through the incorporation of strands of augustinian thought into his exposition, Bernard has protected himself from an exclusive use of one line of imagery by interweaving complimentary concepts into a

16. Ibid., following the unpublished dissertation of P. Simon, *Sponsa Christi: Die Deutung der Braut des Hohenliedes in der vornizänischen griechischen Theologie und in der lateinischen Theologie des 3. und 4. Jahrhunderts* (Bonn, 1951) p. 68.

17. Ep 117.12 (CSEL 55:302–303).

cumulative synthesis. Augustine, therefore, is to be viewed as a counterpoise to the prevailing marital metaphor, opening the door to the development of other equally important aspects of the Christian's ascent to God.[18]

More certain is the likelihood that Bernard knew Gregory's *Super Cantica canticorum expositio* and its continuation by Robert of Tombelaine.[19] Gregory's treatment follows the precedent set by Origen, interpreting the canticle as an allegory of the soul's union with God, and making use of its obscurities to allege points of practical instruction in good living. Although Gregory's writing is no more wooden than usual, it seems heavier by contrast with the spirit of the book itself. Its influence on Bernard's own presentation must be adjudged general and diffuse rather than a matter of literary dependence.

The intervening centuries saw a gradual increase in the selection of the Song of Song as a text for comment. By the twelfth century it was by no means uncommon to find an author of solid theological reputation willing to dedicate himself to this task.[20] In this matter, as in others, Bernard seems relatively unfamiliar with or uninfluenced by the writings of his contemporaries. Even William of St Thierry, his close friend and associate over many decades, does not seem to have been one of his principal literary sources. Of course, it is possible to suggest a more subtle and less formal process of mutual formation. Bernard may have encouraged his stolider companion to greater verve and fervour in his writing, and in return may have received not only a constant

18. There are at least twenty-five references to the augustinian corpus in Leclercq's listings of sources and allusions, *Recueil 1:* 281–295; the debt is probably greater than these literary signals convey.

19. PL 79:471–548.

20. Cf. Ohly, *Hohenlied-Studien*, pp. 92–120.

briefing (tendentious though it was) on theological movements, but also something of William's dominant augustinianism to balance his own passionate lyricism. The hypothesis of reciprocal influence is attractive, but on present evidence remains in the sphere of conjecture. The first thing, therefore, that can be said about the literary precedents of the *Sermones super Cantica canticorum* is that they can be understood in terms of traditional origenist exposition on the Song of Songs which was enjoying something of a second spring at the time Bernard was writing. The fact that Bernard moved further away from the normal genre of scriptural exposition, however, means that other forces also shaped his medium.

A supplementary line of influence may help us to understand the literary quality of Bernard's masterpiece. Bernard opted not to write a commentary, but to write a series of sermons. Here, Bernard's models are those Fathers of the Church whose sermons were recorded for posterity. It was a genre with which the Abbot of Clairvaux was increasingly familiar during the latter half of his literary career.[21] Taking as his starting-point the work of such great western preachers as Leo the Great, Augustine, and Caesarius of Arles, Bernard was able to address himself to the sacred text in such a way that he was not rigidly bound to it. Instead he was able to include the conditions and reactions of his imagined audience and so open to involve himself in any theme which attracted him. Such digressions are not

---

21. Cf. J. Leclercq, 'La tradition des sermons liturgiques de S. Bernard', *Recueil 2:* 203–260; 'L'art de la composition dans les sermons de S. Bernard', *Recueil 3:* 137–162; 'Sur le caractère littéraire des sermons de S. Bernard', *Recueil 3:* 163–210; 'Introduction' in SBO 4:119–159; *Love of Learning,* pp. 168–170. See also Alberich Altermatt, 'Christus pro nobis: Die Christologie Bernhards von Clairvaux in den "Sermones per annum"', ASOC 33 (1977) 3–176.

accidental aberrations in an otherwise polished presentation; they are deliberate modifications made possible by the looseness of a (pseudo-) oral format.[22]

The sermon is a typically monastic genre, drawing its inspiration from those models of patristic preaching relayed to the monks in liturgy and *lectio* and institutionalised in the conferences given in chapter and elsewhere by the abbot and his delegates. The form assumed by such addresses was often that of the commentary — the speaker would take as his theme a scriptural text, or the Rule of Benedict, or some other traditional writing which had just been read. Perhaps there was an element of humility in this, the abbot did not presume to teach of his own authority, but simply expounded existing doctrine, aiding its comprehension and applying it to the lives of his listeners. Perhaps it was simply an adaptation of normal pedagogic method. In any case, the monastic sermon came to be a distinctive form of discourse which would take its beginning from a text already sown in the minds of the listeners and could include any development judged suitable for their spiritual profit.

Of course most such compositions were evanescent. Few would have been written out beforehand and the most we can hope is that the more outstanding examples would have been preserved in summary form, either by their authors or by those who heard them. This is a likely explanation of many of Bernard's *Sententiae* and some of the shorter sermons *De diversis*. Despite the quality of their contents, such familiar discourses were not, for the

22. Cf. J. Leclercq, 'Were the Sermons on the Song of Songs delivered in Chapter', Introduction to CF 7. On Bernard's deliberate mimicry of an oral style see E. Stiegman, 'The Literary Genre of Bernard of Clairvaux's *Sermons super Cantica canticorum*', in *Simplicity*, pp. 68–93, especially pp. 73–77.

most part, considered sufficiently finished to be circulated in written form. If they were published, they had
to be re-written according to literary criteria.

In Bernard's case the process of perfecting even his
literary sermons continued till the end of his life. It is also
possible that instead of the published sermons being more
polished versions of what was preached, the process could
have worked in the opposite direction; the oral presentations
were simply the by-products of a primarily literary endeavor.

It was chiefly the liberty inherent in the sermon
genre which attracted Bernard; it offered him the
possibility of powerfully imprinting his own personality
on what he was writing. Berengar's outrage that Bernard
should have interrupted his discourse with an expression
of personal grief (SC 26), can be rebutted with a
reminder of the sort of writing which Bernard was attempting.[23] It offered him the opportunity of giving expression to himself in a way almost no other genre could.

Thus, the sermons of Bernard are unique because he
made of them vehicles of his own self-expression. This seems
to have been recognised by Robert of Basevorn when, in
1322, he wrote his treatise *The Form of Preaching*.

> Now about St. Bernard. It must be realized that his
> method is 'without method', execeeding the style
> and capability of almost all men of genius. He more
> than the rest stresses Scripture in all his sayings, so
> that scarcely one statement is his own which does not
> depend on an authority in the Bible or on a
> multitude of authorities. His procedure is always de-
> vout, always artful. He takes a certain theme or
> something in place of it — i.e., some matter which he
> intends to handle — and begins it artfully, divides it
> into two, three or many members, confirms it, and

23. *Liber Apologeticus* (PL 178:1863d–1864a).

ends it, using every rhetorical color so that the whole work shines with a double glow, earthly and heavenly; and this, as it seems to me, invites to devotion those who understand more feelingly, and helps more in the novel methods which we are now discussing.[24]

Bernard's art is such that his eloquence overflows the categories of standard presentation and he is able to communicate something of the fire of his own devotion.

The *Sermons on the Song of Songs* are best approached through his other sermons, most of which are contemporaneous with the major work and mirror some of its pre-occupations. These sermons relate naturally to the patristic tradition of pastoral preaching and to the specific monastic mode of text-exposition. Bernard was not interested in writing a commentary on the Song of Songs, as such an endeavour would later be understood. Instead he was engaged in giving a synthetic presentation of his vision of the ascent of the soul to God through the medium of a series of sermons based on the biblical book which seemed to epitomise that ascent, the Song of Songs.

Comparing monastic commentaries on the Song of Songs with those produced by later scholastics, Jean Leclercq signals six characteristic typical of the former and certainly present in Bernard's work:

1. Monastic commentaries manifest a preference for the personal over the collective interpretation of the text.
2. Monastic commentaries tend to concentrate on love rather than on faith or revealed truth.
3. Monastic commentaries emphasise the presence of Christ in the soul rather than his presence in the

24. Translated by Leopold Krul in James J. Murphy (ed.) *Three Medieval Rhetorical Arts* (Berkeley: University of California Press, 1971). The text quoted is from Chapter XII of the treatise, p. 131.

Church through the Incarnation.

4. Monastic commentaries place greater emphasis on the human response to God's love rather than on divine love itself.

5. The tone of monastic commentaries is usually more ardent and the language more poetic than in scholastic commentaries.

6. It usually happened that monastic commentaries were incomplete at the time of the author's death.[25]

Bernard did not write with a view to providing an exegesis of the text or a theological synthesis. He aimed, rather, 'to teach thirsting souls how to seek the one by whom they are themselves sought'.[26] His fundamental motivation was the *propositum aedificandi*, the intention of building up and strengthening the lives of his readers.[27] It is in this sense that he spoke about the 'moral' meaning of the text.[28] This is not so much 'ethical theory' as a practical guide to the living of the realities about which the text speaks.[29] He hoped that his readers would find in his words instruction in living,[30] that their understanding would be seasoned with a 'moral salt'.[31]

Accordingly, in searching for literary antecedents to Bernard's *Sermones*, it is important to remember also their uniqueness which stemmed from the author's particular endowments as much as from the wealth of solid

25. Jean Leclercq, 'Le commentaire de Gilbert de Stanford sur le cantique des cantiques', *Analecta 1:* pp. 205–230, especially pp. 206–207.

26. SC 84.7(SBO 2:306,28–29).

27. SC 27.1 (SBO 1:181,17).

28. SC 16.1 (SBO 1:103,5), SC 86.1 (SBO 2:317,7).

29. The phrase is drawn from William O. Paulsell, 'Ethical Theory in the Sermons on the Song of Songs', *Chimaera*, pp. 12–22.

30. SC 39.1 (SBO 2:18–19). Cf. PP 1.3 (SBO 4:189, 28–190,2).

31. SC 80.1 (SBO 2:277,10).

teaching which he was determined to cram into his exposition.

> In writing the *Sermones in Cantica* [sic], St Bernard
> has created a genre. His first originality has been to
> produce a commentary which, unlike all the ancient
> and medieval Latin commentaries, does not follow
> the text word for word. The only earlier commentator
> who resembles him in this is Origen, and this parallel
> does his great credit. The second originality of Ber-
> nard, one which distinguishes him from Origen, has
> been the introduction into a commentary which is
> already loose, of a large number of digressions which
> have nothing to do with the Song. It is these digres-
> sions which make it an absolutely unique commen-
> tary, without precedent or following.[32]

CONTENT

In attempting to grasp the breadth of Bernard's doctrinal and ascetical teaching, it is important to remember
that he was not a systematic thinker. Trying to draw a
logical map of the ground he covered in his *Sermons on
the Song of Songs* is not an easy task, since there is much
in these sermons which evades classification. If some
aspects of Bernard's thought are obscure and some connections tenuous, it still remains possible to say a little
about the fundamental patterns of presentation.

The key concept of the *Sermons on the Song of
Songs* is love. This is evident not only from the centrality
of love in christian theology but also from the content of
the biblical book on which Benard was commenting and
from his own predilection for the topic. In particular,
Bernard was concerned with the *experience* of love which
is dominated by the dialectic of presence and absence.

32. Translated from J. Leclercq, *Études*, p. 122.

The love which Bernard regarded as primary is divine love, so that the principal focus throughout the *Sermons on the Song of Songs* might be described as the vicissitudes of the soul's love for the Word.

The theological basis of Bernard's approach is to be found in the absolute primacy of God's love over any human merit (SC 83) and the all-pervading presence of divine grace (SC 67).[33] It is God who has taken the initiative in the Incarnation (SC 6) and who has sent the Holy Spirit to stimulate human beings to seek him (SC 8, 14). Christ continually acts for the good of the soul, nourishing it and sustaining it in its search (SC 21, 33) and modifying his interventions to conform to its needs (SC 31, 45). Whatever love is experienced by the soul is God's gift.

To sustain this position, Bernard includes a number of christological developments which are among the most beautiful in the entire series of sermons. He speaks of the Holy Spirit as the kiss of the Father and the Son (SC 8), of the mutual inherence and glory which is theirs (SC 71, 76). He develops the theme of the beauty of Christ, 'the flower of the field' (SC 45, 47), and how much he is beloved of the angels (SC 19). Christ as Word incarnate does not fear to empty himself out of love for humankind (SC 70, 28) and to endure grave sufferings (SC 43, 61) so as to demonstrate that he has care not only for angels but also for human beings (SC 53). Thus he is the mediator between God and humanity (SC 2), the source of all virtues and knowledge (SC 13), of wisdom justice, holiness and redemption (SC 22), of life and fruitfulness (SC 48). The love of the Word is powerful enough to heal human ills (SC 83) and the name of Jesus is light, food, and medicine (SC 15).

33. Cf. M. Casey, 'Nature and Grace in Saint Bernard of Clairvaux', *Tjurunga* 23 (1982) 39–49.

It is also important for the recipient of grace to be possessed of self-knowledge (SC 35–37), and thus Bernard includes in his presentation a number of anthropological developments which view humanity as located between material creation and the spiritual world (SC 5), formed in the image of God (SC 24–26) and enjoying, through the innate nobility of the soul, a certain natural affinity with the divine (SC 80–83). But Bernard also clearly recognises that the spiritual potential of the human being is not yet fully realised, since he dwells in a region which does not foster spiritual growth (SC 38). Hence it is to the future that both the individual and the Church must look for consummation (SC 68), allowing present struggles to be set in perspective by the remembrance of heaven (SC 27, 31, 33, 59, 62).

The tension between the human being's earthly condition and his heavenly destiny means that there is variation in spiritual experience and progress. This *alternatio* or *vicissitudo* (SC 17, 21, 32, 51, 74) is present at all phases of growth and is understood as the constant switching, in spiritual effort, from the doing of good and the delight in virtue, on the one hand, to the struggle against vice, the endurance of suffering and the repentance of evil done, on the other. There is a dialectic between fear and hope (SC 6). Furthermore, Bernard recognises that there are different stages in the spiritual pursuit which must be understood and their sequence respected (SC 3–4, 10, 19–20, 23, 33, 57, 78). The soul has its seasons which direct which efforts are most likely to foster growth (SC 58).

Bernard takes occasion, during the *Sermons on the Song of Songs,* to speak of the good works in which he would see his readers abound. Repentance and the practice of virtue precede close union with God (SC 6); hence there is a need to avoid complacency (SC 8), to grow in the knowledge both of God and of self (SC 35–36) and to be permeated by discretion (SC 50). For this, guidance and correction are required (SC 19, 42). Furthermore one has to remain vigilant (SC 57), with pure intention (SC 40, 70), one's outlook on life shaped by the twin forces of memory and hope (SC 62). One needs perseverance (SC 23) in order to keep cultivating one's vineyard and preventing its deterioration (SC 63). Among the various virtues, humility is given special emphasis. It is present-ed in its relationship to modesty (SC 86), innocence (SC 45), patience (SC 34), and gentleness (SC 69). Such meekness is supplemented by a zeal for justice (SC 70, 30) and expressed in a will for peace with those among whom one lives (SC 29) and the avoidance of sterile debate (SC 22). It is a matter of compassion, encourage-ment, and gratitude (SC 9–12). Above all, Bernard recommends to his readers a life that is characterised by faith, works, and contemplation (SC 51) in which there is an active searching after God (SC 33, 75, 84–85) and a genuine love which carries the searcher towards full union (SC 9, 79).

Bernard speaks also of the negative elements in spiritual growth, the necessity of fear to complement hope (SC 6–7, 54), a recognition of the reality of divine wrath (SC 35) and the prospect of judgment (SC 55). He understands clearly how the flesh acts as a barrier be-tween humanity and the realisation of its hopes (SC 56) and how the native nobility of the soul can be progress-ively eroded (SC 26). He speaks with great vigour about the onslaught of enemies (SC 39) and the dangers and temptations which each must confront (SC 30). Thus he details excessive care for one's own well-being (SC 30, 33), a tendency to extremism (SC 64), unworthy pastors (SC 77), slanderers and flatterers (SC 63), heretics and philosophers (SC 22, 32, 33, 36–37, 65–66, 80) and the attacks of malign spirits (SC 17, 29).

Thus, even within the apparent disorder of Bernard's unmethodical presentation, a substantial body of teaching is communicated, with a minimum of repetition, except where the author wished to approach a subject from a different angle. Each reader will have his own list of omissions; these can, however, be explained by the unfinished state of the work as well as by inferring blindspots in the spiritual vision of the author.

What is interesting, granted the fictional monastic scenario in which Bernard has set his sermons, is the fact that the doctrine proposed is not esoterically monastic. Like much else in the tradition of latin monasticism, the *Sermons on the Song of Songs* attach themselves to the mainline of christian theology. With one or two minor exceptions, Bernard does not address himself to the particular problems of monks and monastic Orders. Instead he concentrates on the more universal theme of proposing a theoretical framework for the soul's ascent to God. It is true that Bernard does not write explicitly about what has become to be called 'the lay state' nor, apart from his rejection of heresy in SC 65–66, much about marriage. But his diatribes against what he terms the 'world' and the 'flesh', understood in the light of traditional usage, apply also to those who are not monastics. The problem of applying the teaching of the *Sermons on the Song of Songs* to other vocations within the Church is not with the content of the sermons but with the initiation required for understanding the language Bernard employed. It was not a language exclusive to monks, it was common to the whole Church; its sources were not arcane monastic documents but the writings and sermons of the great pastors of the souls, intended for the general body of the faithful.

Bernard's teaching is monastic, but not in the narrow sense later assigned to this term. It is an experiential, communitarian, and traditional re-formulation of standard christian teaching. It is not necessary to be a monk to understand it, but it is necessary to enter wholeheartedly into the world of thought of which it is a part. Perhaps the most efficient way of doing this is to study one theme in detail.

THE THEME OF DESIRE FOR GOD

The purpose of this present study is to explore Bernard's understanding of the nature and working of human desire for God. As will be seen, this is not a peripheral notion in his view of spirituality, but one of the most familiar ways of understanding that spark of unfulfilled love which divine grace causes to exist in the human heart. It was a concept already familiar from the Scriptures, especially the Psalms, developed in monastic texts such as the *Conferences* of Cassian and the *Rule* of Benedict, and reaching something of a climax in the writings of Augustine and Gregory the Great.[34] What Bernard did was simply to embrace the theme of desire and to allow it to exercise a dominant influence on his explanation of the dynamics of spiritual life.

The Song of Songs, particularly in its interplay of presence and absence, was seen by Bernard and his contemporaries as a dramatic presentation of the dialectic of desire. This is one of the reasons for its popularity at this time, as Jean Leclercq notes.

> But in reality, what we know of eschatological desire in milieus consecrated to a life of prayer, sufficiently explains their special affection for the Canticle of Canticles. What they saw in it above all was the expression of that desire. The Canticle is the poem of

34. Cf. M. Casey, 'Spiritual Desire in the Gospel Homilies of Saint Gregory the Great', CS 16 (1981) 297–314.

the pursuit which is the basis for the whole program of monastic life: *quaerere Deum,* a pursuit which will reach its end only in eternity but which already obtains fulfilment here in an obscure possession; and the latter increases desire which is the form love takes here below.[35]

In the chapters which follow we shall study Bernard's use of *desiderium* and its equivalents in his *Sermons on the Song of Songs,* with a view to arriving at some general understanding of the notion. From this basic fund of data we shall move into the principal aspect of desire, as Bernard understood this, together with the images he used to evoke its reality. This will lead us to an exploration of the themes of love, feeling, devotion, compunction, and others. Taken together, this will enable us to formulate a comprehensive picture of the linguistic field surrounding desire and thus begin to form some basis on which a theological synthesis may be built.

The anthropology of desire must then be studied. For this it is necessary to appreciate Bernard's theology of human nature. The fact is that he traces the origin of human desire for God to his creation in the divine image. Because God formed humankind with a capacity for and compatibility with himself, it follows that any human movement toward God is a direct result of this gift. It is not a consciously-willed initiative from the human side, nature — as it were — apart from grace, but a grace-inspired assent to a pre-elective tendency of being which impels him toward final glory. The significance of this approach is that it elevates desire above the level of an affective experience of yearning for the absolute and accords it an ontological reality; it is the movement of an incomplete being toward its divine completion.

35. *Love of Learning,* p. 92.

Thus is evoked the object of desire. If the human being is made with a deep inner void which can only be filled through an intimate interpersonal relationship with God, then spiritual desire necessarily leads to divine union. The traditional metaphor for this, which Bernard takes over, and which is already prompted by the text of the Song of Songs, is that of spiritual marriage. The soul thirsts for union with the Word. All its strivings are directed to becoming, in the words of 1 Cor 6:17, 'one spirit' with him. Such a union is not possible during our time of exile and pilgrimage, but is to be realised in the future. Thus is introduced the theme of heaven, one of Bernard's strong emphases. He speaks of citizenship in the heavenly Jerusalem, of having the capacity to see God, of following the ascended Christ into glory, there being transformed and initiated into a life of rest and delight. All this is what the soul desires, as Bernard understands it.

But that is all in the future. Bernard had much to say about how desire is experienced in this present life. The key concept in his understanding is that the form in which desire is experienced is subject to change. Authentic desire for God is not exempt from the *vicissitudo* or *alternatio* typical of all human endeavours in this life. Sometimes it will be strongly coloured by the evil and limitation which sin has brought into the world and then it will take the form of a great yearning for liberation from constraining forces and have a practical expression similar to 'fear of the Lord'. At other times desire will have a more positive hue. It may be suffused by the progressive realisation of grace within it. In such cases it will be experienced as reformation of life, self-transcendence, and wisdom. Bernard understood desire as a dialectic which is fed by both the experience of the presence of its object by the apprehension and dread caused by estrangement. Desire is alternately delighted love and fearful emptiness. Neither one pole nor the other can be dispensed with if there is to be genuine growth. Like the bride in the Song of Songs, the soul has to be prepared to cope with a range of varied experiences in its search for God. What matters is not which species of experience is paramont at any given time, but that the search continue.

It will be possible for us to conclude, as our investigations proceed, that Bernard's *Sermons on the Song of Songs* contain a complete and coherent teaching on the subject of desire for God. Understanding this theme in its broad meaning, we must affirm that it is the key to the comprehension of Bernard's treatment of the *Song of Songs,* a unifying factor in a bewildering display of spiritual riches. At the heart of Bernard's practical, ascetical, and mystical teaching is the conviction that the human being finds fulfilment only in coming close to God. Desire for God is the experiential grasp of this truth.

CHAPTER THREE

THE VOCABULARY OF DESIRE

I N A WRITER as sensitive to style as Bernard of Clairvaux, word choice is a valuable guide to the direction
of thought. By a process of analysis and re-assembly,
it is possible to arrive at a first appreciation of the extent
and composition of a particular strand of thinking in relationship to his total vision. Where a theme is linguisti-
cally linked to most of an author's major pre-occupations, and where it occurs throughout the whole range of
his publications, the presupposition must be that such a
theme is a key-element in his personal philosophical synthesis.

It cannot be emphasised too strongly, in beginning
this analysis, that the words chosen by Bernard are not
specific to him. For the most part they belong to a traditional vocabulary of desire which had its roots in the
writings of John Cassian and came to a climax in the

works of Augustine and Gregory.[1] It was standard ecclesiastical vocabulary, in direct continuity with secular
usage, which became normative for the mystical writers
of the early Middle Ages,[2] and eventually moulded the
vernacular expressions employed, in a different context,
by the troubadors.[3]

Notwithstanding the fact that Bernard availed
himself of this common fund of language, he remained
the master of his own words. He used the tradition
creatively, so that it is possible to gain an insight into his
personal synthesis by examining his choice of words and
the associations between them. He is, for example, quite
different in style from John of Fécamp, although the two

1. On this, see the data provided under *desiderium* in ThLL vol.
5: cols 697–702. Jean Leclercq gives a list of terms in Gregory in 'Un
centon de Fleury sur les devoirs des moines', *Analecta 1:* pp. 7–90;
cf. p. 90. It is important, in this matter also, to appreciate the formative role of the latin Vulgate, where one may find the foundations of Bernard's vocabulary, especially in the Psalms. Another key
source was Augustine's much-read *In Iohannis Evangelium Tractatus CXXIV,* Corpus Christianorum Series Latina #36 (Turnhout,
Brepols, 1954). Perhaps more than any other of Augustine's works,
this series of treatises repeatedly raises the issue of desire for God and
discusses it in a manner both profound and lyric. Many of its pages
were familiar reading to monks of the Middle Ages, both in the liturgy and elsewhere, who found it a means both of reading the
Gospel of John and of being formed by another great master of
spiritual life. Some illustrative references to texts from both
Augustine and Gregory the Great will be made in what follows in an
effort to demonstrate something of the provenance of Bernard's
vocabulary and thought.

2. Cf. J. Leclercq, *Vocabulaire,* pp. 117–121: 'La contemplation
de désir'.

3. Much remains to be clarified concerning the possibility or
probability of influence or reciprocal influence between the world of
monastic theology and that of the literature of the court. Cf. J.
Leclercq, 'Champagne as a Garden of Love', *Monks and Love,* pp.
109–136.

authors wrote from within the same tradition about the same topics and employed the same traditional expressions. The end product is manifestly distinct, reflecting in each case something of the particular philosophy of each author.[4] The same could be said about many of the works falsely attributed to Bernard; they do not stand up to close scrutiny; Bernard's style and way with words is hard to reproduce.

Let us now examine in detail the range of vocabulary used by Bernard with reference to desire for God.

DESIDERIUM

The most general term used by Bernard for desire is its direct Latin equivalent, *desiderium*. He also uses the corresponding verb and other cognates.[5] It cannot be said that *desiderium*, as such, becomes a technical term. It is a descriptive word: the value of the reality it describes is neutral in itself; it becomes possessed of either positive or negative qualities according to its object. A desire for good things is good; a desire for evil is itself evil. Although Bernard often uses the bare word with implicit spiritual connotations to be gleaned from the context, other texts demonstrate that he is aware of the primitive meaning of *desiderium*, that of needing or calling out for. Thus he can write *Sermo finem desiderat*

4. Cf. J. Leclercq, *Fécamp*, pp. 105–106. The author qualifies the style of John of Fécamp as quieter, less passionate, more sober, and more restrained than Bernard's.

5. While it is true that the verb *desiderare* is met less frequently than its noun, both in Bernard's writings and generally throughout the literature (except in the Vulgate), it is difficult to accept the statement of Jacques Blanpain that the verb is 'very rare' in the *Sermons on the Song of Songs*. Cf. J. Blanpain, 'Language mystique, expression du désire', COCR 36 (1974) 45–68, 226–247; 37 (1975) 145–166. The statement occurs in the first part of the article, p. 53.

with the meaning, 'It is time to finish this sermon' or 'This sermon needs to be finished'.[6] Far from regarding desire as such as an unqualified good, he sees clearly that it can be good only when it is directed toward appropriate objects. In many cases he sees desires as obstacles to the soul's growth, when they are directed toward things which are evil, illicit, carnal, or wordly.[7]

Bernard understood spiritual desire as something coming from the very heart of human being. The 'organ'

---

6. SC 69.8 (SBO 2:207,7).

7. Cf. SC 31.6 (SBO 1:223,7-8), SC 35.1 (SBO 1:249,5-8). *Desiderium* is simply an objective lack which is sometimes mirrored in a subjective want. Its neutrality is best indicated in VNat 5.7 (SBO 4:234,3-5): 'Our desires appear to be especially directed to three objects, to what is proper, to what is convenient and to what is delightful (*quod decet, quod expedit, quod delectat*). These are the things for which we yearn, all of us for all of them, though some of us desire one more, others another.' On *carnalia et sacularia desideria* cf. Dil 13 (SBO 3:129,23), Div 69.1 (SBO 6a:303,13-14), Div 69.2 (SBO 6a:304,11-12). *Saecularia desideria* seems to have Tit 2:12 as its immediate provenance, cf. Div 54 (SBO 6a:279,5). On *carnalia desideria* cf. Dil 23 (SBO 3:139,7-8), *In celebratione adventus* 3, 4, 7, 10 (SBO 6a:12-19), Div 12.2 (SBO 6a:128,9), Div 14.4 (SBO 6a: 117,7), Div 28.4 (SBO 6a:206,19 and 22), Div 28.5 (SBO 6a:207,21). In Div 32.3 (SBO 6a:220,14-15), Bernard sees carnal desires as the result of original sin: *Carnalia desideria sunt peccati poena*. Other texts include Div 32.4 (SBO 6a:221,8-11), Div 77 (SBO 6a:316,13-15), Div 101 (SBO 6a:368,15). On *desideria carnis*, which seems to be a reflection of Gal 5:16, see Div 123.1 (SBO 6a:400,3). On *illicita desideria* see Div 72.2 (SBO 6a:308,11-12). On *desideria mala*, Div 75 (SBO 6a:313,17). On *desideria prava* see VNat 2.3 (SBO 4:206,9-10). See also Div 9.3 (SBO 6a:119, 19-20), Div 13 (SBO 6a:75,6); Div 85 (SBO 6a:327,4-5). It should be noted that the whole issue of discernment between good and evil inner processes had preoccupied monasticism from the very beginning. The works of Evagrius and John Cassian clearly spelled out the need for monks to distinguish between what was genuinely spiritual and what had a more mundane origin. We

of desire, often indicated by a subjective genitive, is
habitually designated as either the soul, *anima*,[8] or the

---

find an awareness of the duality of thoughts and desires also present
in the *Rule* of Benedict; spiritual desires are mentioned in 4.46 and
49.7, *desiderium carnis* in 4.59, 7.12, 7.23 and *malum desiderum*
in 7.24. In other examples the word has a neutral tone.

8. Many modern readers, formed in Cartesian dualism or influenced by the sentimental internalism of the Pietist movement
have difficulty in understanding what Bernard means by the term
anima, and feel that he has adopted a Platonic or Neo-Platonic viewpoint which fails to take seriously the bodily aspects of the human
condition. This is a concern which is evident throughout Emero
Stiegman's *Language of Ascetcism*. It is not, however, possible to
give a short answer to such a weighty question, except to say that
Bernard's viewpoint must be considered in relation to his own situation. When he uses *anima* he does so in a variety of ways.
Sometimes, in passage taken from or framed about the Scriptures,
he uses *anima* in place of the personal pronoun, but with a
heightened affective coloration; this is a Semitic usage preserved in
the Vulgate. Thus SC 32.2 (SBO 1:234,17). More commonly, *anima*
is used when the spiritual aspect of the human person is to be emphasised (SC 45.7; SBO 2:54,15), original rectitude (SC 24.5; SBO
1:156,10–14) and dignity (SC 81.4; SBO 2:286,7). It is through the
soul that the human being has an affinity with the Word (SC 81.1;
SBO 2: 284,9, SC 81.11; SBO 2:291,21–22, SC 83.1; SBO
2:298,11–12). *Nullus enim Deo vicinior gradus inter omnes . . .
creaturas quam anima humana* (Div 9.2; SBO 6a:119,6–7). There is
no doubt that Bernard gives priority to the soul over the body, and
sees it as the link between concrete human existence and God. God
is the *anima animae* (Div 10.4; SBO 6a:123,25). 'Just as the soul is
the life of the body, so God is the life of the soul' (Div 47; SBO
6a:267,18). This is simply a recall of an augustinian theme: *In Ioan*
23.5 (CChr 36:234), 47.8 (408). The nearest Bernard gets to a
definition of the soul is the following not very satisfactory statement. 'The soul is that non-bodily and unseen substance which is
neither distinct from the bodily members nor formed by visible col-
ours', (SC 40.1; SBO 2:24,19–21). The soul is, for Bernard, the
dynamic factor in human existence, the source of all spiritual poten-
cy. 'To the soul alone belongs that love by which one loves anything

heart, *cor.*[9] This traditional usage indicates something very important about the nature of desire for God. It is an inner movement, in no way limited to experienced emotional stimulation. This it why Bernard could see no inconsistency in attributing desire to the angels.[10] Desire has its origin deep within, but it is characterised by an externalising force which envelops the whole of human being. Bernard used a traditional phrase to indicate that he was carried along by desire, *desiderio feror.*[11] It is not a matter of following rational conclusions,[12] nor of being constrained by outward necessity,[13] but of consenting to be moved from within by a powerful spiritual force.

---

spiritually' (SC 75.9; SBO 2:252,11–13). It is the basis of the human capacity for God and the source of the appetite for the spiritual things (SC 80.2; SBO 2:278,4–6). It is true that Bernard often speaks slightingly of the body, in comparison with the soul, but this is usually in passages where he is pursuing a moral theme and arguing that spiritual values are not to be allowed to be submerged under the demands of the world and of the flesh. In his more reflective moments, he speaks of it as a boon, (SC, 82.3; SBO 2:294,7) and does not hesitate to draw on its several functions as analogies for the operations of the soul (SC 36.4; SBO 2:6,11, SC 63.6; SBO 2:165, 14–15). On this whole subject cf. Hiss, *Die Anthropologie,* pp. 66–137. On the soul as the subject of desire, cf. SC 1.8 (SBO 1:6, 13–16), SC 28.13 (SBO 1:201,25–26), SC 31.4 (SBO 1:221.27–30), SC 31.5 (SBO 1:222,3–5), SC 62.2 (SBO 1:155,16).

9. Cf. SC 7.8 (SBO 1:35,20), SC 32.2 (SBO 1:227,12), SC 74.7 (SBO 2:244, 6–8) Div 11.1 (SBO 6a:124,11), Div 28.5 (SBO 6a: 207, 20), Div 69.1 (SBO 6a:303,13).

10. Cf. SC 27.7 (SBO 1:187,10), OS.4.2 (SBO 5:356,8), Div 123.2 (SBO 6a:401,14).

11. SC 74.7 (SBO 2:244,4). Cf. SC 74.4 (SBO 2:242,7): *anima amans votis fertur, trahitur desideriis.* Cf Div 25.4 (SBO 6a: 190,12–13), Dil 31 (SBO 3:146,1), Div 70 (SBO 6a:305,16–17), Div 14.3 (SBO 6a:136,13).

12. SC 9.2 (SBO 1:43,11): *desiderio feror, not ratione.* Cf. SC 75.1 (SBO 2:247,19–21).

13. Cf.Asc 1.1 (SBO 5:123,12).

Thus the person assents to be passive under the influence of desire. It is the free choice of the will which makes concordance with spiritual desire different from being overwhelmed by carnal passion. But once the will has shaped the response, there is a similar sense of impulsion. Desire has drawing-power,[14] It is able to bear the soul aloft on its wings.[15] It is characterised as bold,[16] impatient,[17] vehement.[18] Moreover, desire has the capacity to increase its force. It grows,[19] and will continue to grow without restriction, even in eternity. It is an all-consuming appetite[20] which knows no satiation and never leads to a sense of having indulged too much.[21] Thus desire has, for Bernard, an element of *epektasis* noted in the teaching of Gregory of Nyssa.[22]

14. SC 58.1 (SBO 2:127,23–24): *trahi a sponso est ab ipso accipere desiderium quo trahatur.* Div 70 (SBO 6a:305,16):*trahor desiderio.*

15. SC 32.2 (SBO 1:227,22–23). The metaphor is traditional, cf. Gregory the Great *In Ezekielem homiliae* I.3.2 (PL 76:806c).

16. SC 83.3 (SBO 2:299,26–27): *audax desiderio.*

17. SC 28.13 (SBO 1:202,1–4), SC 51.3 (SBO 2:85,17).

18. SC 32.3 (SBO 1:227,25–26), SC 58.2 (SBO 2:128,1), SC 72.6 (SBO 2:229,20), OS 5.5 (SBO 5:364,22).

19. SC 75.1 (SBO 2:247,7–8).

20. SC 31.7 (SBO 1:223,22–23).

21. Cf. SC 57.6 (SBO 2:123,9); the word used to signify over-indulgence is *fastidium.*

22. No suggestion is being made that Bernard is dependent on Gregory of Nyssa for his teaching on this matter: Gregory the Great is a more proximate source. On Gregory of Nyssa's teaching, cf. Daniel O'Donovan, 'Gregory of Nyssa's *Epektasis*', *Colloquium* 4 (1970) 54–61. André Ardouin, 'Desire for God according to Gregory of Nyssa', *Tjurunga* 17 (1979) 89–108. Placide Deseille has written three columns on the subject in DSp 4:785–788. The theme also occurs in the West, for instance, Augustine, *Sermon* 369.29 (PL 39:1633a) It is more extensively developed in the writings of Gregory the Great. *In Evangelia homilia* 36.2 (PL 76:1267a): 'Even while spiritual delights bring satisfaction, they increase desire in the mind, since the more their savour is appreciated, the more the object

On the other hand, there is a strong undercurrent of the conventional sense that desire is necessarily connected with the experience of absence or privation: *desiderium est rerum absentium concupiscentia.*[23] Love and joy are what one feels when a loved one is present; in absence this love expresses itself through yearning and desire. Such a view is found several times in the *Sermons on the Song of Songs.* Some examples follow.

> Love grows strong when its object is near; when it is absent, love languishes. This is evident in the case of one who loves passionately. He necessarily experiences a restlessness in his mind due to impatient desire, whenever the one whom he loves is absent. So wholly taken up with waiting is such a one that even speed itself seems slow to him.[24] When the promise of the kingdom of heaven was given, human beings came to understand that they had here no abiding city, and then they began with all

---

of such intense love is grasped'. Cf. *In Ezekielm* I.8.15 (PL 76:860b), where Gregory is speaking of the joy of the angels in heaven: 'It may be asked how it is that the desire for the vision of God co-exists with such repletion, and how such repletion co-exists with desire. Such desire does not lead to pain nor does such repletion lead to a sense of having over-indulged'. The same idea is discussed at greater length in *Moralia* 18.91 (PL 76:94b): 'The angels both see God and yet desire to see him; they thirst to catch sight of him yet they do catch sight of him . . . But there is no anxiety in their desire, for even while they desire they experience repletion, but in this repletion there is no sense of having over-indulged, since even though they experience repletion, yet they still desire.'

23. Augustine, *In Psalmo 118.*8 (PL 37:1522). See also *In Ps 62.*5 (PL 36:750d–751a). The thought is also found in Cicero, *Tusc* 4.21: *desiderium sit libido eius qui nondum assit videndi.* In similar vein, Bede, *De grammatica* 7.270.24: *Desiderium est rerum absentium et nondum adeptarum concupiscentia utrorumque.*

24. SC 51.3 (SBO 2:85,15–19).

their energy to seek a future state. It was at this time that the voice of the turtle-dove first sounded in our land. For while the holy soul even now sighs for the presence of Christ, it bears the delay of the kingdom with poor grace and from afar calls out to that desired homeland with groans and sighs. . . . Why should not the absence of Christ move me to many tears and daily groaning? 'O Lord, all my desire is before you, and my groans are not hidden from you.'[25]

Bernard recognised that such apparent frustration of a keen desire is not an accidental condition deriving from interior or external mishaps. In line with the firm augustinian-gregorian tradition, he affirmed that such delay and deprivation is the normal means used by God to increase the intensity of the soul's yearning.

In so far as presence is experienced as a source of pleasure, so it must be expected that being deprived of this presence will cause pain. However, the result of the withdrawal of the object of love is an increase in desire. The more ardently you desire something, the more keenly you experience its absence.[26]

25. SC 59.4 (SBO 2:137,16–26). Cf. SC 31.6 (SBO 1:223,12–13), SC 33.11 (SBO 1:241,29–30), Ep 18.2 (SBO 7:67,20–21).

26. SC 51.1 (SBO 2:84,6–9): *subtractio nempe rei quam amas, augmentatio desiderii est.* The idea is often found in Augustine, for instance, *In Psalmo 123*. 3 (PL 37:1641), *In Ps 83*. 3 (PL 37:1057), *In Ps 148*.4 (PL 37:1940), *Sermo* 61 (PL 38:411), *Sermo* 170 (PL 38:932). It often recurs in the writings of Gregory the Great. *In evangelia homilia* 25.2 (PL 76:1190d): 'First one seeks what has not been found so that having found it, one will cling to it more tenaciously. As we have said previously, holy desires grow through delay *(dilatione crescunt)*.' See also *In Ev* 22.5 (PL 76:1177a). The approach is supplemented and reinforced by Bernard's teaching on the theme of *alternatio*, which will be discussed in a later chapter. Two important statements of this theme are SC 17.1 (SBO 1:98) and SC 74.7 (SBO 2:243–244).

As has already been said, it is the object of desire which determines its moral character. Human beings are differentiated, in Bernard's eyes, according to what they seek. One cannot live altogether without desire, since such a feeling is a necessary effect of the incompleteness of concrete human existence in this life. In fact, desire is an important element in growth, since the experience of incompleteness motivates the human being to see a greater fullness and richness of life. Desire becomes spiritual when one directs one's energies toward spiritual realities. When a human being desires God, he seeks the highest of possible goals, and the very nobility of his purpose has the effect of transforming his life, rendering it progressively more godly and open to the divine.

The appropriate objects of spiritual desire are expressed variously by Bernard. Sometimes he is quite general in fixing desire's terms of reference. 'All of us make an effort to go upward, we all tend to the top. It is above to which we all aspire; we all make an effort to reach the heights.'[27] 'The highest desire of the soul here on earth (*interim*) is . . . to see good things.'[28] Elsewhere he notes that notwithstanding the variety apparent in the objects of desire, all fundamentally are in quest of a richer and fuller life. It is life that is sought, above all, in everything that is pursued.[29] He speaks of the desire of becoming better and making progress, or of being fruitful in good actions.[30]

In other texts Bernard is more specific. Desire may be appropriately directed toward the future, to death,[31] to

27. Div 33.1 (SBO 6a:222,4–6).
28. QH 8.3 (SBO 4:427,24).
29. Div 29.2 (SBO 6a:211,15–16).
30. Cf. SC 49.7 (SBO 2:77,30), SC 58.1 (SBO 2:127,23–25), Div 25.4 (SBO 6a:190,14–15), Div 28.4 (SBO 6a:207,2).
31. PP 2.6 (SBO 5:195,24).

heaven,[32] or to the hope of eternal rewards.[33] In one text he speaks of an *appetitus gloriae*, employing an objective genitive,[34] in another, taking his cue from Phil 1:23, of longing 'to be dissolved and to be with Christ'.[35] But, fundamentally, desire aims at fuller experience,[36] to be gained from the presence of the Word,[37] from seeing Christ,[38] from finding God.[39] It is the prospect of union with God in his Word — described by Bernard in so many ways — which is the immediate cause of spiritual desire.

In a subsequent chapter we shall be discussing Bernard's view that the capacity for desire is not something earned, but something with which God has gratuitously endowed human nature. Desire for God is not something that a human being may generate for himself through the use of the intellect and the deployment of will. When Bernard speaks about desire for God, he rarely does so in the context of human effort and achievement, but nearly always with the implicit understanding that when a human being desires union with God, he is

32. SC 27.4 (SBO 1:184), Quad 6.1(SBO 4:378,7), Div 3.9 (SBO 6a:93,17–18), Div 8.6 (SBO 6a:115,5–6), Div 22.8 (SBO 6a:176, 11), Div 25.4 (SBO 6a:190,11), Div 29.2 (SBO 6a:211,13–18), Div 33.1 (SBO 6a:222,8), Div 103.1 (SBO 6a:371,15), Div 111.1 (SBO 6a:385, 8–9), Dil 30 (SBO 3:144,20–21). The theme is beautifully developed in Augustine, *Tractatus in evangelium* 30.7 (CChr 36:293). It is extremely common in Gregory the Great, for instance *In Ev* 11.2 (PL 76:1115c), *In Ev* 18.1 (PL 76:1150b), *In Ezekielem* I.3.9 (PL 76:809c). In a passage of *In Ev* 17.14 (PL 76:1146c), he reflects on the fact that there is a direct proportion between the growth in desire for heaven and the quenching of unspiritual desires; this will often appear in subsequent tradition.

33. SC 33.11 (SBO 1:241,27–28), Div 15.4 (SBO 6a:142,13).

34. Ded 4.6 (SBO 5:388,2).

35. SC 32.2 (SBO 1:227,7–8).

36. SC 1.11 (SBO 1:7,29–30): *inexperti inardescabt desiderio.*

37. SC 33.1 (SBO 1:234,10).

38. SC 28.13 (SBO 1:202,3). Cf. Div 115 (SBO 6a:392,14).

39. SC 84.1 (SBO 2:303,12).

aiming for something above his own range of accomplishment. His desire is, however, not unreasonable. It is the effect of the nature God has given him, and is, itself, an indication of God's ultimate plans for humanity. Human desire for union with God is but a mirroring of the divine desire which created the human race with no other purpose in view than that such a union should result. *Illius desiderium tuum creat.*

> No saying which can contribute to goodness, the practice of virtue or excellent behaviour, ought ever to be listened to carelessly, since this is the means by which the salvation which comes from God is revealed. When a pleasing and acceptable word comes your way, put aside all repugnance and listen to it with desire, for in this word the bridegroom himself is believed to come, and to come quickly. This is to say that he himself desires to come, for *it is his desire which creates yours.* The fact that you rush to give the word entry derives from the fact that he himself is in a hurry to come in. We were not the first to love but, as Scripture says, 'He first loved us'.[40]

Bernard returns to this theme in the following sermon.

> To be drawn by the bridegroom is to accept from him that desire by which he is himself drawn, the desire for good actions, the desire of producing fruit for the bridegroom. For such a one the bridegroom is the whole of life and to die is gain.[41]

The theme of God actively desiring close union with humanity is recurrent throughout Bernard's writings and

---

40. SC 57.6 (SBO 2:123,6–12).
41. SC 58.1 (SBO 2:127,23–25). Cf Dil 1 (SBO 3:119,19): *Causa diligendi Deum, Deus est.* Dil 21 (SBO 3:137,16): *Ipse facit ut desideres, ipse est quod desideras.* Dil 22 (SBO 3:137,18–21): *Ipse dat occasionem. Ipse creat affectionem; desiderium ipse consummat. Ipse fecit, vel potius factus est ut amaretur . . . Eius amor nostrum et praeparat et remunerat.*

has been called 'the supreme explanation of his spiritual teaching'.[42] It is an emphasis which is not found as strongly in Bernard's principal sources, and so must be regarded as somewhat characteristic. It certainly underlines the grace-filled character of desire, as something which rubs off on contact with Christ and grows stronger as the relationship is prolonged. It also ties in with the traditional idea that desire is already an indication of at least a partial possession of God, that in someway it contains within itself the seeds of its own fulfilment.[43]

Even this superficial examination of Bernard's employment of *desiderium* in continuity with traditional usage reveals something of the importance this concept played in Bernard's view of spirituality. A closer analysis of related linguistic strands permits us to view this synthesis in increasing detail.

ASSOCIATED METAPHORS AND IMAGES

As with Gregory the Great, the most persistent image used by Bernard to illustrate the nature and force of desire for God is that of heat. Desire is a flame, a fire which sears the soul, the most intense experience possible for a human being.[44] It is not merely an end in itself, but such burning desire has a purifying effect; it causes a change to take place in the person so that the desire itself

42. P. Dumontier, *S. Bernard et la Bible*, p. 39.
43. Cf. Augustine *In evanelium Ioannis* 18.7 (CChr 36:184), Gregory *In Ev* 30.1 (PL 76:1220c), OS 1.11 (SBO 5:336,8–9).
44. SC 84.1 (SBO 2:303,15). Cf. OS 5.5 (SBO 5:364,22). We also find the expression *inflammamur desiderio* in Augustine, *In evangelium Ioanis* 37.5 (CChr 36:338). Gregory the Great explicitly connects the flame of desire with the workings of the Holy Spirit, for instance, *In Ezekielem homiliae* I.2.12 (PL 76:800d), *In Ezek* I.5.8–10 (PL 76:824–825).

is progressively less mixed with selfish motives and the possibility of receiving God within is continually expanded.

It is right that the warmth of holy desire should go before God's face to each soul which he himself is about to visit. It consumes all the rust caused by vicious actions and thus prepares a place for the Lord. Hence the soul knows when the Lord is near when it feels itself set alight by that fire.[45]

Desire is often qualified by cognates of *ardere*, to burn. The epexegetical genitive *desiderii ardor* is frequent both in Bernard and in his major sources.[46] Desire causes the soul to become warm, *inardescant desiderio*.[47] *Fervor* can be used to replace *desiderium* or to qualify it.[48] Occasionally, stronger terms are employed such as *aestuare*,[49] *flagrare*,[50]

---

45. SC 31.4 (SBO 1:221,27–30) Cf. SC 74.6 (SBO 2:243,14).

46. SC 28.13 (SBO 1:202,1–4), SC 2.1 (SBO 1:8,20), SC 31.4 (SBO 1:221,27). Cf. *In celebratione adventus* 1 (SBO 6a:9,8), Dil 32 (SBO 3:146,15–16). Dil 37 (SBO 3:147,22): *ardens Deo;* SC 51.1 (SBO 2:84,9), SC 74.7 (SBO 2:244,7), SC 75.1 (SBO 2:247,19), SC 75.5 (SBO 2:250, 17). Div 4.3 (SBO 6a:96,1), Div 16.5 (SBO 6a:148,1–2), Div 16.6 (SBO 6a: 148,17). The suggestion made in ThLL 2:482,34 that *ardere* is linked to *aridus,* dry, parched, may point to some intrinsic relationship between desire and 'aridity' or desire and the image of thirst. But this is a question for the etymologists.

47. SC 1.11 (SBO 1:7,30). Cf. SC 57.5 (SBO 2:123,20), Div 1.3 (SBO 6a:75,6)—this text refers to evil desire—Div 23.3 (SBO 6a: 180,15).

48. SC 23.1 (SBO 1:138,23): *desiderium et fervorem,* an example of hendiadys. Cf. Div 14.4 (SBO 6a:137,6), in connection with carnal desire. Also Div 123.2 (SBO 6a:401,14).

49. SC 49.4 (SBO 2:75,15): *Mox redeat divino amore vehementissime flagrans et aestuans iustitiae zelo . . .* Cf.Dil 32 (SBO 3:146,15–16). Precedents can be found, for example, in Augustine, *In evangelium Ioannis* 3.20 (CChr 36:30), *In Ioan* 19.10 (CChr 36:191), *In Ioan* 19.11 (CChr 36:194). Gregory the Great, *In Ev* 24.6 (PL 76:1188d), *In Ev* 25.4 (PL 1192b), *In Ev* 40.2 (PL 76:1304a).

50. SC 41.2 (SBO 2:29,17), SC 52.6 (SBO 2:94,14), SC 67.3 (SBO 2:190,14 and 19), SC 67.8 (SBO 2:193,20), Div 89.2 (SBO 6a:

and their cognates.

Change in temperature seems, therefore, to be an indication of desire; so too is the change in the rate of breathing. Desire is also signified by a word-set which includes *adspirare* and *suspirare*.

> We usually find this word (*adspirare*) when we describe a desire that is vehement. For example, when we say 'He aspires to this honour or to that position'. Hence, this term designates a wonderful but not yet realised enrichment (*mira affutura affluentia*) and a certain vehemence of spirit for that day when not only our hearts but also our bodies will, each in its own way, become spiritual.[51]

It is difficult to find an adequate english equivalent for *suspirare* which is sufficiently void of foolish sentimental overtones to permit it to serve as a vehicle for Bernard's meaning. It can, of course, be translated by 'sighing' or 'yearning', so long as the reader bears constantly in mind that the sigh in question is not an indication of depressed resignation in the face of disappointment, but a strong and virile movement of desire which exerts enough force over the whole being of the individual as to effect modifications in respiration. It cannot be stressed too strongly that *suspirare* is associated more with spiritual exaltation and depth of feeling than with the weary acceptance of an eventless existence.

> To such a sighing soul, who prays frequently and without interruption and who distresses itself because of its desire, he comes sometimes who is the

---

336,4), Mart 5 (SBO 5:402,22): *provocatio flagrantissimi desiderii.* Cf. Augustine, *In Ioan* 62.6 (CChr 36:485).

51. SC 72.6 (SBO 2:229,18–23). Cf. Div 1.4 (SBO 6a:76,9–10), Div 2.8 (SBO 6a:85,25). Augustine *In Ioan* 34.7 (CChr 36:315), *In Ioan* 35.9 (CChr 36:320).

object of that desire. For he takes pity on the one who was seeking him so earnestly.[52]

The image of grief, introduced here, was also used by Bernard to convey something of the nature of desire for God. The sustained experience of living without the object of one's love causes the soul to grow weak and to lose its drive.[53] It becomes sad and upset at having to wait so long,[54] and bears the intervening period with poor grace.[55] So strong is the force of its desire that, even in the absence of the object of its attachment, alternative sources of satisfaction cannot take the place of the beloved. The soul is unsatisfied in its desire, yet it cannot find pleasure in giving itself to more proximate gratifications. That these progressively lose their appeal is one of the signs that, feelings notwithstanding, spiritual growth is taking place. But the process is painful and testing and the soul, in its emptiness, experiences long spells of ennui and *taedium*.[56]

Love that is strong and yet unable to receive fulfilment causes tears of frustation to flow, *flet ex desiderio*.[57] 'Why should the absence of Christ not move me to many tears and daily groaning? "O Lord, all my desire is before

---

52. SC 31.5 (SBO 1:222,3–5). Cf. 35.1 (SBO 1:249,9–11), Dil 12 (SBO 3:129,3–4), Div 2.8 (SBO 6a:85,25), Div 3.5 (SBO 6a:89, 25), Div 8.8 (SBO 6a:117,4): *suspirare ad haereditatem;* Div 14 (SBO 6a:148,1–2), where the expression *suspiria* is linked with ardent desire: Div 111.1 (SBO 6a:385,8–9), *In cel adv* 1 (SBO 6a:9,12).
53. SC 28.13 (SBO 1:201,25–26). *Languere* can be used in a pejorative sense to signify a loss of fervour. Cf. SC 14.6 (SBO 1:79,29), Dil 10 (SBO 3:126,26).
54. SC 31.5 (SBO 1:222,4).
55. SC 59.4 (SBO 2:137,19–21).
56. SC 28.13 (SBO 1:202,1–4), SC 51.3 (SBO 2:85,16–18). The idea occurs with some emphasis in Gregory the Great and will be discussed at greater length in a subsequent chapter.
57. SC 58.11 (SBO 2:134,25).

you and my groans are not hidden from you".'[58] It is at this point that the theme of desire overlaps with that of compunction—a matter to be discussed later in this chapter. The image of hunger occasionally surfaces in reference to desire for God, but it is not a frequent usage.[59] Occasionally it occurs with reference to the Beatitude: *Beati qui esuriunt* . . . and sometimes in connection with the eschatological banquet.[60] There is, however, a little more evidence to associate the concept of eating with the experience of God. Such words as *palatum cordis, dulcedo, sapor, gustum,* occur frequently, and the fact that the life of the soul is maintained by feeding upon God is described through cognates of *nutrire* and *pascere.* Bernard willingly speaks of the *ructus* which follows the repletion of a good meal.

Thirst is a much more frequent carrier of the meaning of desire. The bride of the Word is identified as *anima sitiens Deum,* another precise formulation borrowed from Gregory the Great, in dependence, it seems, on a passage from John Cassian.

> The text says, 'Let him kiss me with the kiss of his mouth'. Whose words are these? The bride's. And who may she be? The soul athirst for God . . . And if, therefore, it is especially and principally the characteristic of brides and bridegrooms to love, then it is not inappropriate that the name 'bride' be given to a soul who loves.[61]

58. SC 59.4 (SBO 2:137,25–26).
59. SC 74.3 (SBO 2:241,8). Cf. Dil 21 (SBO 3:137,8) where the phrase *animi famem* is used. Typical antecedents are Augustine, *In Ioan* 15.1 (CChr 36:151), Gregory, *In Ev* 36.2 (PL 76: 1267a), and *In Ev* 36.7 (PL 76:1269d).
60. OS 1.11 (SBO 5:336,6).
61. SC 7.2 (SBO 1:31,17–18 and 32,5–6). *Anima sitiens Deum* is an echo of Gregory the Great's *Deum sitiens anima* which occurs, for instance in *Dialogues* 3.34.2 (SChr 260:400). This passage is itself

The theme is restated in an important passage toward the end of the *Sermons on the Song of Songs*.

> Rightly, then renouncing all other affections, and giving herself entirely to love, the bride responds to Love himself when she returns love. And even if she were to pour herself out wholly in love, there would be no comparison between this and the never-ending streams emanating from that source. For it is obvious that there is not the same abundant outflow from the one who loves as there is from Love himself, from the soul as from the Word, from the bride as from the bridegroom, from the creature as from the Creator. More does not flow from the one athirst than from the wellspring.[62]

Much of the imagery employed by Bernard to designate the dynamics of the soul's movement toward God is spatial. In a later chapter the important theme of *peregrinatio* will be raised. For Bernard, in line with a tradition stemming from the earliest christian centuries, human life is not an end in itself, but a long, weary journey toward the heavenly homeland. The ethic derived from this perspective is that of the wayfarer: one

---

strongly influenced by John Cassian's *Conference* 9. 26–30, and it is noteworthy that in *Conf* 9.29 (SChr 54:64) in a passage which links together compunction, contemplation and future desire, Cassian speaks in a similar vein: *dum sitit anima nostra ad deum fortem vivum*, 'while our soul thirsts for the strong and living God'. This is, of course, a quotation of Ps 41:3 which, together with Ps 62:2, is the obvious source of the theme of desire as thirst. Cf. SC 23.2 (SBO 1:140,17–18), SC 32.2 (SBO 1:227,8), QH 9.9 (SBO 4:441,28), Div 41.13 (SBO 6a:254, 15), Ep 18.2 (SBO 7:67,25–26). See also Augustine *In Ioan* 5.1 (CChr 36:40), *In Ioan* 13.8 (CChr 36:135), *In Ioan* 15.30 (CChr 36:162), *In Ioan* 21.14 (CChr 36:220), *In Ps 41* 2–5 (CChr 38:461–463), *In Ps 62* 5–8 (CChr 39:796–799), which includes in #5 the lapidary expression, *ipsum desiderium sitis est animae*.

62. SC 83.6 (SBO 2:302,1–5).

must keep up one's plodding progress, maintaining the momentum of the journey and not allowing oneself to be diverted by the sundry attractions available along the way. The various verbs signifying movement which are used in this connection usually have biblical or patristic precedents. Bernard himself demonstrates that, on at least one occasion, he is aware of something of the pedigree of his vocabulary. *Velle enim, teste beato Gregorio, mente ire est:* 'For to will, according to blessed Gregory, is mentally to go there.'[63] He also speaks of going toward God, tending to him, hastening in his direction.[64] Bernard also makes use of the biblical idea of following Christ and of being drawn by him.[65]

A very important theme traditionally linked with that of desire for God in the benedictine tradition is the idea of seeking God. The search for the beloved is also an important sub-theme in the Song of Songs. 'To seek God' is one of the most popular perennial formulations of the benedictine ideal, ever since it was first proposed.[66] It is true that the concept of seeking God does not coincide exactly with that of desire, but the two notions are related and there is a considerable area of overlap. Desire is probably the more fundamental reality, since the search is undertaken in response to this inner prompting. 'God is not sought by the movement of

63. Div 72.4 (SBO 6a:310,5–6). Cf. Gregory the Great, *In Ev* 27.5 (PL 76:1207).

64. Dil 30 (SBO 3:145,3): *transire in Deum;* Dil 19 (SBO 3:135, 22), Div 8.9 (SBO 6a:117,17–18): *Tota pergit [anima] in Deum, unicumque ei ac perfectum desiderium est;* Div 10.3 (SBO 6a:123, 12–13), Dil 27 (SBO 3:142,10–11), Div 18.1 (SBO 6a:157,4), Div 33.1 (SBO 6a:222,5), Dil 29 (SBO 3:144,10–11).

65. Cf. SC 21 (SBO 1:121–129).

66. Cf. RB 58.7. See also G. Turbessi, *'Quaerere Deum: Variazioni Patristiche su un tema centrale della Regula Sancti Benedicti'*, *Benedictina* 14 (1967) 14–22 and 15 (1968) 181–205.

the feet but by desires . . . and because there will never be
an end to desiring, so the search will also continue.'[67]

It is a great and good thing to seek God. I regard it as
second to none of the good things of the soul. It is the
first of gifts and it is the last stage of development. It attaches to none of the virtues, nor does it yield
precedence to any of them. For how can it be attached
to one of the virtues when it is preceded by none of
them? And how can it yield precedence to any when it
is itself the consummation of them all? For what virtue
can be thought to exist in one who does not seek God?
Is there any conclusion to his seeking of God? For the
Scripture says, 'Seek his face always'. It is my belief
that, even when he is found, there will be no halt to the
seeking.[68]

Thus the search for God precedes all good action and all ac-
quiring of virtue, though it is itself initiated and animated
by desire. Seeking God seems, to an extent greater than
desire, to follow upon a conscious decision on the part of the
seeker to allow the desire welling up from his heart to shape
the course of life, notwithstanding the exertions and hardships which such a decision will eventually involve.[69]

The theme of the search is discussed at great length
in Sermon 75, where Bernard is commenting on the text

67. SC 84.1 (SBO 2:303,12–16). Cf. Ep 18.2 (SBO 7:67,14). On
the equivalence of seeking and desiring see Div 8.9 (SBO 6a:117,
10). Also Div 40.6 (SBO 6a:240,12), Div 41.5 (SBO 6a:248,3), Div
42.2 (SBO 6a:256,15); Augustine, *In Ioan* 38.2 (CChr 36:338), *In
Ioan* 101.6 (CChr 36:594). The sentiment expressed in the first half
of this quotation is very augustinian and occurs frequently and continues to be cited throughout the Middle Ages, although with some
slight variation in its formulation. See, for example, from the
treatise *In Ioan*, 22.3 (CChr 36:224), 26.3 (261). 32.1 (300), 36.8
(329), 48.3 (415), 56.4 (468); also *Ep* 155 (PL 33:672).
68. SC 84.1 (SBO 2:303,5–7).
69. SC 35.1 (SBO 1:249,9–11), SC 75.5 (SBO 2:250,17).

of the Song of Songs, *In lectulo meo quaesivi per noctes quem diligit anima mea.*[70]

Indeed, this is the bridegroom who is not found when he is sought, even though the search is made with so much energy and zeal—now in the bed, now in the streets and squares of the city. Yet he is the same one who said, 'Seek and you will find' and 'The one who seeks, finds'. It was to him that the Prophet addressed the words, 'You are good, O Lord, to the soul which seeks you'. Again, Isaiah said, 'Seek the Lord while he is to be found'. How will the Scriptures be fulfilled? Is it to be inferred that she who is seeking in this present instance is one of those to whom it was said, 'You will seek me and you shall not find me'?

In this life there are three things which can cause the seeker to be frustrated; if he seeks out of time or in an inappropriate manner or in an unsuitable place.

If it were true that every time is suitable for seeking, why did the Prophet say in the text already quoted, 'Seek the Lord while he is to be found'? This surely means that a time will come when he is not to be found, and this is why the text adds that he is to be called upon 'while he is near'. For a time will come when he will no longer be near and then everyone will seek him, according to the text 'Every knee shall bow . . .' At that time, however, he will not be found by the wicked, since the avenging angels will surely prevent it. They will take the wicked away so that they shall not catch sight of the glory of God. Likewise, the foolish virgins will cry out in vain, for once the doors are closed there is no hope of his going outside to them. It is such people who may consider the text, 'You seek me but you shall not find me' appropriate for themselves.

---

70. Song 3:1. The Vulgate reading is *per noctes quaesivi.* On this inversion see J. Leclercq in *Recueil 1:* 289–319.

The acceptable time is, therefore, the present. The day of salvation is here. Now is the time for seeking him and for calling out to him. Now is he often experienced as being with us, even before we call upon him. As the Scripture says, 'Before you called upon me I said, 'I am here'. Nor were his kindness and the suitability of the present time unknown to the Psalmist who said, 'The Lord has heard the desire of the poor, and your ear has paid attention to the expectations of their hearts'.

If it is true that it is by good actions that God is sought, then let us do good to all while we have the time, especially because the Lord has openly proclaimed that the night is coming in which no one is able to work. Perhaps you are hoping for a second period in which to seek God and to do good, a time in the future world over and above what God has ordained in the present as the basis of your examination? The answer is no. These present days are the days of salvation, because it is in them that God himself, who is our king before all ages, accomplishes salvation upon the earth.[71]

Thus we see an example of how a major text built around the theme of seeking is paranetic in character. Bernard develops the theme of seeking God as a means of encouraging his readers to give voluntary assent to the Godward orientation of their lives, to let desire find expression in the way they live. This in an important aspect of Bernard's total teaching on desire. He did not develop his doctrine as a private anthropological indulgence, but rather as a basis on which to build sound moral teaching, yet without proposing an external moral code with no relationship to inner sense and feeling. This concern for building bridges between subjectivity and objective behaviour often surfaces. In quoting the text of Ps 37:10,

71. SC 75.3–4 (SBO 2:248–249).

ante te est omne desiderium meum, he added a gloss, *et propositum cordis mei,* as if to suggest that the pre-elective movement of desire needs to be seconded by the assent of the will.[72] Elsewhere we find *opus tuum, studium tuum, desiderium tuum,* yoked together as through some inner affinity.[73] Finally, Bernard affirms the closeness of desiring, seeking God and prayer: *orare, hoc est Verbum quaerere:* 'to pray is to seek the Word'. He continues,

> Therefore you do not pray correctly if, in praying you are seeking anything beyond the Word; or if it is not because of the Word that you are seeking it. This latter is possible because in him all things have their being.[74]

The theme of the search is extremely important to Bernard's approach to the notion of desire for God. Seeking God is, for him, merely an accidental state necessitated by the fact of his absence. To seek God in an active and personal sense is already the effect and sign of the inner presence of God. This Bernard states very lucidly in a much-quoted passage from the *De diligendo Deo.*

> No one has the strength to seek you unless he has first already found you. For it is a fact that you will to be found in order that you may be sought and you will to be sought in order that you may be found. It is possible, therefore, to seek you and to find you, but it is not possible to anticipate you.[75]

72. SC 20.1 (SBO 1:114,20–21). Despite its biblical assonance, the addition does not appear in the Vulgate; the nearest to it is the expression in Acts 11:23: *in proposito cordis permanere.*

73. SC 71.1 (SBO 2:214,20).

74. SC 86.3 (SBO 2:319,11–14).

75. Dil 22 (SBO 3:137–138). Cf. Csi 5.11.24 (SBO 3:486,17–18): *solus est Deus qui frustra numquam quaeri potest, nec cum inveniri non potest;* Div 4.2 (SBO 6a:95,3–4). For background see

To seek God is a good thing, but to find him is even better. Thus in a passage echoed in the pseudo-bernardine
hymn, *Jesu dulcis memoria,* Bernard writes: 'We seek
God, we wait for God . . . and if he is good to the one
who seeks him, how much more so is he to one who
finds.'[76]

These are the principal images with which Bernard
surrounds his teaching on desire for God: temperature,
respiration, grief, hunger, thirst, movement, seeking.
There are other expressions which appear from time to
time. Desire is described as *immissa aviditas* in one
place.[77] It is often imaged by *inhiare,* to long after with
an open mouth.[78] There are also occurrences of the near-
synonyms *cupire,*[79] and *concupiscere,*[80] themselves qualified by the same expression as *desiderare* itself. Occasionally, *desiderium* is used interchangeably with
votum, although the latter often has a far more circum-
scribed meaning.[81]

The imagery used by Bernard to convey the several
aspects of his rich vision of the nature of desire for God is
never systematised. There is considerable overlap in the
metaphors employed, and often a single passage will

Augustine *In Ioan* 7.21 (CChr 36:79): *quaerimus quia quaesiti
sumus; In Ioan* 63.1 (CChr 36:465–486).

76. Div 4.1 (SBO 6a:94,4 and 15–16).

77. SC 58.2 (SBO 2:128,9). Some MSS have *immensa* instead of
immissa.

78. SC 67.7 (SBO 2:193,18: *avidius inhiare*), SC 38.3 (SBO
2:32,4). See also Gregory the Great, *In Ev* 40.2 (PL 76:1304a): *in-
hianter aestuabat.*

79. SC 33.2 (SBO 1:235,6): *vehementer cupiat;* SC 7.8 (SBO
1:35,23), SC 32.2 (SBO 1:227,8), Asspt 5.4 (SBO 5:253,13–15).

80. SC 7.2 (SBO 1:32,4), Div 103.1 (SBO 6a:371,7), Div 15.1–2
(SBO 6a:141,3–4), VNat 2.3 (SBO 4:206–207).

81. For instance, SC 74.4 (SBO 2:242,3–7).

contain a series of different images, brilliantly combined to evoke multiple resonances in the mind of the reader. A single example may perhaps serve to demonstrate this point.

If there is anyone among us for whom, as the Prophet says, 'it is good to be close to the Lord' or, to speak more clearly, if any among us is 'a man of desires' to the extent that he wants to be dissolved and to be with Christ — that he ardently thirsts for this and earnestly sets his mind to it — then such a man is surely one who will welcome the Word as his bridegroom at the time of visitation.

At that hour he will find himself interiorly constrained by the arms of Wisdom, as it were, and he will experience the sweetness of the holy love which is poured into him. To such a one 'the desire of his heart is granted' even while he is still a pilgrim and in the body.

This, however, is but a partial realisation, temporary and very brief. Suddenly the one who was sought with vigils and prayers and with a great flood of tears is at hand. Then, just when it was thought to hold on to him, he slips away. But then he comes again to the one who pursues him weeping, and he permits himself to be grasped. If the devoted soul continues with prayer and with weeping, then he returns again and does not disappoint the prayer of its lips. Then he disappears again and is not seen unless, once again, he is sought with all the force of desire.

Thus, even in this body, it is possible to experience the joy of the bridegroom's presence, but it is never freely available. For while his visitation brings gladness, the change in fortune is a source of trouble. For the time being, therefore, it is necessary for the beloved soul to have suffering until having once and for all laid aside the burden of this bodily mass, it will fly, raised up by the wings of its desires. Then it will browse unencumbered in the fields of contemplation, and will by its mind follow the one whom it loves, wherever he goes.[82]

The linguistic field surrounding the notion of desire includes within its ambit much of the rich theme of love: *amor, dilectio, caritas*. For Bernard, love and desire appeared as complementary realities: love being more appropriate as a response to the presence of the object of one's affection; desire being especially a consequence of his being absent. With his usual flexibility, however, he often uses the words interchangeably and without precise definition. Or he may use them in parallel as a convenient repetition or to balance the flow of a sentence. So it happens that much of his teaching about desire for God is to be found in passages which speak principally of love. It is important, therefore, to establish the relationship between these two themes and to demonstrate that, for Bernard, desire was not so much a selfish movement of spiritual acquisitiveness as a specific aspect of that self-giving which finds expression in charity in all its forms.

AMOR, DILECTIO, CARITAS

Twelfth-century France was in love with love. It was a principal theme both of popular culture and of the intellectual world. It is clear that monks were not immune from its attraction.[83] Cistercian monasticism, with its

---

82. SC 32.2 (SBO 1:227,6–13). The *vir desidiorum* mentioned is the scriptural description of Daniel. Cf. Div 9.3 (SBO 6a:119,21).

83. Cf. Jean Leclercq, *Monks and Love in Twelfth Century France: Psycho-Historical Essays* (Oxford: Clarendon Press, 1979). There are very rich bibliographical indications given in the notes to the various essays. To be read with some reserve is John C. Moore, *Love in Twelfth Century France* (Philadelphia: University of Pennsylvania Press, 1972).

emphasis on adult recruitment and its success in drawing thousands of former knights to its ranks, was substantially influenced by the concern these young men brought into monastic life that monasteries be genuine 'schools of love'.

Of course, there were difficulties in adapting the austere monastic approach to love, with its emphasis on solitude, self-control, and celibacy, to the less disciplined expectations of these young enthusiasts. Yet, a determined effort was made to harness the secular momentum toward love with a view to reaching monastic goals.

Some purification was necessary. The popular work of Ovid on *The Art of Love* (*Ars Amatoria*) was left aside in favour of deeper and more philosophical strands within the same author's thought. Cicero's treatise *On Friendship* also served as a foil to the less desirable aspects of Ovid. From published works we can determine that there was at this time, in religious circles, a revival of interest in the Song of Songs and in the Johannine writings which served to bring to the fore the strong christian tradition in this matter.

There was the problem that the biblical books seemed far less immediate to the experience of young men than the products of popular culture. This is where the various commentaries and expositions had a role to play. Making use of the symbolic approach,[84] the medieval commentators were able to draw from the pages of the Bible a doctrine on love which was both doctrinally sound and yet appealing to their contemporaries. In this way a manly and monastic approach to the subject was possible even while a necessary purification of absorbed beliefs and values was accomplished.

The Song of Songs played an important role in this process. The fact that the love of the bride and groom

84. See, for example, John Morson, 'Symbolic Theology: The Cistercian Fathers, Heirs to a Tradition', *Ideals*, pp. 245–261.

seems to have been unconsummated was a great help in explaining something of the specific character of love in a monastic sense. Love, as Bernard and his contemporaries taught, when it is directed to God, is unfulfilled in this life. It awaits consummation in the next. This is why the experience of love takes the form of desire, since all its energy is directed toward the future.

Accordingly, much of Bernard's teaching on desire will be found in his description of the vicissitudes of love in the life of the monk. Throughout the bernardine corpus love and desire are presented as companion realities, with many themes and allusions common to both concepts.

It should be noted, at this stage, that Bernard's vocabulary of love fluctuates between *amor, dilectio,* and *caritas,* as does latin tradition generally. In one sense, *caritas* is the easiest to isolate. It habitually (but not exclusively) has a spiritual sense irrespective of its object, since it is inevitably related to God, or at least to good. This connotation is certainly moulded by the Vulgate usage in the text of 1 Jn 4:16: *Deus caritas est.*[85] *Amor* and *dilectio* were often used indiscriminately in the twelfth century.[86] Despite the general assumption that *dilectio* has a less instinctual and more rational connotation than *amor,* it was the latter expression which came to used for mystical love. This is because the word *amor* seemed to have a note of greater intensity and warmth than *dilectio* which, in certain cases, has a cool, calculating angle to it. Following Origen-Rufinus and Ambrose, and against some strands of augustinian usage, *dilectio* came to have a generic meaning, whereas *amor* was used for a strongly-felt affective

85. Cf. Helène Petré, *Caritas: Étude sur le vocabulaire latin de la charité chrétienne* (Louvain, 1948). Jacques Farges et Marcel Viller, art. 'Charité', DSp 2/1: cols 523–570. ThLL vol. 3, *sub voce.*
86. Moore, *Love,* pp. 2–3.

experience, such as ordinary sexual love, but also mystical love.[87] In the context of the Song of Songs, *amor* seemed especially appropriate.

Another nuance of difference may be detected. *Dilectio* seems more often to be part of a willed response; a programme of benevolence to which the individual has given conscious, and perhaps sacrificial, assent. *Amor*, on the other hand, appears as pre-voluntary, being paradoxically at once more passionate amd involving the whole person. In many contexts it seems as though *amor* represents a spontaneous force which energises life, whereas *dilectio* seems to be a more controlled, willed and conscious reality. It is as though the person is active in *dilectio* and passive in *amor*. *Amor* is, accordingly, in need of direction and ordering, as Gilson remarks: '*Amor* is a natural affection which, when duly ordered toward its end, is *caritas*, and when turned away from its end, *cupiditas*.'[88]

The distinctions between *amor*, *dilectio*, and *caritas* represent preferences or tendencies in language rather than an inflexible semantic rule. In a writer like Bernard they are not to be pressed rigorously. Nor should such verbal differences serve to form a foundation for a system, such as Anders Nygren attempted in his book *Agape and Eros*.[89] The observations made above,

87. Cf. C. Mohrmann, 'Observations sur la langue et le style de saint Bernard', SBO 2:xx.

88. E. Gilson, *Mystical Theology*, p. 224, note 39.

89. Translated by Philip S. Watson (Philadelphia: Westminster Press, 1953). A satisfactory exposition of many of the inadequacies of Nygren's book is M. C. D'Arcy, *The Mind and Heart of Love: Lion and Unicorn, A Study in Eros and Agape* (London: Faber, 2nd edition, 1954). For a discussion of Nygren and Bernard, see N. Perrier, 'Agapè ou la charité chrétienne selon Anders Nygren et selon saint Bernard', *Homme d'Eglise*, pp. 170–179.

however, have some significance in discussing the relationship between love and desire, since *amor* is often used interchangeably with *desiderium,* whereas *dilectio* is used far less frequently in this way.

John Morson has demonstrated that among the cistercian authors of the twelfth century there was a practical equivalence of love and desire. Of Bernard he writes, with special reference to Sermon 9 *De diversis,* 'It is difficult to maintain that the author makes a real distinction between desire and love'.[90] Jacques Blanpain nuances this somewhat by the observation that the reality 'love-desire' is more often described as 'desire' in the early stages of growth, when the person is more acutely aware of his own incompleteness and needs. Later, when this same 'love-desire' becomes more spiritualised and disinterested, it is more frequently described as 'love', although both love and desire are present throughout the process.[91]

The fact that *amor* and *desiderium* together with their cognate verbs and related concepts operate in a single linguistic field has been demonstrated in many of the texts already cited.[92] We see that both terms are consistently employed in the same word-sets, surrounded by the same qualifiers and parallels. The images applied to desire are also used with reference to love. Love also is vehement.[93] The words associated with heat are applied

90. John Morson, 'Seeking God by Desire', CS 2 (1967) 175–185; p. 175.

91. Blanpain, 'Language mystique', pp. 231–232.

92. See, for instance, SC 7.2 (SBO 1:31–32), SC 28.13 (SBO 1: 202,3–4), SC 51.1 (SBO 2:84,6–9), SC 51.3 (SBO 2:85,15–19), SC 57.6 (SBO 2:123,9–12). See also Augustine, *In Ioan* 3.20–21 (CChr 36:30), *In Ioan* 26.5 (CChr 36:262).

93. For instance, SC 49.4 (SBO 2:75,15), SC 51.3 (SBO 2:85, 18), SC 67.3 (SBO 2:190,14).

to it: *flagrare,*[94] *ignis,*[95] *fervor,*[96] *aestuare,*[97] *ardere,*[98] and *inardescere.*[99] In a single paragraph the bride of the Word is successively described as *anima sitiens Deum* and *anima quae amat.*[100] Love also causes the soul to languish[101] and, like desire, it is subject to growth.[102] Its source is God himself,[103] to whom it ultimately returns.[104]

The explicit connection between love and desire is made in a number of places. 'If you have not desired, then you will not love perfectly; for, just as understanding is the fruit of faith, so perfect love is the fruit of desire.'[105] Just as faith leads to understanding, so the

94. For instance, SC 49.4 (SBO 2:75,18), SC 67.3 (SBO 2:190, 14), SC 67.8 (SBO 2:193,24); Augustine *In Ioan* 32.9 (CChr 36:305).

95. SC 21.4 (SBO 1:124,10): *ignis . . . amoris tui.*

96. For instance, Epi 3.8 (SBO 4:309,23), Div 59 (SBO 6a:289, 19–20), Div 92.2 (SBO 6a:348,3).

97. Cf. Div 29.5 (SBO 6a:214,3).

98. For instance, SC 3.5 (SBO 1:17,3), SC 18.6 (SBO 1:107,21); Augustine, *In Ioan* 34.7 (CChr 36:314).

99. For instance, SC 18.6 (SBO 1:107,19); SC 57.5 (SBO 2:123,20).

100. SC 7.2 (SBO 1:31–32).

101. SC 51.3 (SBO 2:85,15–19).

102. SC 51.1 (SBO 2:83,24): *crevit amor.* Cf. SC 83.5 (SBO 2:301.12): *magna res amor, sed sunt in eo gradus . . .* Bernard is very interested in the phenomenology of love's development and its stages; it is the primary focus of his early treatise *De diligendo deo.*

103. SC 69.7 (SBO 2:206,21–22), SC 83.4 (SBO 2:300,12), SC 83.6 (SBO 2:302,15).

104. SC 83.4 (SBO 2:300,2).

105. Ep 18.2 (SBO 7:67,23–24). In the first clause the verb *amabitis* is used; in the last, the noun *caritas. Caritas* is often used; in referring to the perfect or ultimate form of love. In the various examples quoted above, all three expressions occur but with a preponderance of *amor.* Often the choice of terminology seems to depend on the immediate context, especially if it is a matter of commenting on a particular scriptural text.

love-content of desire becomes stronger and more explicit as development proceeds. Bernard speaks of the waters of desire being drawn from the well of charity,[106] and of desire reaching its culmination in the fullness of love.[107]

This is not the place to speak about the nature and development of love in Bernard's view, nor about the other important question of how love is to be ordered with reference to its ultimate goal, the *ordinatio caritatis.* These areas have been examined already.[108] In any case the last word on the subject must be Bernard's own treatise *On the Necessity of Loving God.* Our limited aim in this section has been simply to demonstrate an overlap between the concepts of love and desire in Bernard's writings, with a view to expanding the basis of our ongoing discussion of Bernard's doctrine of desire.

AFFECTUS, AFFECTIO

Affectus is a fourth declension noun derived from the verb *afficere* (*adficere* = *facere ad*). The verb means 'to do something to somebody, to exert influence, to affect someone or something'. *Affectus* denotes the state produced in the recipient of such influence. It it often used as a synonym for the positive emotions such as love, desire, fondness, good will, compassion, and sympathy.

106. Div 117 (SBO 6a:395,4–5).
107. Ep 18.2 (SBO 7:67,23–24. 'Just as faith leads to full knowledge, so desire leads to perfect love.'
108. Cf. Gianni Dotti, 'Le "caritas" come principio di vita e di dottrina in S. Bernardo', *Studi,* pp. 349–358; Pacificus Delfgaauw, 'La nature et les degrés de l'amour selon saint Bernard', *Théologien,* pp. 234–252; Maur Standaert, 'Le principe de l'ordination dans la théologie de saint Bernard', COCR 8 (1946) 178–216; Robert Walton, Introduction to the treatise *On Loving God* in CF 13:85–92.

In some contexts it is used with the philosophical meaning of 'passion'. *Affectio* primarily denotes the active process of influencing, the action which results in the state of *affectus* in the one influenced. By extension, it came to be associated with its effect, and thus was given a meaning closely akin to that of *affectus*.[109]

109. Cf. ThLL 1: cols 1176–1192. *Affectus* and *affectio* are words used with a practical synonymity in the cistercian tradition, although, on close examination, some theological divergences can be noted between different authors. In general, Aelred, Bernard and William of St Thierry are inclined to use the terms interchangeably, even though they are aware that they are theoretically different. 'The *affectiones*, taken in the true sense, are complex emotions made up of the fundamental *affectus*. However, St Bernard often enough uses *affectiones* in the sense of *affectus*, and then follows the received usage; when he classifies the *affectiones* in the manner above set out, he follows none but his own.' (Gilson, *Mystical Theology*, p. 101, note 131.) Bernard clearly affirms the theoretical distinction based on the fact that *affectio* is active in form whereas *affectus* is passive. Thus he distinguishes between the phrases *in affectu* and *in actu* (SC 50.2; SBO 2:279,5) and strongly denies the ascription of *affectus* to God: *Non est affectus Deus, affectio est* (Csi 5.17; SBO 3:400,23). An earlier statement in the same work confirms and reinforces this orientation of his thought: *Deus sic inest ut afficiat* (Csi 5.12; SBO 3:476,12). In his article, '*Cordis affectus*', DSp 2: cols 2288–2300, Jean Chatillon notes that Bernard's choice between the alternatives is often dictated by the assonance of the phrase. When there is a comparison with *intellectus*, he tends to use *affectus*; where *ratio* occurs, he is more likely to employ *affectio* (col 2288). In Bernard, both *affectus* and *affectio* are habitually used in a generic sense. A specific meaning is to be inferred only on the basis of added qualifiers of the context. Thus *affectus* is used by Bernard to describe his feelings at the time of the death of his brother, Gerard (SC 26.3; SBO 1:171,10). A dry heart in one in which there is no *affectio* (Asc 3.1; SBO 5:134,26–135,1). The words of the bride have the effect of soothing or delighting the *affectus* (SC 67.1; SBO 2:188,23). The words are especially used in the sense of compassion, whether with reference to human beings or (anthropomorphically) to God. Thus SC 57.1 (SBO 2:119,17), SC

The terms *affectus* and *affectio*, as they appear in Bernard's writings, are principally shaped by their long history in christian usage. In general, the Fathers of the Church used both terms, together with such others as *passio* and *perturbatio*, to render standard greek philosophical terms as *diathesis*, *ethos*, and *pathos*, with the general meaning of feeling, emotion, passion, although this general meaning was restricted and applied in particular contexts.[110]

The side of affective response was variously given as the *animus* or *anima*, the *mens*, and the *cor*. This is true of most of the latin Fathers although, as Bernard McGinn notes, 'there is rarely a standard terminology found within a single author'.[111] Statistically, the heart figured

---

44.4 (SBO 2:46,19–20), SC 12.1 (SBO 1:61,2–3), Dil 40 (SBO 3:154,19), Div 50.1 (SBO 6a:271,7–8), Div 58.1 (SBO 6a:288,12). Two definitions of Aelred are significant in demonstrating the kinship of *affectus* and *affectio*. *Est igitur affectus, spontanea quaedam ac dulcis ipsius animi ad aliquem inclinatio* (*Spec Car* 3.11; PL 195:587d). *Affectio est, ut mihi videtur, spontanea quaedam mentis inclination ad aliquem cum delectatione* (*Sermones inediti*, p. 18). Thomas Davis has appended a note on the meaning of *affectus* to his translation of *The Mirror of Faith* (CF 15:93–95) and there is a good listing of occurences in the index to his translation of *The Nature and Dignity of Love* (CF 30:119).

110. Cf. Châtillon, '*Cordis affectus*' DSp 2:2288–2300. Some texts seem to indicate that the *affectus cordis*, in Bernard's view, was a feeling or sentiment coming from the inmost depths of the spritiual person (Div 41.9; SBO 6a:250,16). As such, it was the opposite of any form of enslaved emotion, of feelings dictated by factor external to the heart, of *necesitas cordis* (Div 12.1 [SBO 6a:127,15], Div 14.3 [SBO 6a: 136,5]). Likewise there is a certain emphasis on the intensity of feeling, it is opposed to unfeelingness, thus *toto affectu* is constrasted with *tepide* in Div 25.5 (SBO 6a:190,21).

111. Bernard McGinn, Introduction to *Three Treatises on Man: A Cistercian Anthropology*, CF 24 (Kalamazoo, Cistercian Publications, 1977) p. 83.

most often, especially in the phrase *cordis affectus*, and Bernard himself remarks that 'affections are properly attributed to the heart'.[112]

Many authors note the difficulty of finding a single, consistent translation for *affectus* and *affectio*.[113] Unless the context seems to warrant an alternative usage or a paraphrase, we shall employ the psychological term 'affect' in the general sense of 'feeling, emotion, desire'[114] but with the added connotations which the word enjoyed in the Middle Ages. 'The concept of *affectus* can cover the whole field of varied manifestations of the affective nature and is equally capable of expressing the highest act of will.'[115]

In the monastic theology of the twelfth century, the distinction between faculty and function was not always observed. The later scholastic precision of the *actus primus* and *actus secundus* was, at this time, unknown. As Gilson observes, 'The constant refusal to admit any real distinction between the soul and its faculties or between the faculties themselves is noticeable throughout the history of this school.'[116] Bernard used *affectus* equally for the

112. Div 123.3 (SBO 6a:406,20–21).

113. Thus Thomas Davis, Appendix to William of St Thierry's *The Mirror of Faith*, CF 15 (Kalamazoo: Cistercian Publications, 1979) 93–95. Amedée Hallier, *The Monastic Theology of Aelred of Rievaulx*, CS 2 (Spencer: Cistercian Publications, 1969) p. 29. As a translation of *affectus*, the latter proposes 'love-tendency' which gives a good sense but is stylistically cumbersome.

114. Thus the *Concise Oxford Dictionary*, 5th edn (1964) *sub voce*. When in the translation of bernardine texts in the rest of this section I use 'affect', I do so only to alert the reader to the ocurrence of *affectus* or *affectio;* in most cases 'feeling' would be a better and smoother rendering, although perhaps something of the bernardine sense of the word may be in jeopardy.

115. Hallier, *Monastic Theology*, p. 29.

116. Étienne Gilson, *The Christian Philosophy of Saint Augustine* (Random House: New York, 1967) p. 219.

fundamental dynamic principle within the human being
and for the range of emotions and activities in which this
underlying reality finds expression.[117] Unlike William of
St Thierry and Issac of Stella, Bernard was not greatly interested in an analysis of the parts of the soul. His concern was more often drawn to the experience of *affectus*
than to its cause or source.

There are three extended treatments of aspects of
the affective experience in the human being which are
particularly important for understanding the feeling-
component in desire for God, as Bernard preceived it.[118]
The extent to which this affect or love-tendency is linked
with desire is indicated by the following extracts.

Basing himself on the latin translation of *astorgoi* in
Rom 1:31 and 2 Tim 3:3, *sine affectione,* Bernard affirms the necessity of feeling and affective experience in
spritiual growth, but stipulates that the affects must, like
love itself, be ordered. This is accomplished by their being subjected to God's law.

> I am not saying that we should be without any feel-
> ing in this, that we should put our hands to work
> while all the time our heart remains dry. I have read
> that among the other great and serious human evils
> described by the Apostle, there is one which is
> described as affectlessness.
>
> Affect is something that is begotten of the flesh,
> but it is ruled by reason and given flavour by
> wisdom. It is begotten of the flesh since the Apostle
> notes that it is not subject to God's law — nor can it
> be. It is ruled by reason, as he asserts from the op-
> posite viewpoint, when it consents to the law of God

117. Cf. Hiss, *Die Anthropologie,* pp. 98–105, Blanpain,
'Langage mystique', p. 62. E. von Ivanka, 'La structure de l'âme
selon S. Bernard', *Théologien,* pp. 202–208, see p. 204.

118. See SC 50, Asc 3, and Div 50, all cited below.

as to something good. Thus affect contains within itself two contrary attitudes to the law, one rejecting, the other accepting.

Its third quality, that of being given flavour by wisdom, is far removed from the other two. This is concerned with tasting and experiencing that the Lord is sweet, thus countering the first quality and crowning the second. For the affect of the flesh is sweet but vile; the affect of reason is dry but strengthening, but the affect of wisdom is both rich and pleasing to the taste. Whereas the second is the source of good actions, the third is the very throne of charity.

It is not merely a matter of affect alone which, when enriched and given flavour with the salt of wisdom, brings to the mind the experience of the abundant sweetness of the Lord. It is, rather, a matter of fact. Even when it does not refresh the soul with the pleasant experience of love, it does, nevertheless, vehemently set it on fire with the desire for such love.[119]

What Bernard seems to be saying in this text is that the natural affective tendency of the human being is unruly and unproductive in itself. It needs to come under the guidance of reason by its subjection to the law of God. This state is an improvement on the first, objectively speaking, but on the subjective level—being without much pleasure—it is dry and unrewarding. If one is to persevere with objective good, then something needs to

---

119. SC 50.4 (SBO 2:80,8–22). the distinction in the last paragraph is between *affectualis* and *actualis*. The final phrase is literally translated 'with love for such love'. In the translation and in the remarks which follow, it should be noted that I am interpreting SC 50 on the basis of Bernard's teaching on the three liberties in his treatise *On Grace and Free Choice*. The *liberum complacitum* differs from the *liberum consilium* in that it finds pleasure in doing good. It is, however, perfected only in the next life.

be added so that the path of virtue becomes less dry and feelingless. Thus the doing of good has to be seasoned by the salt of wisdom, so that goodness becomes not only a worthy goal to be pursued, but also a source of good feeling. The subjective state mirrors the goodness of external behaviour. A wise person is one who enjoys being good. The final phase of the progression is reached when the affect enjoys both the spontaneous *élan* of the wild, natural tendency, and the objective goodness of the reasoned response.

The fundamental meaning of affect is that it is a faculty or power of the soul, the counterpart of *ratio, sensus,* or *intellectus.*[120] 'It is the affect which speaks, not the understanding, hence its words are not directed to the understanding.'[121] In many cases Bernard seems to give preeminence to the affect at the expense of cognitive functions, a fact which has caused many cataloguers to label him a 'voluntarist'. The question is, however, more complex than is realised by many whose competence is in later, more systematic, generations of thinkers. The gregorian axiom, *amor ipse notitia est,*[122] was taken seriously by the monastic authors of the twelfth century, to the extent that it was generally taken for granted that love was not without cognitive effect, on the one hand, and, on the other, that perfect knowledge was impossible without love.[123]

Even while affective experience was taken to be distinguishable from understanding, so separation of the two orders was intended. This is to be borne in mind

120. The constrast between *sensus* and *affectus* is strong in Asc 3. Cf. Bernard McGinn, *The Golden Chain: A Study in the Theological Anthropology of Isaac of Stella,* CS 15, (Washington: Cistercian Publications, 1972) 145–152.

121. SC 50.3 (SBO 2:190,3–4).

122. Gregory the Great, *In Ev* 27.4 (PL 76:1207a). Bernard quotes this text and names Gregory as its author in Div 29.1 (SBO 6a:210,10–11).

123. Cf. R. Javelet, 'Intelligence', p. 287, and 'Psychologie', p. 31.

when considering Bernard's view on the two forms of *ex-cessus,* one intellective and one affective.[124] Bernard consistently had in mind the human being as a whole; he emphasised that both powers needed to be activated, each in its own mode. 'This is what reason teaches and it is to this that affect draws us.'[125] If a person is to be stable in virtue, it is not enough that he understands what is required of him, he must also will to give himself to the pursuit. Conversely, good will, by itself is not enough; it needs to be supplemented by such qualities as reasonableness, discretion, and common sense. One must understand.

Because of primal sinfulness, both reason and will are impaired. In the process of restoration, accordingly, it is to be expected that both cognitive and affective faculties will be subjected to progressive purification.

> There are two powers within us which need cleansing, the intellect so that it may know and the affect so that it may will. . . . This is so because the intellect is disturbed and maybe even completely blinded and because the affect is soiled, and soiled badly. Christ will, however, bring light to our intellect, and the Holy Spirit will cleanse our affect.[126]

Bernard often simply identifies the affect with the will: *affectus, id est voluntas.*[127] Such an equivalence, however, is not to be interpreted in the light of a nineteenth-century emphasis on will-power as distinct from feeling. Will was not, for Bernard, a matter of unfeeling compliance with reason or duty. [*Amor*] *affectus est non*

124. SC 49.4 (SBO 2:75,20–23).
125. Div 16.3 (SBO 6a:146,14–15).
126. Asc 3.2 (SBO 5:132,2–3 and 8–10). The role of the Holy Spirit in cleansing the affect is much emphasized by William of St Thierry. See also Bernard's Pent 1.6 (SBO 5:164,6).
127. Asc 3.2 (SBO 5:135,11–12), SC 42.7 (SBO 2:37,24).

contractus: 'love is a feeling, not a contract'.[128] For him, there was always present in will some element of sweetness.[129] In the restored human being doing good and feeling good progressively coincide.

It is, however, important to note that affect is not merely an automatic, sense-generated reaction to stimuli outside the control of the will. It is, rather, a movement coming from within.

> It is necessary to emphasis that the *affectus* in Bernard, as in the patristic tradition, is not to be confused with the *affectus* of the scholastic authors. These understood the phrase *affectus cordis* exclusively as a movement of sensibility or sentiment, according to the current use of these words. If this distinction is not appreciated, then Bernard will be seen wrongly as the initiator of an affective piety which developed in the Middle Ages and which has lasted until the present.[130]

The trivialisation of *affectus,* particularly after Pietism, is paralleled by the change in meaning which the Middle English word 'feeling' had undergone in the last six centuries.

Although Bernard never attempted a systematic analysis of the powers of the soul, he does incorporate, in his presentation, the traditional divisions of affective response.

> There are four well-known affects: love and joy, fear and sadness (*amor et laetitia, timor et tristitia*). Without these the human soul cannot subsist.[131]

128. Dil 17 (SBO 3:133,23). Cf. SC 83.3 (SBO 2:299,28): *parum dixi, contractus: complexus est.*
129. Cf. Div 29.1 (SBO 6a:210,15): *dulciter diliges sive affectuose.*
130. Translated from Blanpain, 'Language mystique', p. 59.
131. Div 50.2 (SBO 6a:271,16–18). Cf. Div 72.4 (SBO 6a:310, 14–22).

Bernard thus affirms that the soul is unable to exist independent of its functioning and thus intimates that, in the process of spiritual growth, there is question not so much of transcending the feelings or affects, as of progressively assuming them more fully within the ambit of spiritual experience.

> The whole heart is contained in these four affects: (namely, *amor, timor, gaudium* and *tristitia*). I consider the saying that you must turn to the Lord with your whole heart must be understood as including all these affects.[132]

Toward the end of the *Sermons on the Song of Songs* he proposes a different listing, limiting his remarks in this case to the carnal affects, which he lists as anger, fear, greed and joy (*ira, metus, cupiditas, gaudium*).[133]

Feeling is, according to Bernard, 'natural, spiritual and good'[134] and, as such, is naturally attributed to Christ. He took upon himself both the *sensus* and the *affectus* of the human condition in order to understand something of the 'necessity' by which human beings are constantly constrained.[135]

Affect is a universal feature of human existence, although the object of the feeling can and does vary from mother-love[136] to friendship.[137] It is not the fact of feeling which requires scrutiny and discernment. What needs to be examined is, rather, the object of this tendency to love. Affect becomes disordinate to the extent that it attaches itself

132. Quad 2.3 (SBO 4:361,11–13).

133. SC 85.5 (SBO 2:310,24–26).

134. Cf. Hallier, *Monastic Theology,* p. 30. See also Dil 30 (SBO 3:138.6–7): *Amor est affectio naturalis.* Cf. SC 44.4 (SBO 2:46, 25–47,2).

135. SC 56.1 (SBO 2:114,20–115,2).

136. SC 10.1 (SBO 1:48,23), SC 10.2 (SBO 1:49,22).

137. SC 44.4 (SBO 2:46,26).

to an inappropriate object. This can happen easily; hence, in Bernard's view, the re-orientation of the affect is a constant task. It is a matter, not of violently supressing a wandering affect, but of gently and intelligently redirecting its growth.

Speaking of the Lord's washing of the feet of the disciples, Bernard noted that it is possible to be pure in head (*intentio*) and in hand (*operatio et conversatio*). Common experience reveals that it is impossible to be pure in feet, that is, as regards the *animae affectiones*. They are always in need of further cleansing. Contrary imaginations and feelings remain throughout the process of spiritual restoration as a reminder that our wholeness is God's gift and not our achievement.

> For as long as we walk in the dust of this earth, the feet, that is to say the affects of the soul, cannot possibly be completely clean. They will always be soiled; somethimes by vanity, sometimes by the pursuit of pleasure, sometimes by curiosity, when the soul, on occasion, gives in to such things.[138].

The affects remain fundamentally good, notwithstanding this accidental taint of concupiscence.[139] As a tendency toward love, they are the direct effect of God's creation of the human being in his own image,[140] and they provide the first, rudimentary stirrings of the movement which terminates in perfect charity.[141] As such they are certainly not to be despised. In one of his sermons for the feast of the Ascension, Bernard refers to the need for carnal beginnings to spiritual growth:

138. V HM .4 (SBO 5:71,19–22).
139. SC 50.5 (SBO 2:80,23–24).
140. Cf. R. Javelet, *Image*, vol. I:44.
141. This is the starting-point as conceived in Ep 11 and the treatise *On the Necessity of Loving God.*

For the cloud is not without meaning and substance. It also has a function in bringing about salvation. It provoked an affect on the level of the flesh in the souls of the disciples who were not yet able to advance to the understanding of the faith without some change on the affective level. They were not yet able to reach up to the spiritual and so, in this way, they were enabled to cleave to a man who had said and done such wonderful things, by means of a love that was still at the level of the human.[142]

Affect becomes reprehensible for two reasons: if it refuses to accept the unfolding of its own spiritual latency and insists on remaining at an inchoate level, and if it attaches itself to an inappropriate object.[143] As a person advances in spirituality, he is subject to the obligation of progressively bringing his affective powers under the control of reason. 'The *affectus* attains its human perfection when it is united with the mind and with the will'[144] This involves a vigorous renunciation of alternative attractions in order to give oneself entirely to the pursuit of the one thing necessary.[145] What is, perhaps, most difficult is relinquishing a hold on those sensible attachments which were permissible and perhaps even helpful at a previous stage of growth and the recognition that each phase has its own specific demands. Thus the process of ordering the affects continues throughout life. The theme parallels that of the *ordinatio caritatis*, as one

142. Asc 6.11 (SBO 5:156,11–17). Cf. SC 20.6 (SBO 1:118, 12–15): 'Note that the heart's love is somewhat carnal since . . . the human heart is affected by the flesh of Christ. When it is filled with love in this way . . . compunction comes easily.'

143. Cf. SC 26.8 (SBO 1:176,26–27).

144. Hallier, p. 117.

145. Cf. SC 83.6 (SBO 2:302,1): *cunctis renuntians affectionibus aliis, et tota incumbit amori.*

of Bernards' sermons entitled *De affectionibus recte or-dinandis* indicates.[146] Such ordering is a grace for which one prays,[147] since it is God alone who disposes all things sweetly and strongly and is able to introduce some order into the naturally unruly feelings.[148]

Affectus is vitiated and in need of purification to the extent that the will applies itself to what is unspiritual.[149] The process of purification or ordering is simply the gradual reversal of this preference, as painful as the willed component of the disordination is strong. Thus Bernard says, 'You have to lose yourself somewhat . . . and live a life based on heaven and not according to human feeling'.[150] 'Reflect, therefore, how, when these feelings are duly ordered, they become virtues, but when they are not so ordered they are simply sources of trouble (*perturbationes*).[151]

> Discretion is not so much a virtue as the moderator and controller of virtue, that which orders the af-fects and gives instruction in right behaviour. Take away discretion and virtue becomes vice and the very inclination of nature (*ipsaque affectio naturalis*) is changed to disturbance and thus becomes the destroyer of nature.[152]

The process of growth which such ordering in-troduces begins with the experience of fear and gradually moves to its culmination in love.[153] As love is purified,

146. Div 50 (SBO 6a:270,12).

147. SC 50.8 (SBO 2:83,15): *Dirige actus nostros . . . et dispone affectus nostros.*

148. SC 50.8 (SBO 2:83,14).

149. Cf. Div 6.3 (SBO 6a:107,14), Div 13.4 (SBO 6a:133,8).

150. Dil 27 (SBO 3:142,16–18).

151. Div 50.3 (SBO 6a:272,4–5).

152. SC 49.5 (SBO 2:76,9–12).

153. Div 50.2 (SBO 6a:271,21–23).

the affect is more and more concentrated on God,[154] and comes to long for the completion of his plan of salvation. 'For he desires to mix with the wine of divine love the sweetness of natural affect in resuming his own body, and that in a glorified state.[155] Thus, we see, Bernard's view on the role of the affect and the conditions for its ordering was determined by his appreciation that in the resurrection of the body, all the components of human nature will find their glorious fulfilment. This outcome is what God has willed in creating us, so that his plan is incomplete without the prospect of our inclusion. Bernard reminds us of this in one of his sermons for the feast of All Saints.

The holy souls whom God has sealed with his own image desire you. They are waiting for you, since without you their joy cannot be full, nor can their glory be complete nor their happiness made perfect. This natural desire still flourishes in them somewhat and, therefore, not all their affect flows in the direction of God. It is, somehow, constrained, so that it makes a fold, bending itself over in desire, also, for you.[156]

At this point it becomes possible to establish that a linkage exists between the concept of desire for God and the theme of *affectus*. We have seen that, according to Bernard, affect is a natural endowment which, when guided by reason and seconded by an upright will, can, under grace, serve as a dynamic factor in the spiritual growth of the human being.[157] Three concise descriptions of *affectus* by modern writers could easily be applied also to desire. Dumontier refers to affects as 'tender and profound movements of the soul'.[158] Blanpain

154. Asc 3.7 (SBO 5:135,25–26).
155. Dil 32 (SBO 3:146,13–15).
156. OS 3.2 (SBO 5:350,14–19).
157. Cf. Hiss, *Die Anthropologie*, p. 106.
158. Translated from P. Dumontier, *S. Bernard et la Bible*, p. 114.

writes, '*Affectio* is a movement of the heart in the direction
of a value which is the counterpart of a desire within the
human being.'[159] Finally, Jean Leclercq makes this more explicit by simply explaining that *affectus* is 'the attachment
experienced by the human being for God'.[160]

There are a few bernardine texts in which affect is explicitly linked with desire. When 'a soul desires nothing else
and seeks nothing else from God except God himself', this is
referred to as a more worthy *affectus*.[161] Prayer should be
made *in summo affectu et desiderio*.[162] We read *affecta
vehementius ad desideratos affatus*,[163] and there is a parallel
between *desiderio feror non ratione* and *affectio urget*.[164]
The conjunction of the two themes is, however, relatively
rare, notwithstanding the fact that desire is a feeling, and often the subjective state referred to by *affectus* is clearly, from
the context, one of desire.

We do find, however, that desire and affect often share
the same qualifiers. Both *suspirare* and *inhiare* are used of affect,[165] as are *vehementer* and *devotio*.[166] Affect also is qualified by *ferventior*,[167] used equivalently to *non tepide*.[168] The

159. Translated from Blanpain, 'Language mystique', p. 66.
160. Translated from Jean Leclercq, 'S. Bernard et la théologie
monastique du XIIe siècle', *Théologien*, p. 14.
161. Div 8.9 (SBO 6a:117,9–11).
162. Div 107 (SBO 6a:380,16). Some manuscripts, as well as the
edition of Mabillon, have an epexegetical genitive here instead of
the reading employed above from the critical edition, that is, *in
summo affectus desiderio*. Not only in the reading of the critical edition more likely on extrinsic grounds, but the alternative is weak in-
trinsically; such a word order is unexpected in such a construction,
especially in a sermon which has affectus as its principal theme.
163. SC 67.3 (SBO 2:190,5).
164. SC 9.2 (SBO 1:43,11–12).
165. SC 9.3 (SBO 1:44,2–5).
166. SC 20.1 (SBO 1:115,5–7). Cf. Div 62 (SBO 6a:295,15).
167. SC 26.7 (SBO 1:175,2–3).
168. Div 25.5 (SBO 6a:190,21).

heart's love is characterized as *affectuosa*.[169]

Desire and affect are not synonymous designations. Generally the theme of desire occurs in more theological contexts, where the language is more biblical. Affect is more likely to appear in passages where the primary interest is experiential or psychological, though obviously there is considerable flexibility needed in defining such areas. Often the terms are used interchangeably, though improperly. Such examples of synedoche were far more frequent in ancient and medieval texts, especially when there was a question of interpreting the Scriptures or patristic literature, than is customary today.[170] The modern reader has sometimes to adapt to the ancient ways.

The dynamic aspect of affect is derived from the fact that it is closely related to *appetentia*. It is because the human being is in a process of becoming and has actively to seek to sustain that process that it is susceptible to the range of affects. To the extent that one seems to be attaining the object of one's pursuit, love and joy are experienced; where such attainment is blocked, fear and sadness intervene. Thus the various affects are to be seen as dependent upon a more basic ontological movement or *appetentia* toward a goal.

Desire depends also on that fundamental teleology and, in Bernard's broad view of the dynamic of desire, is far more wide-ranging than the experience of conscious yearning and willed seeking. The experience of desire, as we will discuss it in a subsequent chapter, is the discovery of an already-existing ontological movement, not the inducement of a psychic state by the manipulation of the

169. Div 29.2 (SBO 6a:211,3).

170. *Synedoche* is a figure of speech by which a part is put for the whole, the cause for the effect, a proper for a common noun, or vice versa.

organs of consciousness. It is this underlying desire, this
pre-elective movement at the level of being which closely
corresponds to the basic *appetentia*, which is the tendency to love and which lies at the root of all affect.

It is only when desire and affect are discussed in a
secondary or derivative sense that a divergence is noted in
meaning. The *experience* of desire is a species of affect,
closely akin to love, but also containing elements of the
other emotions. It is this plural usage of both terms
which makes it difficult to propose the elements of a
clear equation of their relationship. Jacques Blanpain
writes thus of the connections between the two ideas:

> Another concept which is very close to that of desire,
> and which is found on nearly every page of St Ber-
> nard, is that of *affectus* or *affectio*. The analysis of
> this term should enable us to perceive something of
> the significance, the origins, and the life which
> belongs to desire in a human being who orients
> himself toward God. The notion of *affectus* or *affec-
> tio* is, in fact, linked with that of desire, though it is
> very difficult always to define their relationship ex-
> actly.[171]

His introduction to the topic may, perhaps, serve as our
conclusion.

DEVOTIO

Devotio is a common Latin term for a wide range of
religious attitudes, as well as for the external actions and
offerings which stem from these.[172] The word was readily
taken over from pagan usage by christian authors.It was a
concept which seems to have won special favour for itself
among the more 'roman' of the ecclesiastical writers. For

171. Translated from Blanpain, 'Language mystique', pp. 58–59.
172. A survey of usage is found in ThLL vol 5: 878–880.

them it evoked a religious service which was characterised by objectivity, sobriety, gravity, and even a little stateliness. At first, *devotio* was used to designate all forms of divine service but, with the passage of time, there was a change in emphasis. The frequent christian homiletic theme of contrasting interior attitudes with the external forms of worship led to a renewed insistence on the personal and inward aspect of devotion. Once again, the subjective disposition of the worshipper came to be the principal area in which *devotio* was exercised.

The authors of the Middle Ages, perhaps under the influence of Cassian's usage, took up this accent and heightened it. Devotion was seen principally as a subjective state of religious feeling; not mere sentiment, but the appropriate interior concomitant of the virtuous and religious actions of the person. It even came to be regarded as a sort of reward for or confirmation of the dedication which preceded it.[173] Because Bernard associated *devotio* with intense religious feeling, he often used it in association with *desiderium*, and with many of the words which he used as alternatives or supplements. Once again, it is clear that the two words are not synonymous. *Devotio* applies only to desire as consciously experienced. This means that it is not linked with desire as a reality which precedes and goes beyond experience. There is, however, considerable overlap. When the experience of desire is strong, it is often described in terms of *devotio*. Thus, in one text, we read *ingens devotio et desiderium vehemens et praedulcis affectus*.[174]

---

173. This is based on the article of Jean Châtillon, 'Dévotion' in DSp 3: cols 702–716. The value of the author's remarks with regard to Bernard is diminished by his apparently exclusive reliance on Mabillion's index, rather than on a wide reading of the works themselves.

174. SC 32.3 (SBO 1:227,25–26).

Devotion belongs to the affective rather than to the cognitive order. This is demonstrated by a text in which Bernard is discoursing on the wings by which the seraphim are borne aloft.

For my part I believe that these wings can readily be understood as knowledge and devotion. These are the means by which the seraphim are lifted up toward the One who is above themselves. Whoever tries to fly with only one wing falls down, and the higher his attainment, the heavier he falls. The philosophers of the nations were expert at this, for although they had the knowledge of God, they did not render to God the glory that was his due. So, as a result, their knowing was emptied of content and their foolish hearts became clouded. . . . Enthusiasm without knowledge is in the same condition. The more vehemently it presses forward, the more serious its collapse, for it crashes hard and rebounds. Where charity accompanies understanding and devotion goes with knowledge, there a person flies securely.[175]

Devotio is used to describe the same reality as desire;[176] it is regarded by Bernard as a gift of God,[177] and the effect of grace.[178] Devotion is described as a consolation and attributed specially to the work of the Holy Spirit,[179] so often that its outcome is tears.[180] Devotion is often linked with the idea of fervour. Good works are to be done 'with the fervour of devotion and with the sweetness of spiritual grace'.[181] Likewise, Bernard speaks about the

175. I Nov 4.2 (SBO 5:316,3–14). Cf. SC 49.4 (SBO 2:75,20–24).
176. SC 28.10 (SBO 1:199,2).
177. SC 74.8 (SBO 2:244,28–29).
178. SC 74.8 (SBO 2:244,12–19), Div 8.6 (SBO 6a:115,21).
179. SC 20.7 (SBO 1:119,14–15).
180. Epi 3.8 (SBO 4:309,18).
181. Nat 1.5 (SBO 4:248,20–21). Cf. Div 82.2 (SBO 6a:323,9).

'devotion and fervour of the fast'.[182] It is aligned with charity and in the expression *gratia scilicet devotionis et fervor caritatis*.[183] And, speaking of this reality as the object of the human pursuit, he writes, 'These desire devotion, they ask for wine, they clamour for fervour'.[184]

Devotio is found in the same context as *dulcedo* and even *delectatio*,[185] where the dental assonance must have pleased the author. In one case we find *ex pinguedine devotionis* used in parallel with *animi intentio*.[186]

The suggestion that the experience of devotion may have a special role to play in the earlier stages of spiritual development which will be transcended as progress is made, is intimated in one of Bernard's Easter sermons.

For some people Christ has risen, but he has not yet ascended. Indeed, he still dwells with them on earth through the experience of his kindly sweetness. Such people spend their whole day in devotion, they weep at their prayers and they sigh with yearning during their meditations. For them everything is festive and a source of joy, and during these days, Alleluia is their constant song. But it is necessary that this milk should be taken away from them so that they might learn to derive their nourishment from solid food. And so it is good for them that Christ goes away and that this temporary devotion should be removed from them.[187]

Devotion is, as far as Bernard was concerned, an experience of fervour which is expressed in a certain enthusiasm

182. Quad 3.1f (SBO 4:364f).
183. P Epi 2.4 (SBO 4:322,10–11).
184. P Epi 2.8 (SBO 4:325,19).
185. Quad 1.4 (SBO 4:346,13).
186. Quad 9.2 (SBO 4:436,24). The notion of *intentio* as it appears in monastic tradition and in the writings of St Bernard will be discussed in the next section of this chapter.
187. Pasc 4.2 (SBO 5:111,5–8).

for good works and for prayer. Such devotion needs always to be harnessed to understanding and prepared for the inevitable changes which development brings. The joy and consolation typical of devotion are also experienced, from time to time, by someone under the sway of a powerful feeling of desire. Desire is, however, a larger reality, since it comprehends not only the positive feelings characteristic of devotion, but also the negative emotions which follow the discovery of the extent of personal sinfulness and the realisation of just how far away is the goal.

Devotion appears with more weight in the writings of Aelred of Rievaulx. That it was accepted in the monastic ambience of the twelfth century as conveying something of the experiential reality of desire is illustrated by one lyrical passage in his rule for anchoresses. 'Whatever you have of devotion, of love, of desire, of feeling, pour it all out on the head of your bridegroom.'[188]

INTENTIO

Intentio is a word endowed with rich connotations in the writings of latin monasticism, although this is not always recognised. It is a difficult word to translate sensitively since, although Middle English retained the breadth of the older usage,[189] contemporary English restricts the meaning of 'intention' to the narrow ethical sense which *intentio* came to assume in the moral

---

188. Aelred, *De Inst Incl* 31 (SChr 76:128): . . . *quicquid habes devotionis, quicquid amoris, quicquid desiderii, quicquid affectionis, totum effunde super Sponsi tui caput.*

189. Cf. Hans Kurath and others, *Middle English Dictionary* (Ann Arbor: University of Michigan, 1953) *sub voce* 'entente', part E 2, pp. 183–185.

theology of the scholastic era.

I have examined the history and development of this term elsewhere, taking as my starting point the profound designation of prayer as *intentio cordis* in the *Rule of Benedict*.[190] I have tried to show there that when the word is understood in the light of both antecedent and subsequent tradition, especially as represented by John Cassian and Gregory the Great, the phrase likely includes within its meaning the notion of desire for God. This is particularly true of Gregory the Great, who frequently employs the word *intentio* to designate the movement of the Christian in the direction of heaven, with a meaning parallel to *coeleste desiderium*,[191] for instance, in the expression *pro intentione supernae patriae*.[192] John of Fécamp, a benedictine abbot from 1028 until 1078 and a 'master of the spiritual life' who was very much influenced by the language of Augustine and Gregory, used *intendere* and its congnates exclusively in the sense of desire for or movement toward heaven.[193]

The rich history of the theme of *intentio* makes it important that we inquire whether this was part of Bernard's vocabulary of desire.

Bernard's use of *intendere* and *intentio* is rich and varied, a fact which demonstrates that the theme retained a measure of flexibility, even in the first half of the twelfth

190. Cf. M. Casey, 'Intentio Cordis (RB 52.4)', *Regulae Benedicti Studia* 6/7 (1980) 105–120.

191. Gregory the Great, *In Ev* 11.1 (PL 76:1115b). Gregory's use of *intentio* is discussed in M. Casey, 'Spiritual Desire in the Gospel Homilies of St Gregory the Great', CSt 16 (1981) 297–314; see especially pp. 306–308.

192. Gregory the Great, *In Ev* 9.1 (PL 76:1106c), *In Ezek* I.3.2 (PL 76:811b).

193. John of Fécamp, *Confessio Theologica*, I, line 231; II, line 371; III, line 931; Conclusion, line 1263; *Lamentatio*, lines 187–188. I am citing the edition of Leclercq.

century. Firstly, *intentio* can be used in an ambrosian sense to indicate the inward component of behaviour, the complement of *actio* or *operatio*.[194] Thus Bernard writes 'If [the devil] fails to prevent the action, then he attempts to subvert the intention'.[195] Because it is a component in behaviour, Bernard avers that intention needs to be scrutinised as closely as the outward course of action. It is not enough to look at what is going to be done; one must also examine one's motivation. Here Bernard is anticipating something of Aquinas' formal morality based on intention. 'It is the intention of the heart and the judgment of the conscience which gives the colour to what you do.'[196] In the course of deciding a suitable penance for someone who has been negligent in his celebration of the Eucharist, Bernard stated a firm principle.

It is not the cause of events nor what is involved nor the outcome of actions which can decide whether something is worthy of praise or blame, but only the motivation of the intention.[197]

Elsewhere he repeats this teaching more concisely, 'It is the intention which decides merits'.[198] Thus the foundations of justice and rectitude are to be sought at the level of intention.[199] Living a virtuous life is more than performing the works of virtue. One must be possessed of a certain

194. Cf. Ambrose of Milan, *Traité sur l'évangile de saint Luc*, ed. G. Tissot (SChr 45: 51) Introduction, I.18–20 (50–52), VII.85 (SChr 52:36).

195. SC 54.9 (SBO 2:109,8–9). Cf. IV HM 14(SBO 5:66,10).

196. SC 71.1 (SBO 2:215,23).

197. Ep 69.1 (SBO 7:169,4–6): *intentionis propositum*. This is a strong statement, since *propositum* was often used almost synonymously with *intentio*. The two words are also associated in QH 2.3 (SBO 4:391,19). Cf. SC 16.1 (SBO 1:95,20–21).

198. Gra 46 (SBO 3:216,10).

199. Cf. Div 32.2 (SBO 6a:219,16–21), Div 2.5 (SBO 6a:82,22): *opus est enim ut iustitia sit in intentione . . .* Div 64.2 (SBO 6a:297, 16).

quality of mind,[200] which does not permit the person to beome bent in sin.[201]

This teaching, although it undoubtedly has application to the question of purpose and motivation in particular actions,[202] really has to do with a broader, more fundamental and less immediate orientation. It concerns the basic direction which a person allows his life to assume. The intention is not merely one's purpose in doing a particular act, it is also one's fundamental direction in life. Thus, Bernard insists that the intention be fixed on God rather than on worldly affairs.[203] 'It is to Him that he should direct his intention'.[204] Building on the meaning of *intendere* 'to look upon, to look at closely',[205] Bernard defines or describes intention as 'the face of the soul'.[206] By the way he looks at

200. Div 32.2 (SBO 6a:219,16–21), Div 113 (SBO 6a:391,4–6). On the other hand, Div 72.2 (SBO 6a:308,15): *iustitia est rectitudo voluntatis* is a departure from Bernard's usual way of expressing himself.

201. Div 32.3 (SBO 6a:220,10–11): *Ipsa ratio ad peccatum per intentionem curvatur.*

202. This is especially true in SC 30.1 (SBO 1:210,10–11 and 16–18), SC 45.5 (SBO 2:52,17), SC 72.4 (SBO 2:227,22), SC 65.2 (SBO 2:173,2–3) and many other places.

203. SC 40.3 (SBO 2:26,1–2).

204. SC 64.8 (SBO 2:170,20).

205. Helpful throughout this section is ThLL 6: cols 2112–2124.

206. SC 40.3 (SBO 2:25,11). In this respect a comparison with William of St Thierry's *In Cant* 1 (SChr 82:92) is instructive. See also, Javelet, *Image*, vol. 2: xxxvi note 23. On Bernard's use of *intentio* with connotations of watchfulness, diligence and scrutiny, see SC 32.6 (SBO 1:230,4–6), SC 41.2 (SBO 2:2920–21), SC 49.6 (SBO 2:77, 2–3), SC 50.5 (SBO 2:81,8), SC 50.8 (SBO 2:83,1), SC 62.7 (SBO 2:160,4–5), SC 67.9 (SBO 2:194,13), SC 67,12 (SBO 2:196, 5), SC 68.1 (SBO 2:196,24 and 197,4), SC 68,2 (SBO 2:197,10 and 21–22), SC 69.5 (SBO 2:205), SC 69.7 (SBO 2:206,14 and 22), SC 69.8 (SBO 2:207,10), SC 76.9 (SBO 2:259,15), Div 26.1 (SBO 6a: 194,4). Notice that most of the references seem to be concentrated in the sermons written around 1145.

issues, a person reveals his true inner qualities. Thus, intention is seen as the concrete way in which a person presents himself to the outside world. To grasp a person's intention is a process which transcends a mere appraisal of purpose or motivation in a single act. It is going beyond appearances to make contact with the fundamental inner principle which animates and determines the quality of everything that is done.[207]

In a curious series of images, Bernard asserts that the *intentio* is a far deeper reality than either thought or affect. 'We are saying that thought is, as it were, the skin of the soul; the affect is the flesh, and so we are able to take for granted that the bone of the soul is its intention.'[208] Elsewhere the intention is described as the head of the contemplative, meaning thereby his spiritual understanding.[209] The meaning of the bridegroom supporting the bride's head is that he supports the intention of her mind 'so that it does not become bent (*ne incurvetur*) and so incline toward carnal and secular desires'.[210] On the other hand,

207. SC 40.2-3 (SBO 2:25-26). Two elements comprise the constitutive principles of intention, as far as Bernard is concerned: the *res*, which is the matter in hand, the potential course of action which the doer wills to come about, and the *causa*, which is the reason, purpose, or motivation behind his endeavours. For an action to be virtuous both components must be free from all taint of malice and from lower desires. Bernard often speaks of a 'pure intention' and of the necessity of taking concrete measures to ensure its purifications. IV HM 14 (SBO 5:66,10), QH 9.2 (SBO 4:436,25), V Nat 3.6 (SBO 4:216,10), Adv 6.2 (SBO 4:192,1), O Pasc 1.7 (SBO 5:116,24): *caritas sola purgat intentionem*. A strong statement occurs in SC 7.7 (SBO 1:35,3-7): 'In itself continence is not meritorious in God's sight if it pursues human glory. And because of this, the great task is to obtain purity of intention which is the only means by which your mind may strive to please God and so be enabled to come close to him. For to come close to God is to see him, which is given only to the pure in heart.'
    208. Div 6.1 (SBO 6a:105,13-14).
    209. Div 123.2 (SBO 6a:402,2).
    210. Dil 13 (SBO 3:129,21-23).

intentio seems also to apply to the will, as can be gauged from the following exclamation: *O amor sanctus et castus, O dulcis et suavis affectio, O pura et defaecata* [sic] *intentio voluntatis* . . .[211] It is clear, accordingly, that *intentio* does not have a restrictive meaning in Bernard's writings. That it means desire is rarely as evident as in Gregory or John of Fécamp, but Bernard is too traditional a user of language to have emptied the concept entirely of this element. The theme of desire is often present by evocation and association. It has something to do with the fundamental orientation which a person allows his life to take, whether that life retains its native bearing in the direction of God, in whose image it was formed, or whether it becomes bent and folds back on itself to become fully involved in self-gratification.[212]

To the extent that *intentio* relates to desire, it is in the sense of not so much to desire experience, but to desire as the movement of being toward its goal that it has reference. In this sense it can be viewed as complementing *devotio* which concerns only the experiential aspect of desire for God.

The opposite of *intentio* reveals something of its nature. When Bernard seeks something to contrast *intentio* with he usually lights upon such realities as aimlessness, lack of direction, carelessness, insensitivity to spiritual realities, lack of fervour, or excessive concentration on immediate issues, dispersal of energy. In this light, *intentio* appears to be Bernard's way of describing the fundamental orientation adopted by a person. It is a vision of life which is volutarily applied to particular options. When it is consistently followed, it imprints on that person's life a style which demonstrates the direction

211. Dil 28 (SBO 3:143,12–13).
212. Dil 29 (SBO 3:144,5): *Huic fragili et aerumnoso corpori intenta et distenta.* Cf. Div 124.2 (SBO 6a:403,20–21).

of his movement, whether toward, or away from, God.

Recent use of the word 'compunction' usually restricts its meaning to the area of regret concerning sins committed and mistakes made. This had not always been the case, especially in the West. A stream of thought, developed in the writings of John Cassian and greatly reinforced and strengthened in the works of Gregory the Great, understood compunction not only in the sense of grief for personal transgressions, but also in the sense of the pain and suffering occasioned by being separated form the object of one's love and desire, *quia differtur a regno*, because one is so far removed from the Kingdom.[213]

Compunctio was originally a medical term, signifying a pricking, stinging sensation or a piercing, *punctio*. It is active in form. When, throughout the tradition, the concept is used, God is often said to effect compunction —he does the piercing. The human side of the experience is the passive one of being pierced, although

213. Gregory the Great, *Dial* 3.34 (PL 77:300a). A short presentation of Gregory's teaching is given in M. Casey 'Spiritual Desire', pp. 308–311. Jean Leclercq's 'St Gregory, Doctor of Desire', the second chapter in *Love of Learning*, is also to be consulted. The entries in ThLL are somewhat disappointing in their treatment of this aspect of compunction. The eastern monastic tradition is discussed by I. Hausherr, *Penthos, The Doctrine of Compunction in the Christian East,* CS 53 (Kalamazoo: Cistercian Publications, 1982). As a rule, the Eastern Fathers emphasised that their tears were due to their sins and, in humility, refrained from speaking about them as the result of a personal experience of the divine goodness and as the expression of a deep and intense love for God. Much later, Simeon the New Theologian, who was somewhat less veiled in his reference to personal spiritual experiences, wrote more openly about love-inspired tears which were sweeter than honey. Hausherr avers that the older, more reticent Fathers, should probably be understood in the same sense.

this is often obscured by the form of the word and the loose usage of the various writers.

The primary effect of compunction is stimulation. Its purpose is to arouse the individual from torpor and complacency and to lead him to take positive steps to improve his condition. It has nothing to do with a futile and depressive sense of guilt at the measure of personal failure. Nor is it to be associated with a scrupulous review of actions and hidden motivations. Compunction is an energising force. It is the experience of being stung; its outcome is action. Sometimes a person is motivated to amend his life by the perception of the true status of his past performance and a recognition of the dangers to which he is, even now, concretely exposed. In a moment he sloughs off the accumulated complacency of years and stands vulnerable before the evidence of his own fragility. In such a case it is the sobering estimation of the unlikelihood of achieving a particular goal unless great changes are made which signals the birth of compuntion. He is carried towared conversion by the grace of fear of the Lord. This is the harsher and more negative aspect of compuction and one that is, perhaps, better known.

But compunction also has a positive side. Often a person is drawn to conversion, not so much through the recognition of personal sinfulness, as through the positive appreciation of the love and kindness of God. He is, perhaps, moved, touched, pierced by the realisation that, despite all his sinfulness, he is loved by God. When the depth of the divine compassion penetrates through the hardened husk of habit, the person becomes aware of the inadequacy of his own former level of response. His experience of his continuing resistance to grace is poignant, he becomes regretful of his past and dissatisfied and angry at elements of his present life. He is, thus motivated to change his future, animated by the desire to respond more fully to the love of God which he has experienced. The sustained struggle which amendation involves fills him with the desire to be beyond compromise, and so compunction becomes simultaneously an avowal of inadequacy and a fervent desire for the coming of the Kingdom. This is clearly stated by Gregory the Great.

> There are two main types of compunction. First the soul thirsting for God is pierced (*compungitur*) by fear and afterwards by love. In the beginning, the soul is moved to tears at the remembrance of its evil deeds, and it fears the prospect of eternal punishment. But when, after a long and anxious experience of pain, this fear works itself out, then is born in the soul a calmness coming from the assurance of forgiveness and the soul is inflamed with love for heavenly joys. He who previously wept at the prospect of being led to punishment, now begins to weep most bitterly because he is far from the Kingdom. For the mind contemplates the choirs of angels, the community of the blessed spirits and the splendour of the unending vision of God and it becomes still more downcast at being separated from these eternal goods than it was when it wept out of fear of unending evils. For it is a fact that when the compunction of fear has become complete, then it draws the soul into the compunction of love.[214]

214. Gregory the Great, *Dial* 3.34 (PL 77:300a). The same thought can be found in *Moralia* 24.6 (PL 76:291), *In Ezek* II.10. 20–21 (PL 76:1070), *Ep* 7.23 (PL 77:879), *Moralia* 23.41 (PL 76: 276a). An extraordinary passage is *Moralia* 23.43 (PL 76:277–278), of which the following is part. 'Sometimes he is admitted to a particular, unaccustomed experience of inner sweetness and, for a moment, he is, in some way, a new man, set afire by the breath of the Spirit. And the more he tastes the object of his love, the stronger grows his desire for it. . . . For after he discovers that sweetness, he

We know from the writings of John of Fécamp that this gregorian concept of the dual nature of compunction was still current in the eleventh-century world of monastic theology.[215] The question which must be posed here is whether Bernard was familiar with it and whether some of his teaching on the nature of desire for God is to be found in passages which deal with compunction.

In fact, Bernard wrote a great deal about compunction. He often refers to it as an integral part in the process of conversion.[216] Usually, he regarded it as the first phase in the process of being converted,[217] although

---

becomes capable of perceiving what sort of a person he is without it. He tries to prolong the experience, but he is driven back from its strength because he is still weak. And because he lacks the capacity to contemplate such purity, he weeps sweet tears and then he falls back and lies down on the tears of his weakness. . . . In this state he is filled with yearning and he ardently tries to transcend himself, but each time he is beaten by fatigue and falls back into familiar darkness. When we are thus pierced (*compuncti*), we seek to distance ourselves from what we have made of ourselves, so that we may be refashioned according to what we were originally.' One of Gregory's principal sources in this matter, as in others, is John Cassian. It is interesting to note the breadth of Cassian's view of compunction, regarding both its causes and its forms. A particular point to note is the number of times he stresses the joy of compunction. For instance, 'It often happens that because of the unspeakable joy and the great enthusiasm of spirit, the fruit of such saving compunction bursts forth in cries of unbearable and unmeasurable joy. The result is that the great happiness of heart and the feeling of exalation penetrates even to the cell of one's neighbour.' *Conferences* 9.27 (SChr 54:63). On the text of Gregory, cf. Div 3.6 (SBO 6a:91,1–3).

216. SC 57.7 (SBO 2:123,18).

217. Asc 1.3 (SBO 5:125,9–10): 'The first work of faith working through love is compunction of heart'. Bernard often refers to the sequence: *compunction, devotion, piety,* understanding this last term more in terms of love, *pietas*, or kindness, the quality of being *pius*, than of religious fervour. For instance: Sent 1.9 (SBO 6a:9,15–17). Sent

sometimes he placed fear ahead of it.[218] The connection of compunction with fear of the Lord and Bernard's emphasis on its special role in the early stages of spiritual development are constant features of his presentation. He admits the negative character of these realities and does not dissimulate the pain which they cause.[219]

2.169 (SBO 6b:56,1–4), Div 87.6 (SBO 6a:333,9–12), Div 90.1–4 (SBO 6a:337–340). All the texts cited are explanation of the image of the three unguents and are either sources or tributaries of the development in SC 10–12 where, however, *contritio* is used instead of *compunctio*. Note SC 12.1 (SBO 1:60,9–11): 'The first unguent is experienced as stinging, because it leads to compunction. This is the bitter recollection of sins and it causes pain.' In SC 16, Bernard discusses the seven yawns; the first four of these relate to compunction, the remaining three to confession. Cf. SC 16.4 (SBO 1:91–92). A further sequence is given in SC 18.6 (SBO 1:108,4–6), again with compunction listed first. A different schema appears in p Epi 1.4 (SBO 4:317,1–10), though the sequential relationship of the items listed is less obvious in this case. Cf Div 48 (SBO 6a:268, 10–11), Div 118 (SBO 6a:396,8–11), Div 88.1 (SBO 6a:334,4–7).

218. Sent 1.34 (SBO 6b:18–19) has the following listing: *timor, compunctio, abrenuntio, humilitas, confessio [= purgatio], pullulatio* [sic] *[= virtutes], sapientia [= caritas perfecta]*. Div 40 (SBO 6a:236–243) has *cognitio sui* at the head of the list. This is followed by *paenitentia* (which includes much of the territory normally assigned to *compunctio*), *dolor, confessio oris, maceratio carnis, correctio operis* and *perseverantia*. A different approach again is found in Asspt 4.3 (SBO 5:245–246). Here Bernard is speaking of the four days which preceded Lazarus' return to life. The first he assigns to fear, the second to the laborious contest with evil habit and temptation. The third day is taken up with the painful recognition of wasted years and the fourth with the confusion and shame occasioned by the appreciation of the weight of personal sinfulness. At this point, Bernard believed, the soul is in the right state to be recalled to life.

219. Here the medical imagery associated with the original idea of *compunctio* may return. Compunction is the lancing of the wound of routine, *consuetudo* in SC 18.5 (SBO 1:106,5). See also,

Compunction is similar to *contritio* (which, of course, means being broken),[220] in that both are activated by the remembrance of having sinned.[221] Compunction is a more elementary experience than devotion, although it leads to it.[222] It is a less advanced experience than *affectus*.[223] The role of compunction, as Bernard understood it, is to make the person aware of his concrete sinfulness, and so to discomfort him by this realisation that he is motivated to take steps to amend his life, not for the sake of virtue, but simply to ease the pain. As such, compunction is closely related to penitence,[224] in its effect of countering the influence of sin,[225] so long as compunction's effects are verifiable in behaviour.[226]

The subjective experience of being pierced by compunction finds its characteristic expression in tears.[227]

SC 10.4 (SBO 1:50,21), SC 12.1 (SBO 1:60,9–11), Vict 1.5 (SBO 6a:32,10–11). A dual pain is noted in Div 2.1 (SBO 6a:80,20): *labor in actionibus, dolor in passionibus.*

220. Cf. SC 10.4–5 (SBO 1:50–51).

221. SC 12.1 (SBO 1:60,9–11); *In labore messis* 1.4 (SBO 5:219.7), Asspt 4.3 (SBO 5.245–246), Sent 1.9 (SBO 6b:9,15–17), Sent 2.169 (SBO 6b:56,1–4).

222. SC 10.4 (SBO 1:50,21), SC 18.5 (SBO 1:106,26–27), SC 18.6 (SBO 1:108,4–6), Div 88.1 (SBO 6a:334,4–5). There is a contrast made between compunction and devotion in SC 23.9 (SBO 1:145,4–5).

223. SC 32.3 (SBO 1:227,29–30, 228.1–2).

224. SC 23.9 (SBO 1:145,4). Cf. SC 18.6 (SBO 1:108,4–6), Div 30.2 (SBO 6a:215,19–20), Div 40.4 (SBO 6a:237,5), Div 75 (SBO 6a:314,3–4).

225. SC 48.1 (SBO 2:67,21). Cf. Asc 1.3 (SBO 5:125,14–15).

226. Pasc 1.17 (SBO 5:93,27): 'The sign of true compunction is the flight from opportunities for sin and the removal of their occasions.'

227. SC 54.8 (SBO 2:107,25–26). John Cassian takes a different approach. An outbreak of tears is only one manifestation of compunction (Conf. 9.27; SChr 54:63) and not all kinds of tears are to be sought indiscriminately, lest in the effort to produce them the

The capacity to be moved by tears is diametrically opposed to that hardness of heart which resists grace and, thus, represents a step in the direction of conversion. These tears are seen, according to an ancient precedent, as a sort of baptism. 'There is a kind of baptism involved in compunction of heart and in earnest tears.'[228] The privileged occasion of receiving the gift of compunction is in the reading of the Scriptures and in the exercise of psalmody.[229]

Bernard demonstrated that he was aware that compunction has a dual basis. 'There are two types of compunction. One is grief for many excesses, the other is a celebration for the divine gifts.'[230] He distinguished tears which are associated with devotion from those which stem from repentance.[231] He also recognised that the grief of compunction is the beginning, not the end, of the spiritual life and, as such, it prepares the way for less painful experiences.

> The third kiss takes place when the mind, having been consumed by penitential sorrow and having received the gifts of the virtues, is inspired by heavenly desire, and desires to be led into the secret joys of the inner chamber and is impatient in its love. Then, with sweet sighs, breaking into the words of the soul, it cries out with all the affection of

---

straining after God (*intentio*) is diminished (*Conf* 9.30; SChr 54: 65–66).

228. O Pasc 1.7 (SBO 5:116,7).
229. Div 55.1 (SBO 6a:281,1). The connection between compunction and *lectio divina* is repeatedly stressed in the latin monastic tradition. On compunction and psalmody see Cassian *Conf* 9.26 (SChr 54:62), 10.11 (54.92). Cf. M. Casey, 'The Prayer of Psalmody', CSt 18 (1983) 117–118.
230. SC 56.7 (SBO 2:118,16–18).
231. Epi 3.8 (SBO 4:309,18–20).

its heart, 'It is your face, O Lord, that I seek'. And thus the bridegroom, who is the object of its love and affection and for whom it sighs, becomes present to it because of its vehement desire.[232]

But compunction is more, as far as Bernard was concerned, than a painful prelude to love. It is itself a work of love.[233] The pain is merely the suffering induced by the agony of neutralising the effects of sin and selfishness and of cutting off former sources of gratification. Such a process would never be initiated unless its necessary toil and grief were compensated for by a hope for expectation of a felicitous outcome. Who would willingly embrace such suffering unless there were a reasonable assurance that it would be worthwhile? Thus Bernard noted that it is only when one is already touched by love that it is possible to bear such pain, and even to seek it out.[234]

It is true that the germinal love which animates compunction has to be allowed to grow, that it is of a rudimentary spirituality which will later have to be surpassed, but Bernard saw an advantage in this. Because love begins at the level of the flesh, it is able effectively to counter the influence of concupiscence. 'This sort of love is set against the consupiscence of the flesh.'[235] Thus, also, sharing in the sufferings of Christ is not the highest expression of love, but it nourishes the soul 'with the sweetness of devotion' and causes it to grow strong and thus able for higher things.[236]

Bernard recognised the positive aspect of compunction. Commenting on the reunion of the patriarch

232. Div 87.1 (SBO 6a:330,4–9).
233. Asc 1.3 (SBO 5:125,9–12).
234. SC 20.6 (SBO 1:118,15).
235. Div 29.4 (SBO 6a:212,18–213,1).
236. SC 20.8 (SBO 1:120,11). Cf. Aelred, *Orat Past* 8 (SChr 76:198): . . . *et suavitas compunctionis reficiat mentes eorum.*

Joseph with his brothers, he spoke of tears flowing from the fullness of his heart, *de pinguedine cordis.*[237] The sorrow which is experienced by those who desire God is occasioned not only by their failures to live according to the fundamental direction of their lives, but also from the completeness of their desire, which occasionally overwhelms sensibility and expresses itself in tears: *flet ex desiderio.*[238] The reasons for such affliction are spelled out in terms strongly reminiscent of Gregory the Great.

The grief of the saints is threefold: it is because they have fallen from paradise, it is because they are held fast in a state of exile, and it is because they are still far away from the Kingdom.[239]

Accordingly, Bernard's teaching on compunction must be regarded as being radical continuity with the general acceptance of that theme in latin monastic tradition. There is, in Bernard, a tendency to emphasise its role in the early stages of spiritual development and accordingly more of his teaching on compunction is concerned with the experience of repugnance at past sinfulness than with the positive aspects which we find emphasised in Gregory.[240]

Bernard's acceptance of the realities about which Gregory wrote and the inherent duality of spiritaul experience

237. SC 12.4 (SBO 1:62,9–10).

238. SC 58.11 (SBO 2:134,25).

239. Sent 2.35 (SBO 6b:33,8–9): *Quia differuntur a regno,* is a reflection of Gregory the Great's *Dial* 3.34 (PL 77:300a). Cf. Div 1.1 (SBO 6a:73,20): *longe es a regno Dei.* The reader will have noticed that the great bulk of the references to the theme of compunction in the *Sermons on the Song of Songs* is to be found in the earliest part, written about 1135–1136. The theme assumes less importance as the series (and perhaps its author) develops.

240. Cf. Alberto Gómez, 'Compunctio Lacrymarum: Dottrina de la compunción en el monacato latino de los siglos IV–VI', COCR 23 (1961) 232–240. Joseph de Guibert, 'La compunction du coeur', RAM 5 (1934) 225–240.

is demonstrated by his treatment of other aspects of the theme of desire. Compunction is probably de-emphasised as a factor in desire because Bernard had already an adequate vocabulary which was at once more related to the biblical texts he used to develop his theme and more appealing to the psychological interests of his own century. It must be said, therefore, that although Bernard made no explicit break with his sources, and although he certainly gives evidence of recognising the desire-potential of the theme, he does not exploit it to the same extent that earlier writers had done. At the same time, it remains a latent factor which, perhaps, unconsciously influences his synthesis.

CONCLUDING REFLECTIONS

Desire for God is not a visible, measurable factor within human experience. It is an element of the inner life of every human being, yet it is only glimpsed fragmentarily through successive and disparate manifestations. As such, it cannot be described in the language of ordinary experience; it is forced to rely on abstraction and symbolism. To penetrate to an understanding of desire for God requires 'the gradual construction of a quite different mode of apprehension and of expression'.[241]

There is, therefore, no guarantee that the teaching of any one individual on such a subject is going to be immediately accessible to anyone who is literate. The formation of a new language is necessary if the topic is to be pursued at a level deeper than that attained by conventional parlance. Conversely, to understand what is written requires not only some understanding of the subject, it also demands an initiation into new forms and an apprenticeship in new skills.

241. Bernard Lonergan, *Method in Theology* (London: Darton Longman and Todd, 1972) p. 258.

Thus, to understand the content of Bernard's teaching on desire for God, our first task is to appreciate the linguistic forms which he adopted for his exposition. This means, in fact, appreciating the language of tradition, the particular twelfth-century, french, monastic blend of augustinian and gregorian adaptations of elements handed down from the ages of classical Latin. It means also that we have to enter a symbolic universe different to that with which we are familiar, one which has its own myths and images and literary conventions.

In this chapter we have attempted to explore the words and images which are important in Bernard's meditation on the theme of desire for God. We have attempted to demonstrate something of their reciprocity, without denying the fact that many of these words are also used in other contexts. The result is not easy to summarise in a few sentences. Some objective, statistical correlations are possible, but this is not so important. What really matters is that we have become sensitised to the broad range of concepts which have some bearing on the topic of desire for God, that we understand something of their richness and avow our helplessness before their irreducible complexity.

It is true, as Emero Stiegman notes, that the study of language is a necessary prerequisite for the comprehension of Bernard's teaching.[242] Such a study has the added effect that it introduces us to an aspect of Bernard the writer which is beyond doctrine. Any attention to Bernard's language inevitably leads to an appreciation of Bernard the poet, the skillful artificer of words. Perhaps this brings us closer to the personality behind the writing and allows us to make contact with some of the mystical fire which gave him something to write about when he broached such a subject as desire for God.

242. E. Stiegman, *The Language of Asceticism*, p. 73.

CHAPTER FOUR

THE ANTHROPOLOGY OF DESIRE

IN BERNARD'S VIEW, the basis of the human being's yearning for the Absolute is the nature with
which the Creator has endowed him. It is because he
has been made to God's image — with a natural affinity
with his Maker — that the human being cannot be wholly
engaged or satisfied by realities in his own order of existence. Thus he is driven by a natural tendency to transcend his own order and to seek the divine. Because Bernard believed that union with God was the ultimate goal
of nature, the underlying legitimation of his teaching on
desire for such union must be sought in his philosophy of
human reality, his anthropology.[1]

1. I use the word 'anthropology' in its most general sense of
'science of the human being'. In Bernard's case, this science is
theological and philosophical, not social or cultural. It is a conventional usage, as is indicated by the title of Hiss's book, *Die Anthropologie Bernhards von Clairvaux*.

To limit the concept of desire for God to a complex of affective states is seriously to curtail the breadth of Bernard's understanding of the matter and to risk interpreting him wrongly. For him, desire for God exists at the level of being before it rises to that of awareness and so becomes a factor in one's choice of personal orientation. To seek God and to desire union with him are more than a consciously-willed programme adopted by some individuals as an expression of their particular goals. As far as Bernard was concerned, seeking God is a pre-elective imperative of human nature, assented to in the same moment that one accepts one's own nature and rejected only at the price of fundamental disfigurement.

To a theological mind which is aware of the controversies in the area of nature and grace, a reservation may occur. Is the view which Bernard is espousing a factor in undermining the pre-eminence of grace, since it attributes to human beings such a lofty natural goal? We have discussed the question in another place and hence, here, we need do no more than to recall some conclusions.[2]

There is, in Bernard, a clear awareness of the gratuity of salvation in all its phases, and this is expressed repeatedly throughout his works but especially in his treatise *On Grace and Free Choice* and his *Sermons on the Song of Songs*. His approach to salvation being ontological, he viewed the entire process — creation, redemption, culmination — as a single reality, each phase following the same pattern.[3] This is quite a different approach to that taken these past centuries, which has emphasised more the psychological or subjective aspects of salvation and so concentrated particularly on justification. For Bernard it was

---

2. M. Casey, 'Nature and Grace in Saint Bernard of Clairvaux', *Tjurunga* 23 (1982) 39–49. See also Sr Marie-Bernard Saïd, 'The Doctrine of Grace in St. Bernard', CSt 16 (1981) 15–29.

3. Cf. Gra 49 (SBO 3:201,13–19).

impossible to conceive that what was created by God could, in any way, be opposed to redemption and final glorification. It is sin and human malice which has caused the deformation. Nature and its tendencies were conceived by Bernard as the first manifestation of grace. Because they pre-exist human choice, they are beyond the range of human decision and manipulation and therefore must be attributed to God – they are his gifts.

I have no care for any merit which would exclude grace. I have a horror of whatever comes from myself and remains my own. The only exception is that which is my own because it is the gift of the One who has made me my own.[4]

For Bernard, what is natural is also a gift of grace. A natural capacity is not something which exists and can be satisfied without God, but something which is a necessary, and therefore universal, component of human existence. When Bernard spoke about a 'natural' desire for God, he did so in complete ignorance of the controversies about natural and supernatural which would rage centuries after his death. For him, to describe something as 'natural' was a compliment.

THE IMAGE OF GOD

A widespread appreciation of the subjective aspects of christian faith, existed in the twelfth century. The theology of that period was, in a certain sense, oriented toward experience. There was a renewal of interest in the depth of psychological and anthropological insight contained in the patristic heritage, notably in the works of such cardinal authors as Origen, Augustine, and Gregory of Nyssa. On the pastoral level, many were convinced

4. SC 67.10 (SBO 2:195,9–11. Cf. Div 16.1 (SBO 6a:145,4–5).

that spiritual growth was aided not only by a knowledge of God and of the objective aspects of christian belief, but also by a comparably deep understanding of the nature and functioning of the recipient of grace. The theme of self-knowledge was not only an exhortation to humility, it was also a legitimation for undertaking a closer study of the functioning of the human being. So it happened that the twelfth century witnessed a dramatic upsurge in works of theological anthropology. Apart from a number of anonymous treatises we find tracts *de anima* issuing forth from many of the most important theologians of the time, such as William of Champeaux, Hugh and Richard of St Victor, and Arnold of Bonneval. Many Cistercians wrote in the same vein: William of St Thierry, Aelred of Rievaulx, Alcher of Clairvaux, and Isaac of Stella.[5] Even Hildegard's commentary on the *Hexaemeron* is strongly stamped with this character.[6] Bernard did not write a treatise *de anima*. His work *On Grace and Free Choice* has sometimes been viewed in this light, but this is not really so.[7] As elsewhere in Bernard's writings, the interest in anthropological matters is strong, but the main thrust of the work lies more in the field of theology.

Such anthropological treatises are, for the most part, technical in content and presentation. Their central

5. For a list see Javelet, 'Psychologie', p. 20, note 1. Cf. Bernard McGinn (ed.), *Three Treatises on Man: A Cistercian Anthropology*, CF 24 (Kalamazoo, 1977). *Id.*, *The Golden Chain: A Study in the Theological Anthropology of Isaac of Stella*, CS 15 (Washington: Cistercian Publications, 1972). Aelred of Rievaulx, *Dialogue on the Soul*, CF 22 (Kalamazoo: Cistercian Publications, 1981).

6. PL 207:742.

7. Thus A. le Bail, art. 'Bernard (Saint)', DSp 1:1472. The contrary view is expressed by Bernard McGinn in his introduction to the English translation in CF 19 (p. 5) and also in CF 24 (p. vii), though elsewhere he recognises the importance of anthropology to Bernard and Bernard to anthropology. Cf. *Golden Chain*, p. 236.

concept is that of the soul, its origin, nature, faculties, and functions, and its relations with the body, on the one hand, and with the spirit, on the other. At times there are complex discussions of medical or cosmological matters.

Although they were scarcely intended as works of devotion, even such abstruse considerations were meant for more than idle speculation. The ultimate rationale for such theoretical excursions was practical and pastoral. They sought to provide the resources which would aid in the medical treatment of a sick soul, as a title of a work by Pseudo-Hugh indicates.[8]

> It was the very exigencies of spirituality itself which had drawn the attention of the spiritual masters toward human nature. This subject inspired numerous treatises. Both schoolmen and abbots were dedicated to basing the spiritual dynamism of souls on the real. It was not a case of seeking 'the nature of things'. What held the attention of these masters, who saw themselves primarily as directors of conscience, was human destiny and the journeyings of the interior life.[9]

The theme of the creation of man and woman according to God's image was the most important theological tenet in the picture of human nature which emerged. Aelred Squire describes the fundamental importance of this concept:

> It suffices for the moment to recognise that from the earliest times, whether in the East or the West, the great theologians of the spiritual life are unanimous in the importance they attach to the doctrine of man's imagehood. In the West, the last firm expression of this universal tradition is to be found in St

8. PL 176:1188–1202.
9. Translated from Javelet, 'Psychologie', p. 20.

Bernard and the other twelfth century writers who came more or less directly under Cistercian influence. They were all men involved in a conscious return to the spirit of the Fathers, both Greek and Latin, whose teachings they studied and digested, as far as they could get hold of them, putting them to the test of experience with an integrity impressive in some of its more tangible results.[10]

What really sets these twelfth century thinkers apart from their modern counterparts is the strength of their conviction that human nature is essentially spiritual and that divorced from God and humanity becomes deficient.

Nominally, this approach stems from the text of Gen 1:26 about the creation of man and woman in the image and likeness of God. Exactly what the text means is difficult to say; there is no consensus among modern exegetes, although it can, perhaps, be safely assumed that the text indicates that it is the imagehood of human beings which places them on a plane superior to the rest of creation, whilst they yet remain inferior to God.

Three elements were extracted from the biblical narrative and developed by subsequent theological reflection. The first was the use of a plural verb. This provoked Trinitarian considerations in many of the Fathers and led them into a discussion of the triple imagehood in the human person, each facet or function mirroring a person of the Trinity. This was particularly so in the case of Augustine and also in the non-monastic authors of the first half of the twelfth century. Secondly, the dual expression 'image and likeness' was (incorrectly) thought to refer to two distinct though related features of human life. After centuries of conjecture, a sort of consensus emerged which affirmed that the 'image' was the permanent and fundamental affinity

10. Aelred Squire, *Asking the Fathers* (London: S.P.C.K., 1973) 15–16.

with God enjoyed by human beings; the 'likeness' was the waxing and waning conformity with this basic orientation to God. Thus 'imagehood' could not be lost, but it could be obscured and deformed through the loss of 'likeness'. To speak about human beings as images of God was to indicate their underlying spiritual capabilities, whereas to take up the theme of likeness was to switch from ontology to morality. The final point in the text which occasioned comment was the fact that the Vulgate referred to creation *ad imaginem*. This was often understood in the latin tradition as signifying that human beings were not themselves, individually, the image of God. But they were created with a tendency toward that image, *ad imaginem*. Since it is the Word who is God's Image, humanity must be understood as having an innate tendency toward the Word, since it is only in the Word that it participates in divine imagehood.

In reading medieval texts on this matter, these points need to be borne in mind. The authors of those times were not much interested in providing the exegesis of a biblical text in the manner to which we are accustomed. They were more concerned to develop a rich vein of christian reflection which had, by this time, become standardised in its language and metaphors and in the chains of biblical passages it utilised. To see such expositions merely as defective exegesis is to miss their primary character as theological reflection.

Before beginning our reading of the anthropological texts in the *Sermons on the Song of Songs*, two preliminary points may be made.[11]

11. The literature on the patristic treatment of the theme of the image is vast and cannot be cited here. There are, however, a number of more specialised treatments which have a bearing on our subject. Robert Javelet, 'Psychologie des auteurs spirituels du XIIe siècle', *RechSR* 33 (1959) 18–64, 97–164, 209–268. *Id.*, *Image et*

In the first place, it is necessary to bear in mind that Bernard approached the theme of the image from different angles and with different purposes foremost. This means that it does not necessarily follow that all the references can be jumbled together indiscriminately to form a synthesis. He himself noted that the treatment he gives the theme at the end of the series is different to, though not compatible with, that proposed in the treatise *On Grace and Free Choice*. [12] As Standaert notes, 'Bernard does not have one doctrine but several doctrines of God's image and likeness in human beings'. [13]

The second caution to be observed comes from the nature of the references themselves. Many of them are casual, undeveloped statements of the theme, simply introduced into the course of a sermon with no attempt made to exploit its richness or to futher the work of theological synthesis. Such instances must yield precedence, in case of conflict, to more direct and developed treatments.

Let us first examine the occurrences chronologically, before attempting to draw from them the significance of the theme of the image for Bernard's teaching on the nature of desire for God.

In Sermon 5 on the Song of Songs (SC 5), Bernard seeks to outline the anthropological basis of union with

---

ressemblance au douzième siècle: De saint Anselme à Alain de Lille (two volumes) (Paris: Letouzey et Ané, 1967). S. Otto, *Die Funktion des Bildebegriffes in der Theologie des 12. Jahrhunderts* (Berlin: De Gruyter, 1964). M. Standaert, 'La doctrine de l'image chez S. Bernard', ETL 23 (1947) 70–129. L. Pascoe, *The Doctrine of the Imago in St. Bernard and its Relation to Cistercian Monasticism* (unpublished thesis), Fordham University, New York, 1960). See also the works of Bernard McGinn, already cited.

12. SC 81.11 (SBO 2:291,15). Cf. H. de Lubac, 'A propos de la formule: *diversi sed non adversi*', RechSR 40 (1952) 27–40.

13. Standaert, 'La doctrine', p. 100.

God. He does so without explicit reference to the theme of the image, operating from a more cosmic standpoint. He locates the human being in a middle place, situated between what is highest and what is lowest, combining within himself something of the angelic and something of the bestial. Nevertheless, Bernard's view of the body is entirely positive throughout this sermon.[14]

SC 11 is mainly devoted to the theme of thankfulness for the gift of redemption. In speaking of the concrete effects of grace on the soul, Bernard demonstrates that he was familiar with Augustine's triadic conception of the soul, based on its Trinitarian model. He notes that sin affects each aspect of the *ratio, voluntas* and *memoria* so that they have become defective.[15] On this account the 'noble creature' has become subject to a threefold vanity.[16] Instead of being imprinted with the truth, love and eternity of God,[17] the soul has been corrupted and has lost its likeness. It is now *dissimilis.*[18]

In SC 18, in the course of a discussion of the twofold action of the Spirit, Bernard speaks of the upflaring of love in response to this action and ends by affirming that

14. SC 5.1 (SBO 1:21,21-23): 'Although we are spiritual creatures, we have need of the body, for without it we will in no way be able to attain to that knowledge from which it is possible to progress to spiritual understanding.' He notes that even angels need bodies, though God does not, SC 5.6 (SC 1:23,31-32). This eccentric view is discussed by E. Boissard, 'La doctrine des anges chez S. Bernard', *Théologien*, pp. 114-135. In SC 5.7 (SBO 1:24,23-24), Bernard notes, 'I do not think that knowledge of these things is of much help as far as your spiritual progress is concerned.'

15. SC 11.5 (SBO 1:57,18). Cf. Div 45 (SBO 6a:265,14-15): *Est Trinitas creatrix: Pater et Filius et Spiritus Sanctus, ex qua cecidit creata trinitas: memoria, ratio et voluntas.*

16. SC 11.5 (SBO 1:57,23-24).

17. SC 11.5 (SBO 1:57,26-27).

18. SC 11.5 (SBO 1:58,4-5).

because it has been moulded according to the image of God himself, the human heart can never be satisfied by anything else.

> Having taken food and drink, all that remains for the sick person is that he should rest in the quiet of contemplation after the sweat of activity. And while he is thus asleep in contemplation, God appears, as in a dream; not directly but obscurely, as in a mirror. This is because God is not seen face to face during this life. He is glimpsed rather than observed, and that very briefly, like a quickly passing spark of light. But even such a rapid contact causes the soul to catch fire with love and to say, 'My soul has desired you in the nighttime, as has my spirit which is within me'.
>
> It is appropriate that the friend of the bridegroom and necessary for the faithful and prudent servant whom the Lord has placed over his household, to burn with this love. Such a love fills and grows hot and boils and then safely expands and overflows. . . . For love is the fullness both of the Law and of the heart, at least if it is perfect love. For God is love and there is nothing in all created things which is able to fill the creature who has been made to God's image except the Love which is God. For he alone is greater than the human being.[19]

In this passage the thought sequence is clear. One is able, even in this earthly condition, to experience transiently some traces of the presence of God, and even this inchoate initiation into divine goodness is enough to overwhelm one with a consuming love.

Human being is made for love and only God himself is large enough to be able to satisfy the immense craving for love which the human heart experiences. Being

19. SC 18.6 (SBO 1:107,14–29).

made in the image of God signifies that the person has a capacity for God which cannot be filled by anything else. And until such time as he is fully invaded by divine charity, he remains imperfect.

An anthropological undertone can be detected in the discussion about angels in SC 19. There is one lesson which applies both to angels and to human beings and it is that the service and love of God must follow the exigencies of their specific natures. 'These all love according to their grasp.'[20] The corollary to this is that the response to grace must be in substantial accord with the realities of nature and the level of growth. Desiring to progess beyond one's capabilities is *praesumptio* and thus matter for rebuke.

The same cautionary note sounds in SC 21.6: 'In the day of your strength, do not be too secure'.[21] Bernard is commenting on the text of Song 1:3 *Trahe me post te,* and is making the point that one must maintain 'the image of eternity' while coping with the interplay of good times and bad typical of any human life. To avoid being swept away by the fluctuations of superficial change, one needs to base one's life, not on external factors, nor on the emotions, but on the underlying spiritual stability which characterises the soul.

And so, let hope not desert you when times are bad, nor foresight in good times. Thus you will achieve, in some way, an image of eternity in the manner in which you cope with changing seasons of profit and adversity. You will have the unassailable and unshakable evenness of disposition which comes from a firm soul.

This is the way by which you will win for yourself a permanent state of unchangeableness, even in this

20. SC 19.7 (SBO 1:112,10).
21. SC 21.6 (SBO 1:125,11).

capricious world of doubtful outcomes and certain defeats. For you will begin to be renewed and reformed according to the ancient and distinguished image of the eternal God, with whom there is no change, nor the shadow of alteration. As he is, so shall you be, even in this world; not fearful in hard times nor lacking in discipline when things go well.

This noble creature, who is made in the image and likeness of his Maker, demonstrates that he has received the dignity of this ancient honour and that even now it is effecting his recovery, when he considers it unworthy of himself to conform to this passing world. He aims rather at being re-formed, according to St Paul's teaching, in a newness of understanding and in that same likeness according to which he admits that he was made.

In this way, he duly forces the world to be conformed to him, for whose sake it was made. By such a marvellous reversal, all things begin to work together unto good in their proper and natural form, without any deviance, because they acknowledge as their lord, him in whose service they were created.[22]

In this remarkable passage we see the theme of the image being drawn upon to support a message of constancy in the face of difficulties and in the rejection of worldly standards. The *ordo* established in creation places the earth under human dominion. Sin reverses this order by virtue of the fact that in sinning the human being instead of retaining his superiority, consents to be the slave of material reality. Grace, however, restores the original condition.

We find in this text the affirmation of the human being's independence from temporal determinants; he

22. SC 21.6 (SBO 1:125,14–126,3). I depart from the critical edition, as printed, in reading *dominus* instead of *Dominus* in the last line. Perhaps the capital letter is a misprint.

has a basic freedom of will which is nature's gift. He becomes free from the disatrous effect of sin only through the grace of God, and so is prepared to be totally removed from all suffering when he attains to the state of glory.[23] Submission to grace facilitates this process and causes the human being to become participant in the stability of God. As he becomes more like him, his life is more determined by eternity than by the things of time. The human person is a 'noble creature' by divine institution; he belongs to the aristocracy of creation.[24] It is, therefore, obligatory that his behaviour accord with his high estate: *noblesse oblige*. Far from being a constraint upon nature or a restraint on due freedom, the effort to live a spiritual life works for the liberation of nature from the alien bondage of sin. By grace the primordial order is progressively re-established, so that human beings have the opportunity to live a life that is not characterised by oppression and slavery.

This leads Bernard to the surprising conclusion that the world belongs to the spiritual, since they are the only ones who are not dominated by it. By their victory over the world, they have won the right to be its rulers. Bernard, who was not above using his spiritual status in political byplays—remember that this passage was written in 1135–1136—never developed this theory fully.

23. This is the *leit-motiv* of Bernard's treatise *On Grace and Free Choice*.

24. *Nobilis creatura* (SC 21.6; SBO 1:125,23) is also used in SC 11.5 (SBO 1:57,23–24), Gra 7 (SBO 3:171,8), Div 29.2 (SBO 6a:211,7), Div 40.3 (SBO 6a:236,13), Div 42.2 (SBO 6a:256,16). The human being was created *non sine magnae praerogativa dignitatis:* Div 19.5 (SBO 6a:163,21–22). Cf. Div 12.2 (SBO 6a:128,9): *Memor esto nobilitatis tuae.* . . . On this theme, cf. O Schaffner, 'Die "noblis Deo creatura" des hl. Bernhard von Clairvaux', GuL 23 (1950) 13–57.

His interest, at this point of his exposition, was purely spiritual.[25]

Sermons 24–27 constitute an anthropological bloc, in which Bernard devotes himself to sustained teaching on the human condition. A number of polarisations are noted: between body and soul, between origin and present state, between present state and final destiny, or between deformation and transformation. According to Bernard, imagehood is God's primordial gift to humanity, containing within itself the germ of future promise. This glorious outcome recedes from view with the advent of sin, but begins to shine forth clearly again as the work of grace proceeds.

There are problems associated with the manuscript tradition of SC 24. Two versions exist: a single sermon judged by Leclercq and Rochais to represent the final state of the material after Bernard had finished with it, and a pair of shorter sermons composed of substantially the same material, partly prepared before Bernard's journey to Rome in 1137 and partly after his return in 1138.

After a brief introduction mentioning the defeat of the anti-pope Petrus de Leone, Bernard returns to the text of the Song of Songs and to the point he had reached before the interruption: *Recti diligunt te*, 'the upright love you'. After an animated digression on the subject of

25. The political parallel to this passage is to be found in a celebrated letter written to Pope Eugene III in 1146 in the context of the Second Crusade. This mentions the idea that Christ gave Peter and his successors two swords to wield for the defence of the Church, one spiritual and the other temporal. Ep 256.1 (SBO 8:163,15). Cf. E. Platonia, 'L'azione e il pensiero politico di San Bernardo di Chiaravalle', *Annuario dell' Insitituto Universitario di Magestero 'Maria SS Assunt'*. (1947–1948) pp.75–143. P. Zerbi, 'Riflessione sul simbolo delle due spade in San Bernardo di Clairvaux', *Raccolta di Studi in onore di G. Soranzo* (Milan, 1967) pp.1–18.

detraction, Bernard introduces the key term for the discussion which follows, *rectitudo,* uprightness. This, for Bernard, is a quality of the soul in its original state and is signified concretely by the upright stance of the human body.[26] The opposite quality is that of being bent over, weighed down by the heaviness of the body. This is *curvitas,* the state of the *anima curva,* the bent soul. A bent soul is one which, instead of exercising due dominion over the body, allows itself to become subject to it. It loses its upright posture, whereby it may look up to the heavens, and is doubled over to walk on all fours, like the animals. 'A bent soul changes likeness to God for likeness to the beasts,' says Petrus Comestor.[27] This theme is found both in Gregory of Nyssa and in Augustine and is widely disseminated among the writers of Middle Ages.[28] The theme of uprightness is bracketed between two scriptural texts: Qo 7:30: 'This alone have I found that God made human beings upright', and Ps 91:6: 'The Lord our God is upright and there is no iniquity in him'.[29]

In reading the text, we find it helpful to recall that the object of Bernard's presentation is primarily to motivate his readers to live in accordance with the imperatives of their God-given nature and, thus, to allow themselves to grow in the divine likeness.

26. SC 24.5. I am translating *rectitudo* and its cognates in terms of 'uprightness', wherever possible. The present context demands this. Both Luddy and Walsh use 'righteousness' which obscures the point that Bernard is attempting to make.

27. *Serm* 47 (PL 198:1836d).

28. Thus Gregory of Nyssa, *De hominis opificio* 4 (PG 44:136b), *De hom opif* 8 (PG 44:144b). Heavily dependent on this approach is William of St Thierry, *De natura corporis et animae* 2.5 (PL 180:714b). For Augustine, see *De civitate Dei* 14.13 (CChr 48:434–436), *De disciplina christiana* 5 (CChr 46:211–212).

29. Cf SC 24.5 (SBO 1:156,14 and 1:157,2).

Having called to mind these few things concerning this most malicious vice [of detraction], let us now return to the order of exposition and examine who it is that is referred to in the text as 'upright'.

I am sure that nobody with an upright mind could be of the opinion that those who possess mere bodily uprightness are the ones referred to as loving the bride. It will be shown that, in this context, there is question of spiritual uprightness, which is something which belongs to the soul. It is the Spirit who speaks: he compares spiritual realities with other spiritual realities.

When God is said to have made human beings upright, this is to be understood primarily of the soul, not of the earthly excrement of matter. God created the human being in his own image and to his own likeness. Now, of God is it sung in the Psalm: 'The Lord our God is upright, there is no iniquity in him'. Therefore, the God who is himself upright, made the human being to be upright and, thus, like himself. This is to say that he made him to be without iniquity, since there is no iniquity in himself.

Iniquity is not an aberration of the flesh but of the heart. Hence the likeness to God is to be preserved or recovered, not in the crude clay of matter, but in your spiritual part. God is himself a spirit, and he wills that those who persevere in his likeness or grow in it, should enter their hearts and be active within their spirits about this affair. It they do this, then, when they gaze upon the glory of God, they will be transformed from brightness to brightness by the Lord who is spirit, into that same image.

God also endowed the human being with an upright stature, so that this bodily uprightness in his outer and less precious component, might serve as an encouragement to his inner self which was made to God's image, so that it might maintain its quality of spiritual uprightness. In this way the beauty of clay serves as a reproach for deformity of soul.

Bernard now begins to warm to his theme, showing how disproportionate it is for the human being to have such a beautiful body while he allows his soul to become defiled, disfigured and deformed.

What can be more grotesque than to have a bent soul in an upright body? It is a foul and twisted thing that this vessel of clay, which is the body made of dust, should have its eyes uplifted so that it may freely gaze at the skies and take delight in the heavenly bodies while, meanwhile, the spiritual creature is the opposite. It has its eyes, which are the inner senses and affects, dragged down to the earth. What should be feeding in delicacies is, instead, wallowing in the mud, like a pig covering itself with manure.

'Look at me', says the body, 'and blush, O soul. You have exchanged the divine likeness for that of the beasts. Although you are from heaven, yet you roll around in filth. You were made upright, as your Creator is upright, and you were given a helpmate, similar to yourself, also upright in its own bodily fashion. Wherever you turn, whether to God above or to me below (for no one can hate his own flesh,) you will encounter the familiar admonition of Wisdom's teaching, reminding you constantly of your beauty and dignity.'

Souls bent in this manner are not able to love the bridegroom, since they are not his friends but friends of the world. As it is written, 'Anyone who wants to be a friend of this world makes himself God's enemy'. To seek and take delight in things which are on this earth is to have a bent soul. Uprightness, on the contrary, consists in constantly keeping in mind and in desire, the realities which are above. For this to be complete, an act of the will must follow the choice.

You are truly upright, I say, if uprightness characterises all that is in your mind and is not negated
by what you do. For it is faith and action which
make known the invisible condition of the soul.[30]

This substantial passage touches upon a number of
points which are significant for an understanding of the
theme of the image. First of all, the image of God is to be
found reflected in the *animus* or soul.[31] Whatever good
qualities are possessed by the soul derive from its likeness
to the Creator and hence are his gift. So it follows that
the basis of all human uprightness is God's creative and
self-diffusive uprightness which communicates itself, in
some measure, to all that he has made. When the soul
refuses this gift and allows itself to become disordinated,
it is bent over spiritually, thus negating the divine endowment of uprightness. In such a state, the soul degen-
erates and becomes a slave to bodily necessity, *necessitas,*
and concentrates all its interests and energy on earthly affairs. In this situation, the human being is radically un-
true to himself and to his nature; his upright physical
stance is at variance with the fallenness of his soul. He is
living a lie.

On the other hand, to the extent that the soul works
at keeping the body in subjection, the lost likeness is
gradually recovered. If the human being strives to fix his
gaze on heaven, he is less likely to be dragged down to
the earth. His soul, nourished by such contact, begins to
be transformed into the original image, becoming, as it
were, what it was made to be.

---

30. SC 24.5–7 (SBO 1:156–159). Cf. Div 12.1 (SBO 6a:127,
17–128,2). The constrast between *caelum* and *caenum* in SC 24.6
(SBO 1.158,6) also occurs in SC 26.9 (SBO 1:177,9) and in SC 63.6
(SBO 2:165,27). See ThLL vol. 3: col. 98, lines 72–76 for some other
examples.

31. SC 24.5 (SBO 1:157,4–5): *in spirituali portione tui.*

SC 25 takes up the next verse of the Song of Songs: 'I am black but beautiful, O daughters of Jerusalem' (Song 1:4). After an opening thought on the subject of gentleness, Bernard returns to a consideration of the bride as someone of lowly outward appearance who is, nevertheless, possessed of inward nobility and beauty. He begins by contrasting the soul's condition in exile with that which it will enjoy in its homeland.[32] He then refers to the contrast between St Paul's lowly external appearance and his lofty spiritual attainments and then uses this as a starting-point for a consideration on the fact that the saints were often indifferent to their grooming.

> This is why the saints, having scorned the adorn-
> ment and extravagant care of their outward selves
> (which will certainly perish), give all their industry
> and time to cultivating their inward selves, which
> are images of God and which are renewed day by
> day. They are convinced that nothing is more pleas-
> ing to God than his own image, once it is restored to
> its real beauty.[33]

The theme of the image is thus evoked to provide substance for a reiteration of one of Bernard's major themes: the insistence on the absolute priority of what is inward and spiritual over external and material concerns. One might see another element entering into his presentation and that is his habitual aesthetic preference for nature rather than artifice.

In SC 26, the mention of 'the tents of Kedar' gives rise to a discussion of the interaction of soul and body

---

32. SC 25.3 (SBO 1:164,21–23). Bernard is diffident about applying the text to the disjunction of image and likeness because both parts of the expression are in the present tense, whereas, the transition from the 'earthly image' to 'heavenly likeness' is characterised by temporal sequence. Cf. SC 25.4 (SBO 1:165,3–6).

33. SC 25.7 (SBO 1:167,6–10).

and leads the thought in the direction of eschatological realities—the theme of *peregrinatio,* which will be discussed in the next chapter. However, the presentation is abruptly ended by Bernard's splendidly crafted elegy for his brother Gerard, who died in 1138.[34]

In the following sermon, Bernard develops the complementary aspect. The bride, though oppressed by temporality, still manifests her noble origins. Thus, the soul is compared to 'the curtains of Solomon' (Song 1:4), a metaphor interpreted as signifying its heavenly origin and nature.

> Whatever meets the eye is rightly judged as worthless and foul compared to the inner beauty of the saintly soul. For, I say, what can be found in this passing world to rank with the beauty of such a soul who, having removed the old garments of the earthly self, puts on the beauty which comes from heaven. It is adorned with the jewels of excellence in what it does. It is purer than the ether and more radiant than the sun.[35]

Reverting to themes raised earlier, Bernard traces the origin of this beauty to the fact of the soul's being an 'image of eternity', interpreting this phrase as meaning that the soul is full of charity and all the other virtues. 'But her beauty is on the level of the understanding, her appearance is spiritual, even eternal, since she [the bride] is the image of eternity.'[36] The practice of the virtues is the basis for such perpetuity, since 'there is no place in the soul for the perpetual and blessed life except what is realised through virtue'.[37]

Thus, the soul which seeks God is moving toward heaven, which is where the object of its love is to be

34. SC 26.1–2 (SBO 1:169,–170).
35. SC 27.1 (SBO 1:182,11–16).
36. SC 27.3 (SBO 1:183,11–18).
37. SC 27.3 (SBO 1:183,26–27).

found.[38] This leads Bernard to say that when the bride is wholly occupied with heavenly things, she herself becomes a heaven. But first he has to demonstrate that the soul has sufficient stature to become the dwelling-place of God, and this he does by ascertaining its heavenly origins.

There is no more manifest pointer to a heavenly origin than maintaining one's inborn (*ingenita*) likeness, even in the region of unlikeness, than the glory of the celibate life being lived on earth by an exile, than one living as an angel in a body which is almost that of the beasts. These things derive from heavenly not from earthly power, and they indicate that the soul which is capable of them is truly from heaven.[39]

The capacity for heavenly behaviour is a sign of a heavenly origin. Heavenly origin, for Bernard as for many of the Fathers, is already a pointer to a heavenly destiny. Even though the soul presently dwells apart from its own ambience and is subject to alienating influences, the fact that it maintains its capacity for other-worldliness indicates that it is not simply the product of this-worldly forces. Bernard puns on the similarity between *caelebs* and *caelum*, citing celibacy as a manifest proof that the human being traces his origin to heaven.[40] It is this heavenly or spiritual character of the soul which founds the possibility of a relationship with God and which therefore must be seen as the dominant factor in the emergence of a desire for such a relationship.[41]

The contrast between a soul living according to its own nature and the pattern of worldly existence is considerable. For Bernard, the spiritual person was an exile on earth, an

38. SC 27.4 (SBO 1:184,16–17).
39. SC 27.6 (SBO 1:185,22–26).
40. Cf ThLL vol 2: col. 65. J. Leclercq (*Recueil 1:* 286) refers to an article by P. Grosjean in *Analecta Bollandiana* 72 (1956) 364–365.
41. Cf Yves Congar, 'L'ecclésiologie de S. Bernard', *Théologien*, pp. 136–190; especially pp. 139–140.

angel dwelling among beasts and striving to remain un-
formed by their standards. There is an element of choice
involved. The actual character possessed by an individual
life is partly inborn and partly the result of free choice. If
a human being chooses to assent to his natural movement toward God and to resist the forces drawing him in
the opposite direction, then he becomes, as it were, an
island of heaven in a hostile sea.

> I think that every soul of this sort can rightly be called
> heavenly or even a heaven, not only becaue of its
> origin, but also because it imitates [the heavenly way
> of life]. It is this that clearly demonstrates that its
> origin is really from heaven, when its way of life is
> heavenly. Its sun is understanding, its moon is faith
> and the virtues are its stars.[42]

Because it is heavenly, such a soul makes a worthy dwelling-place for the Word.[43] This leads Bernard to the consideration that, if a soul is able to contain God, its capacity must be vast.

> O how great is the size of the soul, and how amply
> endowed with merits it is that it be found sufficient-
> ly capacious and suitable to receive the divine
> presence within itself! How large is that which is
> able to provide suitable broad avenues for His Ma-
> jesty to walk along. Such a soul cannot afford to
> become involved in law-suits and in other worldly
> cares and causes, nor to give itself over to the belly or
> to sex. It must leave aside idle entertainment, the
> will for universal domination and the pride which
> comes from power. For the soul to become a heaven
> and thus become the dwelling-place of God, it must
> first ensure that it is empty of all these other

---

42. SC 27.8 (SBO 1:187,12–16). Bernard here exploits the fact
that *coelum* means both 'heaven' and 'sky'.
43. SC 27.9 (SBO 1:188,8–10).

things.[44]

In this bloc formed by SC 24–27, the main interest is focussed on the soul, seen by Bernard as presently existing in a state midway between its noble origins and its final glory. Despite appearances and the pressures of earthly existence, the soul has within itself the capability to live a life according to spiritual priorities. It is only to the extent that this potential is realised that its earthly career will have a felicitous outcome in heaven. At the basis of Bernard's exhortations to other-worldliness is a clear perception that such conduct is not a distortion of fundamental human reality, but rather its natural expression. Bernard is appealing to the soul that it remain faithful to its own self.

In these sermons, the connection with the theme of the image is made several times, wherever Bernard felt that it was necessary to provide doctrinal support for his assertions. Implicit throughout the development of his thought, the theme provides the unifying point of origin from which Bernard's reflective and exhortatory conclusions inevitably sprang.

In SC 33, for the first time, we find the attribution of the title *imago Dei* not to the human being but to the Word. The reference is framed around Col 1:15, and is used as a foil to the term *forma servi* taken from Phil 2:7.[45] A further anthropological bloc occurs in SC 34–38, written around 1140, where Bernard is commenting on the text of Song 1:7: 'If you do not know yourself, O most beautiful among women, then go away and follow the flocks of your friends, and pasture your goats near the shepherd's tents'.[46] In accordance with the tradition of

44. SC 27.10 (SBO 1:188,25–189,5).
45. SC 33.3 (SBO 1:235,21).
46. Bernard has *abi post greges sodalium tuorum* in place of the Vulgate *post vestigia gregum*. It seems likely that he, or the version

interpretation initiated by Origen and found in all his tributaries, Bernard used the text as a starting-point for a discussion of self-knowledge.

This theme goes deeper, in the partistic tradition, than introspection and knowledge of character and temperament. In includes elements of humility. It also involves some degree of theoretical knowledge, according to which the role and rank of the human being in the order of existence is understood and accepted.[47] Truth, after all, Bernard affirmed to be the life of the soul.[48]

The theme of self-knowledge was an important one for St Bernard and for all the writers of the cistercian school. His treatise on humility witnesses to his early concern with the subject and the theme can be perceived throughout many of his later writings. Wilhelm Hiss develops at length the suggestion of Étienne Gilson that the teaching of Bernard, in this regard, constitutes a 'Christian Socratism'.[49]

---

he was using, transposed the variant phrase from the previous verse. For a discussion, see J. Leclercq, *Recueil 1:* pp. 312–313.

47. The commentary of Origen has a long development on self-knowledge at this point. See especially, *In Canticum* 2 (PG 13:123bc and 127bc). The necessity of a sound self-knowledge as the basis of desire is indicated in col. 139a. Rufinus' translation has the byplay *egregium . . . in grege,* which Bernard willingly makes his own. Toward the end of the commentary of Gregory the Great, we find a characteristically firm statement of the theme. *In Cant* 1.28 (PL 79:490b). 'Every soul should have as its paramount concern that it know itself. For who knows himself, knows that he was made to God's image and that he ought not to follow the likeness of animals, either in his sexual practice or in his desire for the things of this world.' See also Div 2.5 (SBO 6a:83,6) and Div 40.3 (SBO 6a:236,10).

48. Div 10.1 (SBO 6a:121,18).

49. Thus Hiss, *Die Anthropologie,* pp. 31–41, following Gilson, *Mystical Theology,* p. 103, note 140. A more recent discussion of the *scito teipsum* theme is found in Javelet, *Image,* vol. 1: 368–371. SC 23.9 (SBO 1:144,21–22) demonstrates how Bernard is able to flesh

Sermon 34 is a brief reflection on humility. In the following sermon, Bernard returns to the theme of the body as a tent in which the soul is forced to live for a short time while it is on pilgrimage.[50] He then goes on to contrast the occupations of the soul which are the result of its taking its heavenly vocation seriously with those which come from the instability caused by defective self-knowledge, that is, activities which do not take into account the spiritual character of the soul.

It is at this stage that the picture of Adam is drawn and the delights of the primal paradise evoked.

> Raised above all these benefits, the human being was supreme because of the noble, divine likeness which was his. It was this which give him fellowship with the throng of angels and with the whole array of the heavenly host.[52]

But, Bernard dolefully notes in the words of Psalm 105:20, 'he exchanged the glory of God for the likeness of an ox which eats grass'.[53] Having thus manipulated an extraneous image into the discussion by means of the catch-word 'likeness', he proceeds to develop a complicated metaphor of the Son of God becoming grass (in the manger, as in Lk 2:12), so that set before the animals (deformed humanity) he might feed them with his heavenly life in a form which they were able to absorb.[54]

---

out the philosopher's injunction with a saying from the Scriptures: *Iuxta illud graecorum, scire meipsum ut sciam cum Propheta, quid desit mihi.* The reference is to Ps 38:5. Cf. Dil 4 (SBO 3:122,10), Dil 14 (SBO 3:130,20–21).

50. SC 35.2 (SBO 1:250,10).
51. SC 35.3 (SBO 1:250,17–28).
52. SC 35.3 (SBO 1:251,13–15).
53. SC 35.4 (SBO 1:251,16–17).
54. SC 35.5 (SBO 1:252,12–13).

Thus, the former cultivator of paradise and lord of the earth and citizen of heaven takes on a likeness to the beasts, *pecorina similitudo*.[55] He can be saved only through recognising his own fall from grace and by acknowledging in weakness the One whom he refused to serve when he was strong.

Self-deception was the cause of the fall, coupled with the refusal of the human being to recognise his own lowly status and so to render due acknowledgement of the gifts of God. In his lack of understanding, he becomes like the beasts (Ps 48:13). Playing on the words *egregia . . . grege*, Bernard summarises the effect of the fall in the conventional comparison of angels and beasts. 'This excellent creature becomes one of the herd, changing the likeness to God for a likeness to a beast, and giving up the company of the angels in order to share life with the animals.'[56] Then he goes further: the human being is not the equal of the beasts if he lacks self-knowledge. He is worse than them since, having the capacity to know and spurning its use, he merits condemnation and punishment.[57]

The knowledge to which Bernard refers throughout this discussion is not, of course, academic knowledge, although this also serves a purpose.[58] The knowledge he is advocating is that which enables a person clearly to grasp the underlying orientation of his being. In this way he is protected from the possibility of being led astray by the alien environment in which he lives. Solid positive knowledge and conviction is needed if the individual is to resist the uncreative currents of thought which surround him. This, in turn, will lead to an appreciation of just how false and misleading much of what passes for

55. SC 35.5 (SBO 1:252,13–14).
56. SC 35.6 (SBO 1:253,6–8).
57. SC 35.9 (SBO 1:254,21–23).
58. SC 36.2 (SBO 2:4,14–17).

knowledge really is.

> Is it not so that a person thus seeing himself in the clear light of truth will discover that he is living in the region of unlikeness and, sighing unhappily, will be unable to disguise his discontent at this state of affairs?[59]

Self-knowledge causes a discontent with the range of answers and satisfactions offered by this present life, a sort of *Weltschmerz,* which causes the desire for a better life to arise. To recognise, even implicitly, that one has a transcendent destiny is a necessary pre-requisite for allowing oneself to desire such an outcome.

A necessary part of this self-knowledge is the acceptance of the damage done by the Fall. The loss of the divine likeness caused the human being to degenerate, and the weakness and sinfulness which follow are the source of all suffering. If, in this state of deprivation, the human being recognises his need for God, than all is not lost. If, on the contrary, he refuses to acknowledge the woundedness of his nature, he is prevented from breaking out of the situation which causes the pain. Someone who is complacent never knows his need for salvation. Hence, desire for God begins with self-knowledge, which includes the sober acceptance of the pain of human existence. If this transposes itself into a prayer for forgiveness and rehabilitation, then progress in becoming like God is possible. 'For when a human being understands that he is oppressed, then he will cry out to the Lord and he will hear him . . . in this way knowledge of yourself is a step toward knowledge of God',[60] for the experience of God is impossible without an authentic self-experience. Bernard goes on to say that once a person begins to walk the way of self-knowledge then the divine imagehood in him begins to be renewed

59. SC 36.5 (SBO 2:7,1–10).
60. SC 36.6 (SBO 2:8,1–5).

and restored, day by day, until he is transformed in glory.[61]

The next two sermons continue with the theme of the knowledge which is necessary for salvation. Toward the end of SC 38, Bernard warns the bride to be cautious and to remain ever-mindful of her limitations. She ranks below the angels while she is in this world and hence cannot hope to have a detailed knowledge of all that the divine mysteries involve. This is not obscurantism, but the common-sense affirmation that perseverance is impossible for one who has no tolerance of some degree of darkness: the rhythms of spiritual growth are often surprising. So, Bernard reminds the bride, transcendent experience is, in its fullness, reserved for the last times. Weighed down by its body and oppressed by earthly cares, the soul must learn to be content with a limited understanding. 'Look to your own affairs', he concludes, 'and do not seek what is too high for you.'[62]

The following forty sermons, written between about 1140 and 1148, are not rich in anthropological teaching. The random remarks that do occur are undeveloped, serving only to confirm the major lines of what Bernard had already proposed.

In SC 40, Bernard gives as the basis of spiritual perception the fact that the human being is itself spiritual in essence and origin. Once again he emphasises the spiritual and incorporeal character of the soul.[63] He follows this with a description of the bride's face (which he interprets as the *mentis intentio*) and then goes on to speak of her neck, which he interprets as signifying understanding. This, he affirms in familiar vein, is something

61. SC 36.6 (SBO 2:8,5–7); the sentence is based on the text of 2 Cor 3:18.
62. SC 38.5 (SBO 2:17–18).
63. SC 40.1 (SBO 2:24,19–22).

which is beautifully formed by nature and is in no need of external ornamentation. From this he concludes that sojourners on earth should not devote their energies to seeking outward and alien adornment but, rather, should exploit the innate beauty which is theirs by nature.[64]

The spiritual nature of the soul is again mentioned in SC 45, this time in connection with its compatibility with the Word, a theme that will be powerfully developed in the final sermons of the series. 'The Word is a spirit and so is the soul. They have their own language by which they converse and reveal their presence to each other.'[65] Speaking of the Incarnation of the Word, Bernard marvels at the Word's leaping over the angelic orders to take his place in the world of human beings.

> You have made him a little less than the angels. It is possible to interpret this text as a compliment to human nature, in the sense that the human being was made in the image and likeness of God and endowed with reason, just as the angels are. On the other hand, he is far away from the angels because of the fact of having an earthen body.[66]

Note that imagehood is not, in this text, distinguished from likeness, but jointly they are equated with the gift of reason.

In SC 69, the title 'Image of God' is applied to God's Son, who is the Wisdom of God and the splendour and form of his substance. This concatenation of 1 Cor 1:24, Col 1:15 and Heb 1:3, although it uses the term, 'image of God', does not have an anthropological reference; it has to do with Christology.[67]

64. SC 41.1 (SBO 2:28,14–17).
65. SC 45.7 (SBO 2:54,15–16).
66. SC 53.8 (SBO 2:100,22–26).
67. SC 69.4 (SBO 2:204,15–16).

SC 72 is a sermon of markedly eschatological colouring. The theme of the renewal of the image figures prominently in the context of a presentation of the life of the
blessed. Speaking of the final transformation in terms
drawn from Phil 3:20–21, Bernard notes that the process
has already begun 'according to which our inward self is
renewed from day to day. It is renewed in the spirit of the
mind and thus it moves toward the Image of the one who
created it. In this manner it, also, becomes day from day
and light from light'.[68] Here again it is the Word who is
the Image; the process of renovation undergone by the
human being is one which renders it *ad imaginem;* it is a
continuation or replication of creation. The final phrase
is, of course, modelled on the Nicene Creed; creation
and redemption are seen as being continuations or expressions of intra-Trinitarian processes and relationships.

In another sermon, Bernard remarked that it is the
divine imagehood which enables a person to aspire toward
the embrace of truth, to rest in the love of the Word and so
to come to Glory.[69] Although this is only a brief statement,
it is significant for our purposes in clearly setting forth Bernard's assumptions about the human being as image of God
as the foundation of his teaching on spiritual desire.

The last sermons of the series are remarkable for their
profundity and poetry. There is a subtle change in tone in
Bernard's presentation as he presents some of the loftiest
and most beautiful reflections in the entire body of his
writing. These sermons exhibit the same mellow philosophy
as his *Five Books on Consideration,* but the tone is more
lyrical and the latent political archness and cynicism present in the papal handbook are less in evidence. In some

68. SC 72.11 (SBO 2:232,–233). 2 Cor 4:17 is also influential in
shaping the thought of this passage.
69. SC 77.5 (SBO 2:264,26).

sense, this bloc of sermons may be regarded as Bernard's spiritual testament.

SC 80–83, probably composed between 1148–1152, constitute the third major anthropological bloc in the *Sermons on the Song of Songs* and, of them all, the most thorough. There is a change in emphasis in his thought, as Bernard himself notes, particularly with reference to the strongly augustinian interpretation of the image theme, found in his 1128 treatise *On Grace and Free Choice*.[70] In the earlier work the emphasis was placed on the process of regaining likeness to God through the working of grace and the assent of the will. Granted the subject of the treatise, this is not surprising. In the present group of sermons, Bernard is more concerned to unfold the consequences of the human being's permanent imagehood and to exploit the truth that human beings are fundamentally and dynamically ordered toward God.

Another fact which may have determined the altered shape of Bernard's thought is that Bernard was no longer struggling with a growing simplicity of outlook and clarity of vision, on basic elements within the soul's ascent to God. There is a move away from the practical,

70. SC 81.11 (SBO 2:291,15). In his article 'Saint Bernard et les Pères grecs', (*Théologien*, pp. 46–55), Jean Daniélou argues that the change of emphasis can be explained in terms of a move away from the earlier augustinian position toward that presented in Gregory of Nyssa's treatise: *De eo quo sit ad imaginem Dei: In Scripturam verba: Faciamus!* (PG 44:238–298; SChr 6 critical edition by J. Laplace and J. Daniélou, *La création de l'homme* [Paris: Cerf, 1944]). He believes that the switch was made under the influence of William of St Thierry. Cf. J.-M. Déchanet, *Aux sources de la spiritualité de Guillaume de Saint Thierry* (Bruges: Desclée de Brouwer, 1940), especially pp. 57–58. When first expressed, this opinion met with a degree of enthusiasm. Nowadays it is generally regarded with considerable reserve.

moral, and exhortatory concerns which occupied most of his teaching life in the direction of the mystical. The wonder of divine union was beginning to absorb him, so that when he approached the theme of the image, it was the boundlessness of the divine gift which was paramount to him, not the behavioural consequences of the doctrine.

In SC 79, Bernard discussed the adhesive power of love, the *gluten amoris* which binds the bride and the bridegroom together. He now wished to establish what is the source and origin of such love. In the first place he came to the conclusion that the union of the soul with the Word is not explainable merely in terms of the soul's willing assent and industry. Rather it derives from the power of divine love planted at the centre of its being. Not only does God infuse love into the soul, he continued, but he also prepares for this gift by forming the soul in such a way that it is capable of receiving it.

> Why do you join these two things? What has the soul in common with the Word? The soul has much in common with the Word, and in many ways. In the first place, they are closely related in that the Word is the Image and the soul has its being to-the-Image. Secondly, the likeness attests to this affinity. For the human being was made not only to-the-Image, he was also made to-the-Likeness. You may ask, in what does this likeness consist?
>
> First, listen to what I have to say about the Image. The Word is truth and wisdom and justice. It is in this that the Word's imagehood consists. The Word is, thus, the Image of Justice and of Wisdom and of Truth: justice from Justice, wisdom from Wisdom and truth from Truth, in the same way that he is light from Light and god from God.
>
> Now, the soul is none of these things, since it is not the Image. It is, however, capable and desirous

of them. What a lofty creature it is, in its capacity for majesty and in its preference for seeking what is upright. For we read that God made the human being upright and that he made him great. This confirms that the human being has such a capacity. For it is right that what was made to-the-Image should have some agreement with the Image itself, otherwise it would merely share the title 'image' and nothing else. . . . From God, who is upright and great, the Image has received uprightness and greatness. And it is from the Image that the soul has received these things, because it is to-the-Image.[71]

This very difficult passage makes a number of important points. The soul has nothing except what it receives from the Word, and even having received a participation in his qualities, the soul does not possess them as belonging to it by right. It receives them by a sort of osmosis so long as it clings to the Word; it is not able to participate in such attributes in a state of separation. The soul's capacity to be endowed with what properly belongs to the Word derives from the fact that it has been created with an innate tendency which carries it toward the Word. It is created *ad*.

There is a difference in the manner in which the soul possesses qualities and the way in which they are present in the Word. Such good qualities as the soul possesses are received from an outside agency: through creation by God or through this free gift of grace, working in manifold ways. They do not come from the soul itself, they are gifts, even as human nature and existence are themselves gifts. As the later scholastics would say, only God is *a se*. Hence the soul only borrows the attributes of the Word; possession of them is conditional on maintaining links with their source. The Word, on

71. SC 80.2 (SBO 2:277–278).

the other hand, possesses internally the qualities that are his. They come to him in generation. The Word possesses all such qualities totally and in their fullness. What he has, he has without measure. On the other hand, the soul's concrete capacity for eternal realities, although potentially unlimited, is, in fact, restricted by its present mode of existence and by the degree of compromise always inherent even in its choice of the good.[72]

Thus, Bernard is now saying that the imagehood is realised not in the natural endowment of the human being as a whole, but specifically in its relationship to the Word. The imagehood is identified with that tendency which draws the human being toward the Word, into the Word, and even deeper into him. It is by virtue of this unitive force that the human being is able to participate in the qualities and attributes which are proper to the Word. It is this which makes him desire ever more complete union. The permanent relationship with the Word, initiated at creation and furthered through a life based on spiritual priorities, is qualified by several different expressions which expand on the phrase used earlier, *vicinitas naturae*, 'closeness of nature'.[73] Thus, between the soul and its Exemplar, there is said to be *cognatio* (kinship), *affinitas* (affinity), *propinquitas* (nearness), *convenientia* (compatibility). All these terms witness to how highly Bernard rated the dignity of the human soul.

Recovering his theme after a diatribe against Gilbert of Poitiers for his view that godhead is distinct from God, Bernard began SC 81 by pointing out that, when he refers to the affinity of the Word and the soul, it should be noted that there is subordination in the relationship. It is not

---

72. SC 80.3 (SBO 2:278–279).
73. SC 69.7 (SBO 2:206,23). This is in the context of 2 Cor 3:18. Cf. Div 9.2 (SBO 6a:119,6–7).

the linking of equals.[74] 'For who among you is so feeble-minded that he cannot see that the Image and that which is to-the-Image are bound together?'[75] His purpose in insisting upon the relationship is that, recognising its origins, the soul might be ashamed at its choice of sin and so amend its ways, 'governing itself, by God's gift, and thus boldly approaching the embrace of the Word'.[76] The moral interest is still there, even though it is no longer as paramount.

Suddenly and without warning, Bernard introduces the idea which had been at the heart of all his reflections on this matter, the conclusion to which he had been leading. He affirms that it is the nature of the human soul that it progresses toward the embrace of the Word, mystical union, spiritual marriage, the experience of contemplative *excessus*. Bernard's prime anthropological tenet is that the human being was created for no other purpose than that of spiritual union with the Word. It is only to the extent that the human being becomes one with God's Word that the potentiality inherent in his being created *ad imaginem* is fully realised and he becomes fully alive. And when the human being becomes fully like the Word, they form together one spirit.

Bernard now discusses the qualities of soul which derive from its imagehood and which will become progressively realised as likeness to the Word is achieved. The simplicity, immortality, and essential freedom which characterise the soul's substance must, as likeness proceeds, be impressed on the way the individual acts and reacts. Bernard had earlier noted two generic features of the soul: its greatness and its uprightness, the first deriving from the imagehood, the other from the likeness. The soul is great because it was so created. The

74. SC 81.1 (SBO 2:284,9).
75. SC 81.1 (SBO 2:284,15–16).
76. SC 81.1 (SBO 2:284,23–24).

soul is upright becaue it consents to express its greatness
in behaviour. This is represented schematically in Figure
One.

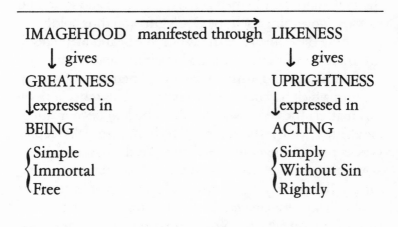

IMAGEHOOD manifested through LIKENESS
↓ gives   ↓ gives
GREATNESS   UPRIGHTNESS
↓expressed in   ↓expressed in
BEING   ACTING
{ Simple   { Simply
{ Immortal   { Without Sin
{ Free   { Rightly

Figure One

The simplicity, immortality, and freedom which characterise the soul's mode of existence constitute its imagehood. These qualities are present irrespective of how a
person decides to order his life. On the other hand, the
likeness is realised only in so far as the soul consents to act
in accordance with its nature: simply, innocently, and according to what is right. When uprightness of behaviour
signals that the soul has accepted to live in accordance
with its innate greatness, then it begins to become fully
what it has been given to be in germ.[77]

In SC 82, Bernard raised the question of the disjunction
of imagehood and likeness cause by sin. His terminology

77. An alternative combination of these factors is given in Standaert, 'La doctrine', p. 91.

is not consistent and, it appears, was in a state of transition. 'Scripture speaks about the unlikeness which has come about. It does not say that the former likeness was destroyed, but that another likeness was introduced.'[78] In place of 'former likeness', 'image' would have been expected, although here it may mean that concrete combination of imagehood and likeness which was found in the human being before the Fall.

The effect of sin was to obscure, cover over, and veil the image, disfiguring its innate beauty with the ugliness of foreign elements. There is still an inchoate likeness which comes as a consequence of the imagehood, but now it has to struggle against a movement in the opposite direction which would cause it to be submerged still more. Bernard's thought is perhaps easier to grasp if we view likeness as a tendency present within the soul rather than a state.

It is not a matter of the soul divesting itself of its native form, but of a foreign form being introduced. It is a question, not of one form being lost, but of another form being added on. It is possible for the new form to obscure the innate form, but it cannot eliminate it entirely.[79]

The human being remains substantially simple, but with the advent of sin, simplicity or singleness of heart becomes duplicity. Continuing a long patristic tradition, Bernard saw this transition and loss of innocence and directness as symbolised by the shame experienced in nakedness. Instead of allowing themselves to be seen for what they were, Adam and Eve were forced to divert attention from their actual state of being 'with aprons of leaves and words of excusation'.[80]

78. SC 82.2 (SBO 2:293,17–18).
79. SC 82.2 (SBO 2:293,19–21).
80. SC 82.3 (SBO 2:294,1): *frondium succinctoriis et verbis excusatoriis.*

In this reversal, all the soul's endowments were turned against the fundamental tendency of the human being. Now they oppose what they had been intended to serve and promote. The soul in such a state experiences an attraction toward what can only debase it; it finds pleasure in what runs counter to its ultimate profit. On the other hand, all that leads to authentic personal growth is experienced as toilsome and without much immediate gratification. As a result, the human being easily tires of following the path toward truth, with it rigours and abstentions, and allows himself to be drawn instead into easier and more pleasant ways. Alternative attractions lure him away from uprightness; in bending over to partake of them he deforms himself, and contradicts the basic direction of his existence.

Sin distorts human being. As a soul recedes from likeness to God, it denies its own nature and becomes also unlike itself. *Inde anima dissimilis Deo, inde dissimilis sibi.*[81] To the extent that sin represents a blunting of nature's thrust toward God, it is a thwarting of nature itself and, consequently, a frustration of its potentialities.

Conscious of a double law operating within his heart, the human being experiences himself as rent asunder. He cries out to God for redemption, his prayer echoing the agony of his being, but even as he attempts to do so, he is inhibited by despair. This is a dangerous time in which one has to opt either to be cast down by the sight of one's own degeneration or to be lifted up by the glad recognition of the gifts of God.

Bernard's response to this crucifying dilemma is a lyric celebration of God's will to save, concretely evidenced in the soul's permanent capacity to receive and be ennobled by the gifts of grace.

---

81. SC 82.5 (SBO 2:295,26).

It is my teaching that every soul
although burdened with sins,
although caught in a trap,
although a captive in exile,
although imprisoned in its body,
although clinging to the mud and stuck in the mire,
although afflicted with sorrows,
   made anxious by many worries
   and unsettled by suspicions,
although it is a traveller in a hostile country
   and thus, as the Prophet says,
   soiled by contact with the dead and
   reckoned with those in hell,
—this is what I say—
that although a soul is so condemned and so
   desperate,
nevertheless it is my teaching that
such a soul is able to find within itself
not only a source of relief in the hope of pardon
   so that it may hopefully seek mercy,
but also it will find a source of boldness
   so that it may desire marriage with the Word,
   not fearing to enter into a treaty of friendship
   with God,
   nor being timid about taking up the yoke of love
   from him who is King of Angels.
For what cannot be safely dared
when the soul sees itself
as his excellent image
and distinguished likeness?[82]

The theology of the image grounds a confidence in the possibility not only of obtaining mercy and, perhaps, a meagre measure of salvation, but also an assurance of attaining the loftiest peaks of spiritual progression. The source of such boldness is not to be found in human

82. SC 83.1 (SBO 2:298,13–299,1).

merit or achievement, but in the inscrutable mystery of God's self-communication to the human race. It is only to the extent that a soul recognises that its movement toward God is itself his gift, that it will have courage and confidence in difficult times. The magnitude of its degradation, instead of forcing it into a depressed denial of spiritual aspiration, can thus serve to fuel its desire for self-transcendence.

As the fundamental imagehood is uncovered and revealed and the soul grows in likeness to God and in fidelity to its own nature, love becomes more and more in evidence in its life, a love deriving from and dependent on God's prior love. So often a lack of love is the automatic result of a failure in self-acceptance or of fear and confusion about one's basic identity and worth. Someone who appreciates that his whole being is the gift of God's love is more likely to love in return. In this way, the soul becomes even more like God, since now it becomes a mirror which reflects the divine charity. 'For God loves only with a view to being loved.'[83] 'Can anyone doubt that the soul is loved by the Word, first and to a greater degree?'[84]

In SC 85, Bernard passes on to the theme of the search for God, noting that the soul should adorn itself with garments that suit its status as image. He then lists the various virtues which constitute the true beauty of the soul, the *animae decor*.[85] This is the final direct reference to the theme of the image and it represents one of Bernard's consistent pre-occupations throughout his presentation, that in some way persons bestir themselves to embody in their way of living the spiritual potential gratuitously granted by God.

83. SC 83.4 (SBO 2:301,9–10).
84. SC 83.6 (SBO 2:302,13–14).
85. SC 85.10 (SBO 2:304,9–19).

THE REGION OF UNLIKENESS

The counterface of Bernard's teaching on human being as the image of God was his conviction that remaining faithful to this gift involves struggling against a predominantly hostile ambience. One is an exile here on earth and so does not receive from the world the sort of support one needs if one is to persevere. Worse than that, in a sense, is the fact that one's sojouring has compromised one's own integrity, so that the body, instead of serving as the soul's helpmate, aligns itself with the forces of the world in working counter to the upward movement.

Bernard's way of expressing himself in this matter is likely to be foreign and even offensive to our modern sensibilities. It is, therefore, all the more important to try and understand something of the background out of which he spoke. Furthermore, he was not enunciating a theorectical or speculative proposition; he was merely drawing from an ancient stream of thought, vocabulary, and imagery to express what, for him, was primarily an experiential reality. He knew from his own struggles and vicariously that spiritual growth is necessarily accompanied by a prolonged wrestling with contrary forces and that the whole of human life on earth is warfare. Irrespective of philosophical niceties, the body *can* appear as an enemy of spiritual growth and the world *does* tend to subvert any attempt at spiritual living. This experience was the primary focus of Bernard's gaze; he was not primarily interested in theory.

The term 'region of unlikeness', *regio disimilitudinis,* may have originated with Plato, but it certainly appears in Plotinus, and it is through him that it passed through Augustine, at least, into christian tradition. This theme emphasised the conviction that existence in the material world is a burden for the human being, whose true homeland is above. If he is to achieve a likeness to his prototype, it is necessary for the human being to struggle against the opposition of his immediate ambience. Christian thinkers saw this unlikeness as the result of the Fall and co-extensive with the reign of sin. The human being was created to God's image and likeness but fell away from this primal perfection and so lost the likeness. Though he retains his imagehood, he is no longer like God, nor like his own ideal self. He was dismissed from Paradise and, like the Prodigal Son, constrained to live 'in a distant region', far from his homeland. And so, progressively, he becomes alienated from himself.[86]

86. The standard studies on this theme are the following. F. Châtillon, 'Regio dissimilitudinis', in *Mélanges E. Podechard* (Lyons, 1945) pp. 85–102. Pierre Courcelle, 'Tradition néo-platonicienne et traditions chrétiennes de la "région de dissemblance"', *Archives d'histoire doctrinale et littéraire du moyen âge* 23 (1957) 5–34: this article includes a ten page inventory of occurrences. *Id.*, 'Témoins nouveaux de la "région de la dissemblance"', *Bibliothèque de l'Ecole de Chartres* 118 (1960) 135–140. J.-M. Déchanet, 'Aux sources de la pensée philosophique de S. Bernard', *Théologien*, pp. 69–77. *Id.*, 'Guillaume et Plotin', RMAL 2 (1946) 241–260. J.-C. Didier, 'Pour la fiche "Regio dissimilitudinis"', *Mélanges de science religieuse* 8 (1951) 205–210. E. Gilson, *Mystical Theology*, pp. 33–59. *Id.*, '"Regio dissimilitudinis" de Platon à saint Bernard de Clairvaux', MedSt 9 (1947) 108–130. W. Hiss, *Die Anthropologie*, pp. 42–65. R. Javelet, *Image*, vol. 1: 266–285; vol. 2: 228–243; the author indicates a further twenty-two occurrences of the expression which had not been included in the lists of Courcelle, vol. 2: 240–243. B. McGinn, *The Golden Chain*, pp. 133–134. L. Pascoe, *The Doctrine of the Imago*, pp. 33–52. M. Schmidt, 'Regio Dissimilitudinis', *Freiburger Zeitschrift für Philosophie un Theologie* 15 (1968) 63–108. A. E. Taylor, '"Regio Dissimilitudinis"' *Archives d'histoire doctrinale et litteraire du moyen âge* 9 (1934) 305–306. A good survey is given by G. Dumeige, art. 'Dissemblance', DSp 3: cols

In Bernard's view, the world, the flesh, and the devil conspire to inhibit the spiritual development of the human being.[87] It is easy enough to understand Bernard's

------

1330–1346. Something should perhaps be said, at this juncture, concerning the question of platonic and neo-platonic influence in the writings of the Fathers of the Church and in St Bernard. To begin with, it would be wrong to give the impression that the Fathers simply absorbed neo-platonic thought uncritically and, in so doing, undervalued the specific and explicit orientation of the scriptural authors. If the Fathers incorporated elements of a platonic philosophy into their reflection, it was not because they were seeking to impose an alien viewpoint on revealed truth, but because they honestly believed that such elements were true and that they conveyed the truth of the Bible, taken as a whole. A particular example is discussed by J. Kirchmeyer in DSp 6: cols 813–814: 'The theme of the human being made to God's image and likeness can be traced in its content and certainly in its language to a double source, part philosophical, part biblical. . . . The doctrinal significance of the theme is, in the writings of the Fathers, much less dependent on hellenisitic philosophy than on those passages of the Bible which, in different contexts, refer to the image of God' (translated). When minds trained in or familiar with the categories of platonising philosophy made contact with the Scriptures, certain meanings of the biblical text became apparent, which would not be quite as obvious to the authors, to the uninitiated, or to modern exegetes. Just as a botanist reading the Bible is more sensitive to information about plant life, so these philosophically oriented readers were eager to seize and exploit the philosophical possibilities which the sacred text offered. The fact that the literal meaning, as they perceived it, was often difficult or irrelevant undoubtedly legitimated such a transposition. It was in this way that many of the Fathers found a 'true philosophy' hidden in the obscure details of the texts before them, and marvelled at the inscrutable ways of God who, in inspiring the Scriptures, placed in them more than even their writers could perceive. As far as concerns the theme of the *regio dissimilitudinis,* it is wise not to become so absorbed in its potential roots that the actual meaning intended by its use is missed.

87. Cf. S. Wenzel, 'The Three Enemies of Man', MedSt 29 (1967) 47–66. The author gives a history of this famous triad. It appears

unfavourable attitude to the devil.[88] but the significance
of his apparent rejection of the world,[89] and the flesh,[90]

periodically in Bernard, through there is some variation in vocabulary, and often one or other of its components is missing. See
SC 1.9 (SBO 1:76), SC 11.6 (SBO 1:58,17–18), modelled on the
baptismal renunciation; SC 20.4 (SBO 1:116,20–24), SC 39.5 (SBO
2:221,11–12), SC 61.3 (SBO 2:150,9), SC 85.3 (SBO 2:309,7–8),
Sent 2.2 (SBO 6a:23,10). Sent 3.9 (SBO 6b:88,13–14), Ep 237.1
(SBO 8:113,18). Wenzel concludes his discussion on Bernard's use
of the triad by saying that it 'had become a pattern which suggested
itself naturally whenever he [Bernard] was thinking of man's temptations' (p. 54).
88. Apart from the texts cited in the previous note, see SC 64.6
(SBO 2:169,10) and SC 72.5 (SBO 2:228,29-229,1). Both of these
speak of the devil in terms of 2 Cor 11:14, as an angel of light. Bernard admits that he sometimes found difficulty in discerning what
was due to the devil and what came from himself, SC 32.6 (SBO
1:230,16–17). At times, the devil seems to be no more than the per-
sonifications of human vices, such as we sometimes find in the
primitive Judeo-Christian texts. See, for instance, SC 38.5 (SBO
2:21,15–23).
89. A special issue of RAM (41/3 [1965] 233–432) was devoted to
the theme La notion de 'mépris du monde' dans la tradition spirituelle
occidentale, included in which was an article by F. Lazzari, 'La con-
temptus mundi chez S. Bernard', (pp. 291–304). R. Bultot has a multi-
volume work on the subject. A convenient summary of his views is his
article 'Spirituels et théologiens devant l'homme et le monde', Revue
Thomiste 72 (1964) 517–548. Reservation about 'the world' is not, of
course a monastic preserve; it is inculcated throughout the New Testament and by the Church in its general teaching. On this see P. Grelot
and E. Pousset, art. 'Monde', DSp 10: cols 1620–1646.
90. Cf. P. Daubercies, 'La théologie de la condition charnelle
chez les maitres du haut moyen-âge', RTAM 30 (1963) 5–54. The
'flesh' often receives the opporbrium strictly reserved for its disordinate inclinations. Cf. B. Stökle, 'Die Konkupiszenz bei Bernard
von Clairvaux: Ein zeitgemässes Steck mittelalterlicher Geistlehre',
GuL 35 (1962) 444–453. Id., 'Amor carnis-abusus amoris: Das
Verständis von der Konkupiszenz bei Bernhard von Clairvaux und
Aelred von Rieval', Analecta 7, pp. 147–174.

is somewhat more difficult to appreciate positively. It is possible, of course to trace the pedigree of his views and vocabulary and to demonstrate that they were not without distinguished precedents. The task of establishing to what extent the terms he used represented his personal philosophy, however, is one that requires great sensitivity. It may be that he was utilising conventional turns of phrase without much thought for the theoretical ramifications of what he was saying.

In this matter, Emero Stiegman's *Language of Asceticism* is of great value. He examines the question at great length and concludes that, taken within Bernard's own cultural, monastic, and literary setting, and viewing his writings in terms of the problematics which confronted him, the bernardine corpus is not negativistic. The negative statements which abound in his works contained positive content, and this was clear to those who read them within Bernard's own environment. To readers of another generation, however, such statements can be misleading.[91]

It is within the context of temptation, struggle, failure, sin, and the sustained laboriousness of the spiritual pursuit that Bernard's teaching on the *regio dissimilitudinis* needs to be interpreted. It was, for him, one among many images which betoken the negative experiences encountered in the process of growth, it blends well with the traditional theology of the image and likeness, and it is itself a striking and euphonious phrase whose use enjoys the weight of precedent since the time of Augustine. There is, accordingly, a strong *a priori* argument that the phrase does not necessarily connote a philosophical stance which is dualist, neo-platonic or non-Christian.

In the twelve uses of the term which I have been able to find in the works of Bernard, *regio dissimilitudinis*

---

91. Cf. E. Stiegman, *Language of Asceticism*, pp. 312–322.

is surrounded by elements of a single linguistic field.[92] Several times it is part of a series of uncomplimentary references to the flesh and to worldly involvement, or it is used to highlight the distance between this present life and the world to come. A typical example is the following.

Nothing is more effective and speedier in bringing a soul to humility than for it to discover the truth in its own regard. There must be no dissimulation or deceit, but the soul should simply set itself before its face, and look without turning aside. If it thus looks at itself in the clear light of truth, it will discover that it exists in the region of unlikeness, and that it cannot hide from its own unhappiness. Then from its unhappiness it will cry out to the Lord with the Prophet, 'In your truth you have humbled me'. How can a soul not be humbled by such truthful self-knowledge? For it perceives itself burdened with sins, entangled with earthly cares, infected with the excremental desires of the flesh, blind, bent, weak, riddled with manifold error, exposed to numberless dangers and fearful of many terrors, made anxious with a thousand problems and beset with a thousand suspicions, afflicted by a thousand constraints, prone to vice and powerless for virtue. Is there, in such a situation, any source of uplift or pride?[93]

Bernard did not want his readers to repress the very real suffering which they experience and which he believed to

----

92. Cf. SC 27.6 (SBO 1:184,22–23), SC 36.5 (SBO 2:7,9), Gra 32 (SBO 3:188,27–28), Div 40.4 (SBO 6a:237,9–10), Div 42.2–3 (SBO 6a:256–258)—this is the most sustained presentation of the theme. The term *regio dissimilitudinis* occurs three times in the two sections. Here it applies simply to worldly existence. It is contrasted with the paradisus *claustralis,* with purgatory, with hell and, finally, with the *paradisus supercoelestis.* Sent 3.21 (SBO 6b:78,17), Par 1.2 (SBO 6b:262,1–2), Ep 8.2 (SBO 7:48,14). Ep 42.8 (= Mor 8; SBO 7:107,25–26).

93. SC 36.5 (SBO 2:7,5–18).

be a significant part of every human life. It is not that he was in favour of suffering, but simply that he recognised that it could not be minimised or endured until first it had been accepted. Thus to grant even a theoretical recognition of the possibility of pain is the first stage in deciding on a conscious attitude to adopt in its regard. So long as the various ills attendant on human existence are regarded as avoidable or accidental, then one is able to postpone taking a stance about ultimate issues. One lives in the deluded hope that, in some felicitous change of circumstances, a painless life is possible. Bernard doubted the practical effectiveness of such groundless optimism. He thought rather, that human beings should be prepared for the *dura et aspera*. If there is negativity in Bernard, it is not because the language or outlook has cast reality in a negative mould, but simply because negativity, whether we like it or not, is an inevitable part of the human exisistence.[94]

Bernard was proposing a way out of this recognised pain, by presenting the christian path to endless joy. There is, however, a condition imposed on those who wish to walk the road that leads to unalloyed happiness. They must begin a process of renunciation of the deceptive pleasures of this life—the world and the flesh—in order to find their joy in the more substantial and lasting pleasures of the spiritual order. This is not something that can be accomplished by a quick decision and an immediate change in direction. Total renunciation is more a process of weaning. The person has to be educated in the appreciation of spiritual realities; as his taste for these develops and he finds himself more attracted to them,

94. 'This aspect of the problem of interpretation may demand, not further philological inquiry, but conversion.' Thus Stiegman, *Language of Asceticism*, following the thought of Lonergan's *Method in Theology*.

his need and desire for lower pleasures slowly recedes. It is a long process, but perserverance in it is helped by understanding what is happening. Even the theoretical recognition of the impermanence of temporal gratification is a step along the way, a loosening of the bonds which will be ultimately flung aside.

Bernard was more sober in his evaluation of the body and the world when he spoke more philosophically about the human condition. He recognised that body and soul form a true unity, even though in his preaching he often spoke of them, as distinct and opposed realities.[95] He acknowledged that the body is a benefit to the soul rather than an impedance.[96] He was not really advocating a philosophy hostile to material reality; what he rejected is the giving of priority and superiority to the non-spiritual. For him, this is the source of all evil.

When the body acts independently of the spiritual side of the human being, disorder results. It weighs down the soul,[97] it renders pure contemplation impossible,[98] because it is continually giving birth to new disturbances,[99] and afflicting the spirit with *torpor, acedia, taedium,*[100] a restless distaste for what is good for it. The sin-related disadvantages of the body can never be entirely neutralised during this life,[101] and so the soul is kept from attaining perfect beauty.[102] It is always somewhat overclouded with darkness,[103] and kept far away from the light.[104]

95. Csi 5.20–21 (SBO 3:483–484).
96. SC 82.3 (SBO 2:294,7). Cf. Div 12.4 (SBO 6a:130,4–5).
97. SC 81.7 (SBO 2:288,10). Cf. Div 47 (SBO 6a:267,17).
98. SC 41.3 (SBO 2:30,16).
99. SC 48.1 (SBO 2:67,8–9).
100. SC 21.4 (SBO 1:124,17–18), SC 21.5 (SBO 1:124,26).
101. SC 58.10 (SBO 2:133,26–28).
102. SC 38.4 (SBO 2:17,25).
103. SC 82.3 (SBO 2:294,11–13).
104. SC 38.5 (SBO 2:17,18).

The soul is a 'vagabond',[105] forced to dwell 'in the region of bodies',[106] bewailing its involvement with the body of this death.[107] 'Woe is me! How vile is the covering you seek, O unhappy soul!'[108] The body is a dung heap, *sterquilinium*,[109] and the soul is described as 'surrounded by the repulsive excrement of the bodily prison', *faeculenti corporis horrido circumdari carcere.*[110] Likewise, the whole world is a prison, where the soul is racked by necessities and impositions.[111] And forced to dwell among the wicked, *in circuitu impiorum.*[112]

The soul is subject to the destructive forces of the concupiscence of the flesh,[113] through which all its accumulated goodness is subject to dissipation.[114] Concupiscence is permanently present in the flesh,[115] and once the soul responds to its incitement or titillation,[116] it freely becomes the slave of sin,[117] thus beginning a

105. Dil 18 (SBO 3:135,5).
106. Div 2.7 (SBO 6a:84,15).
107. SC 21.1 (SBO 1:122,8 and 11–12), Div 26.4 (SBO 6a:196, 20–21). Cf Div 42.2 (SBO 6a:257,1–2). Cf. Rom 7:24.
108. Div 5.2 (SBO 6a:99,14).
109. Div 82.2 (SBO 6a:322,15–16), Div 5.4 (SBO 6a:102,12).
110. Ep 144.1 (SBO 7:344,16–17), Cf. Asc 3.6 (SBO 5:135,6–7), SC 24.5 (SBO 1.156,13–14), *In celebratione adventus* 1 (SBO 6a:9, 14–15), *In cel adv* 2 (SBO 6a:10,6), Div 12.3 (SBO 6a:128,20), Div 14.7 (SBO 6a:139,13), Div 16.3 (SBO 6a:146,7). Cf. V Nat 2.3 (SBO 4:206.2): *de ergastulo huius corporis;* In Div 19.7 (SBO 6a: 164,24), the body is referred to as a *saccum*, which must be rent open, presumably to reveal the soul which is inside.
111. SC 21.1 (SBO 1:122,8–9), SC 20.3 (SBO 1:116,12), Div 14.7 (SBO 6a:139), V Nat 2.3 (SBO 4:206,1–2), SC 68.1 (SBO 2:196,22).
112. Dil 19 (SBO 3:135,17), Div 1.3 (SBO 6a:75,1). Cf Ps 11:9.
113. SC 44.5 (SBO 2:47,14–15).
114. SC 46.4 (SBO 2:58,10–11).
115. SC 56.5 (SBO 2:117,19–20).
116. Div 6.1 (SBO 6a:105,21).
117. SC 56.6 (SBO 2:117,22–23).

process which terminates in the complete destruction of good will and the victory of malice.[118]

It is concupiscence which is the cause of the negativity of the flesh and, in the word of Gen 8:21, makes the human being more prone to evil than to good.[119] This is why even infants are described as 'children of wrath', since they, also, are slaves to the promptings of the flesh.[120] All alike are infected with the pestilence of pride,[121] and forced to live in darkness and in the shadow of death, in ignorance of the truth,[122] with the mark of original sin branded on the whole of their life.[123]

Such, for Bernard, is the recipient of grace; such is the subject of divine attraction. It is of such a one that he speaks when he develops the theme of desire for God. There is a paradox here. The stark picture of human life sold out to sin is balanced by the buoyant optimism occasioned by a recognition of the power of grace. It was only to set off the boundless gratuity of God that Bernard expatiated on the gloom inherent in a life lived without him. Of himself, the human being is nothing; even his best gifts are distorted out of shape unless he re-attaches them to their source. It is this image of the human being, helpless except for God's help, which Bernard was advancing. It was not pessimism which inspires such pictures, but Bernard's desire to communicate a vivid awareness of life before salvation. There is irony in his words; he described human ills with great power, all the while realising that deliverance was at hand.

Without such a recognition of the precariousness of

118. SC 56.6 (SBO 2:117–118).
119. SC 29.4 (SBO 1:206,3–4), SC 44.5 (SBO 2:47,8).
120. SC 69.3 (SBO 2:204,7).
121. SC 54.8 (SBO 2:107,10–11).
122. SC 22.7 (SBO 1:133,9–10).
123. SC 72.8 (SBO 2:230,19–20).

his own position, the human being is prone to thousands of evils.[124] If he recognises the power that sin holds over him, calls out for help and co-operates with it, he is able thereby to neutralise some of the force of evil. 'But to be able to deal with these thorns and not be hurt, is a work of divine power, not of your own virtue.'[125] But the wine of the Spirit acts to negate the attraction of carnal pleasures,[126] so that the image is renewed and the human being progressively becomes more and more like his Creator.[127]

The 'region of unlikeness' is, then, one of a series of images used pastorally by Bernard to indicate the negative forces operative in the process of salvation, the things which the human being must resist on pain of destroying himself. The use of this metaphor need not necessarily indicate that Bernard's view of life was particularly pessimistic or that he himself was exceedingly negative in his view of temporal realities. There is an element of exaggeration and literary licence in what he wrote, which may cause alarm to the literal-minded interpreters of later generations. Strange as it may appear, in relation to such a serious subject, Bernard seemed to *enjoy* heaping scorn on the world, flesh, and devil; his prose is vigorous and his images are strong. There is every indication that he was having fun doing it. At least some of his disgust is over-dramatised. Bernard recognised both the negativity and the relativity of many aspects of human existence and confronted them regularly in his sermons with a view to helping his reader achieve a better perspective on life. No serious attempt was made by Bernard to diagnose the philosophical origins of these realities nor does he seem to

124. SC 35.6 (SBO 1:252,3).
125. SC 48.2 (SBO 2:68,2–3).
126. SC 18.5 (SBO 1:107,10).
127. Div 69.1 (SBO 6a:304,1).

have been concerned about the logical corollaries of some of his more outrageous utterances. He simply made his point, using a variety of images and metaphors, with a view to redressing the balance in a world which gives too little attention to the things of the spirit. In a general way he accepted that the world and the flesh were good, but this was conditional on their keeping their place in the divinely-established heirarchy of being, the *ordo* given in creation and to be realised in all human acts. The problem which he saw around him and which he understood from his own experience was that the world and the flesh tend to get out of control and subvert this order. It was then, after they had removed themselves from the life-giving dispositions of God, that Bernard judged them to be 'vain and empty baubles, the final outcome of which is death'.[128]

This is not to say that Bernard's approach to these matters will suit everybody or that his style of presenting his views will meet with universal approval. There is question here of trying to understand Bernard's position rather than of attempting to evaluate its validity in a different setting. His exaggerated and sometimes extreme symbolism is shocking to our literal-minded world and his frequent faecal references are an affront to well-mannered translators, but it was not always so. Bernard was well enough accepted by his contemporaries, who understood the context out of which he was speaking. For ourselves, it is undoubtedly more difficult. What we have to do is to see this harsh, negative extremism as counter-balanced by the rest of his teaching.

THE ORIGIN OF DESIRE

There are many ways in which it is possible to present the anthropological basis of Bernard's teaching on

128. SC 16.4 (SBO 1:92,13–14).

desire for God. Because he was not a systematic thinker, the elements of his synthesis are to be found scattered throughout his writings in different contexts and combinations. It is left to the would-be expositor to work out his own method of putting them together. It should, therefore, be understood that, if a particular path out of the maze is proposed, no suggestion is being made that other solutions are not possible. There is no doubt that Bernard's thought is so rich, and at times so elusive, that any attempt to pin him down to concrete theological propositions must be approached with suitable diffidence.

A starting point for Bernard's anthropology of desire may, perhaps, be found in a very simple principle. In fact, one of the most recurrent elements in Bernard's preaching is the theme that due priority must always be given to the spiritual. It has an established ascendancy over what is material, worldly, and carnal, and has therefore the first claim on our energies. In Bernard's view, the whole work of spiritual endeavour—and the whole purpose of monastic life—can be understood in terms of restoring the original harmony between all orders of creation by re-asserting the primacy of what is, by nature, highest.

Sin, therefore, for Bernard, was the upsetting of this divinely-established hierarchy and the giving of preference to the worldly and carnal at the expense of what was both closer to God and more conducive to human welfare. It was not that Bernard was antagonistic to the world and the flesh as such, but he understood clearly that often these forces were in revolt against the spiritual and, therefore, against God.

The constant theme of his preaching was that we must not join in the rebellion, but must strive to rediscover that freedom from world and flesh which alone can lead to happiness and growth. This very assertion, however, leads to the question about the basis for such a pre-supposition. What evidence is there that, in fact, the human being is fulfilled only through giving himself to spiritual realities and in fighting against the autonomy of lower powers.

And so an anthropology is formed, composed for the most part of elements drawn from traditional ec-clesial writers, and fused into some sort of unity by Ber-nard's own keen awareness of what was important.

That the human being was made for spiritual life is inferred from the fact that nothing else is able to satisfy his questing heart. Bernard asserts the traditional view that only God is able to fill the vast void which the human being experiences within himself and that it is only in heaven that he will be fulfilled. If this truth is ac-cepted, then it follows that everything else has only a relative value; nothing else is absolute.

Bernard found support for his position not only in the wealth of theological and scriptural reflection on the subject, but also in his own experience and in that of his readers. In fact, neither the world nor the flesh brings more than a modicum of pleasure and that quickly passes. The only way that an individual is kept from a *Weltschemertz* which might lead to the truth, is by be-ing enslaved to the lie that, whereas present gratification is minimal enough, better things lie around the corner. So long as he is thus deluded, he continues to blame his unhappiness on not getting enough of what the world and the flesh have to offer. And so he seeks more and gives himself to the pursuit with greater abandon than ever, only to find his frustration unabated. Bernard wants his readers to be aware of this trap. To recognise in their own lives the feeling that the satisfactions offered by the world and the flesh are inadequate to sustain a person's inner fire.

If one is to be led to make a trial, a double knowledge is necessary. Firstly, one needs the theoretical conviction that spiritual realities are worth pursuing. Secondly, one needs some awareness of the actual dynamics of the pursuit, so that one's expectations may be realistic. Bernard's teaching seeks to cover both these areas. He was constantly exhorting his readers to 'taste and see that the Lord is good', setting before them the values of serving God as he desires to be served, and deploying his considerable powers of invective against unspiritual living. On the other hand, he constantly supported those who struggle to perservere in their service by explaining the rhythms of growth and how present difficulties are, in fact, making things easier for the future. But, above all, Bernard kept returning to the theme that, irrespective of how one feels about present experiences, the path ahead must always lie in following the imperatives of one's own nature.

This leads to the affirmation that the human being is capable of entering into union with God, no matter how much present appearances may *seem* to render this impossible. More than this, such a capacity is not merely the opportunity for the exercise of arbitrary personal choice about whether one will exploit it or not. It is also an imperative of being. The capacity is there; unless it is brought into fullness, the human being will be thwarted of his goal; if it is radically denied, he will be ultimately frustrated.

It is at this point that Bernard had recourse to the traditional theology of the human being as the image of God and to the varied body of thought which was associated with the theme. As far as Bernard was concerned, this was an integral element of faith; it was no more possible to dismiss this truth and remain a Christian than it was to refuse belief in God or the divinity of Christ.

There is, accordingly, a movement in being which carries the human person toward God. This is not the result of any act or choice on the part of the person; it is a tendency present at the level of nature. At the pre-elective, ontological level, human being is defective and incomplete without God, hence there is a *desiderium* present in the human person, whether he knows it or not.

When one becomes, through various experiences, aware of this natural drift, one is faced with a choice; either to allow oneself to be carried by it beyond the range of known gratifications and experiences or to propel oneself in a contrary direction. To go with the stream is to give oneself to a process of continual self-transcendence in the blind faith that, by God's grace, all things will turn out well. To resist and struggle against this tendency, however, does not permit one to remain as one was. Inevitably and secretly, a decline begins and the whole process of human liberation and growth is retarded. Unhappiness increases as complicated processes of compensation and rationalisation intervene, and the individual finds himself more and more caught in snares of his own making.

Even at this unfortunate point, Bernard affirmed that all is not lost. The very agony occasioned by objective decline can be a factor in helping an individual see the truth about himself and motivate him to attempt to reverse the trend. The capacity for God causes suffering when it is frustrated, but remains ready to be filled whenever the heart consents to turn back to God.

Giving oneself to the search for God—whether within the context of monastic life or in another situation —is not primarily a matter of consciously-adopted programme of life. It is, in Bernard's view, simply an assent to the full implications of human being. Often one may seek God for many years without being reflexively conscious of the object of one's quest. Perhaps one would explain it in different categories. The point is, if the seeking is the result of a real effort made to be faithful to the dictates of one's own heart, according to the situation in which one is placed, then it can truly be designated as a search for God. This is what it truly is, even though the seeker himself is unaware of where his struggling steps will lead.

Desire for God may be defined, in the first instance, as that movement of being which carries the person toward God. It is the tendency to self-transcendence, although it is doubtful whether Bernard would have been at ease with such grand language. It is that mysterious force which, when accepted, communicates an inner integrity to a person's life, irrespective of how prominently 'religion' may figure in either outlook or behaviour. Desire for God is, first and foremost, an ontological reality.

Desire has also, as we have seen, its experiential aspects; it is feeling and yearning and fervour. But these subjective manifestations of the more fundamental reality are derivative. They are not the crucial components, but merely external verifications which help the person to recognise what is going on within him and to re-orient himself so that the process is furthered. Divorced from its anthropological basis, Bernard's teaching on desire for God is in danger of becoming mere frothy pietism, a manipulation of subjective states with no visible benefit to behaviour or contribution to the Church and the world. This was not Bernard's view. For him any outward ministry must be an expression of a more fundamental fidelity, to gospel priorities, to the call of grace, to the exigencies of nature.

In the light of the tradition, Bernard's anthropological teaching is standard enough. The importance which he assigned to such understanding is, likewise, typical of his own generation, as we have noted. Hence, the question may be asked about how original his position is.

In general, and not merely regarding his anthropology, Bernard was only accidentally original; he tried not to be. His originality consists not so much in the content of his teaching as in the passion which he expended on it, his mastery of words and images and his stunning capacity to juxtapose two well-known texts or truths in order to intimate a third. I think that he would have seen his task less as the pure establishment of the truth than as the relatively uncritical acceptance of received truth and the application of this to the concrete condition of his readers. Any innovations in content usually came, not from concentrated speculation, but from this process of adapting the truth to particular situations. In such circumstances, experience often suggested alternative interpretations of elements in tradition or new aspects which the past had overlooked.

His anthropology is, according, not really a great contribution to universal theology — if this be considered as an accumulating fund of theological conclusions. In the light of later narrowness, his statement of the universal possibility of spiritual marriage is refreshing, but again it is only the making explicit of existing consensus. Perhaps the wholeness of his doctrine is what is most uncommon, the way in which desire for God is seen in relation to almost every aspect of human life. This, particularly in the centuries after his death, is not widely attested.

But, if it is a fact that his anthropology is not so innovative, it is, at least, not only coherent with his total philosophy of life but even characteristic of his style of teaching. Perhaps it is also something of a universalisation of his own character and temperament, and, even, as Pascoe suggests,[129] an ongoing, defensive legitimation

129. Louis B. Pascoe, *Saint Bernard of Clairvaux: The Doctrine of the* Imago *and its Relationship to Cistercian Monasticism,* (MA Thesis: Fordham University, 1960). See, for example, page 75: 'It

of his own monastic choice. One thing is certain. It is not possible to remove the anthropological component from Bernard's thought and still have a credible basis for any major aspect of his teaching. Above all, his doctrine on desire for God is absolutely unthinkable without his overriding conviction of the paramountcy of the spiritual in the unfolding of human being.

One final point may be made. It seems likely that the ultimate explanation of the importance of anthropology in Bernard's spiritual teaching is that Bernard was one who took seriously the consequences of the Incarnation. His Christology constantly exploited the traditional theme of fully human, fully divine, to the point that he was utterly convinced that humanity was not only compatible with divinity, but incomplete without it. It was his appreciation of the humanity of God which made him place such great emphasis on the divinsation of human beings.

---

was by participating in this dynamic *reformatio* that was Cistercianism that the individual soul as the *imago Dei* most perfectly achieved its own personal *reformatio*.'

CHAPTER   FIVE

THE   CULMINATION   OF   DESIRE

T HE SONG OF SONGS is a dialogue between two
lovers. Its drama devolves upon a dialectic between
the joy experienced when the lovers are together and
the sadness and longing which is their lot when they are
apart. The desire springing from the experience of desolation is directed toward reunion, toward a mutual presence which suffers no obstacle or threat of termination.

In commenting on the Song of Songs, Bernard was
faithful to its general movement. It is a song about love,
about the relationship which exists between Christ and
his Church, and between the Word and the individual
soul. This love is not capable of complete realisation in
this present life and, hence, includes in its basic notion
the idea of movement toward a future in which its
perfect and permanent expression will be possible. Bernard's teaching about the desire which is the keynote of
love for God during this life, necessarily looked beyond

190

the concrete conditions of present existence. It focussed on the world to come.

It is in this sense that is is possible to speak about the 'eschatological' meaning of desire for God. It is oriented toward the future, to heaven. Bernard's approach was not apocalyptic, especially in the *Sermons on the Song of Songs*. He was not a herald of the imminent end of the world, nor was his major imagery drawn from the fiery themes associated with that tradition. He simply expounded soberly and consistently the accepted doctrine on the final things, seeing such teaching as the necessary perspective in which to speak about present realities, and a potential source of motivation and encouragement in practical everyday life.

The goal of desire is a union of love with God in his Word. In this chapter we shall speak of the theme of spiritual marriage. We discuss, in particular, the emphasis given by Bernard to the *spiritual* character of this experience, especially in the light of the text of 1 Cor 6:17, 'He who adheres to God becomes one spirit with him'. We then examine the various complementary aspects of Bernard's teaching on heaven and its relationship with present existence. Then the christological aspect of Bernard's approach is reviewed, particularly with reference to Bernard's great devotion to the mystery of Christ's Ascension.

SPIRITUAL MARRIAGE

From the text of the Song of Songs, Bernard drew a wealth of sponsal imagery with which to convey his teaching on the ascent of the soul to God. He interpreted the object of the soul's longing as spiritual union with the Word, and spoke about it in terms of the interaction of earthly lovers. A number of delicate distinctions need to be drawn before discussing what Bernard has to say in this regard.

In the first place, it is important that sentimental conventions about the 'languishing spouse' which flourished in the seventeenth century and afterwards should not be retrospectively attributed to Bernard. Bernard never forgot that the images he used were images and not reality. Even in his most 'flowery' passages, he can never be ranked with the writers of the sickening insincerity which filled prayerbooks in the last century. The Cistercians of the twelfth century were an austere group of men, deliberately choosing a life of considerable physical hardship. They attracted to their ranks men who were robust and masculine, most of them coming to the monastery as mature adults. Bernard himself wrote strong, vigorous, and manly prose, a fact not always conveyed in translation. His *Sententiae* demonstrate that what was not intended for publication was often spoken plainly, to the point of crudity. If there is a 'feminine' element to be noted in cistercian spirituality, it is not due to an absence of masculinity. It is, rather, an integrating factor in lives that were strongly masculine in character. So manly were these monks that they were not afraid to leave the opposite qualities unrepressed.[1]

Secondly, the marital imagery used by Bernard was not his creation. It has its origins in the Bible and in the writings of the Church Fathers. Bernard never lost sight of the fact that the primary bearer of the title 'bride of Christ' is not the individual soul, but the Church.[2] Far

1. Cf. J. Leclercq, 'S. Bernard et le feminin', *Nouveau visage,* pp. 127–154.
2. Cf. E. Mikkers, 'De kerk als bruid in de Hoogliedcommentaar van Sint Bernardus,' in *Sint Bernardus,* pp. 195–214. T. Moritz, 'The Church as Bride in Bernard of Clairvaux's Sermons on the Song of Songs', *Chimaera,* pp. 3–11.

from being a promoter of an individualist 'God and I' spirituality, he saw clearly the interaction of personal and corporate factors in the way in which a human being relates to his Creator. Bernard's mysticism is never divorced either from theology or from concrete participation in ecclesial and communitarian life.

Thirdly, Bernard wrote with great sensitivity to the issues involved in using sexual love (as in the Song of Songs) as an image of love between the human being and God, especially since the bulk of his readership was vowed to a celibate life. In the first place, as will be discussed in a later section of this chapter, he gave great emphasis to the fact that the relationship between the soul and the Word was accomplished at the level of the spirit, through the elevation of the soul. It was a spiritual experience, not a sensible or carnal affect. It may seem strange that such a point has to be made, yet the fact is that a number of modern writers and speakers have erroneously inferred from misunderstood texts that mystical experience is accompanied by definite physiological effects. In reading Bernard, one must be clear that this is not what he is saying. In the second place, Bernard spoke with great delicacy of the details of sexual intimacy, never permitting his imagery to become prurient and so to distract the reader from the message intended. At the same time, he wrote with a relaxed sense of freedom; his prose exhibits none of the tautness one would expect of mere repression. Jean Leclercq deals with this matter well.

> It is, therefore, normal and easy for a Bernard, a Richard Rolle or a John of the Cross to pass from the language of love to that of charity, from the dialogue between a man and a woman to that between Christ and the Church. How different this is from the erotic language of courtly literature! . . .
> All that has been said leaves no doubt that Bernard

could easily have spoken of a love that was purely carnal. Instead, by a hidden change, he passes into a language that is exclusively religious. It is from the Bible that he derives both languages and also the possibility of blending them: that of the Song of Songs with that of St Paul, that of loving desire with that of prophetic desire. This is because the desire of the Prophets was also that of Bernard, as it is, in the Church, also that of the readers both of the Prophets and of Bernard.[3]

Union with the Word takes place at the high point of human being. There is no question, in Bernard's mind, of its being a mere neurotic or emotional ravishment.

The theme of spiritual marriage has a long history in christian tradition and can be traced back to the Bible itself.[4] In becoming man, the Word of God is seen as entering into a relationship of wedlock with the human race. Those united to him, who form the Church, may be individually and corporately designated as his 'bride'. Although the joining of the partners is legally complete, it awaits consummation, which will take place only in the future life. This symbolism was especially prominent in those writers who were influenced by or who commented on the Song of Songs.[5]

In Bernard's presentation of the theme, the soul enters into a state of spiritual marriage with the Word to the extent that it freely allows its will to be confirmed with that of the Word. When the natural potential of the

---

3. Translated from *Nouveau visage*, p. 147.

4. Cf. Pierre Adnès, art. 'Maeriage', DSp 10: cols 398–408.

5. With regard to the identification of the bride in the Song of Songs, Daniélou (*Origène*, p. 297) states that though Hippolytus had nominated the Church, Origen preferred to add the possibility of applying the text to the individual soul. Cf. Crouzel, 'Le thème du mariage mystique chez Origène', in *Studia Missionalia* 26 (1977) 37–57. See also the surveys of Ohly and Riedlinger, already cited.

soul for likeness to the Word is realised through grace, on the one hand, and through free assent, on the other, then 'such conformity marries the soul to the Word'.[6] They are now in a state of spiritual matrimony.[7] 'Thus to love is to have been married.'[8] 'If love is the principal and specific quality of those who are married, then the soul which loves is rightly given the name "bride".'[9]

Within this spiritual marriage occur all those expressions of love and affection which characterise an authentic married life, but on a spiritual level. Thus, Bernard began his commentary on the first verse of the Song of Songs with nine sermons exploring the significance of the words, 'Let him kiss me with the kiss of his mouth'. Bernard's words, though forthright and direct, remain as chaste as the bride herself. This can be seen from the peroration to SC 12.

> We give thanks to you, Lord Jesus, because you have been so good as to include us in your dearly-loved Church, not only to keep us faithful, but in order that we might be joined to you (*copularemur*) in the bride's joyful chaste and eternal embraces (*amplexus*). In this way, we shall be enabled to look, with face unveiled, upon the glory which you share with the Father and with the Holy Spirit, for ever and ever. Amen.[10]

Bernard's most sustained development of the theme of the spiritual marriage of the soul and the Word occurs in the relatively short SC 83, probably written around 1152, the year before his death.

---

6. SC 83.3 (SBO 2:299,21): *talis conformitas maritat animam Verbo.*

7. SC 85.13 (SBO 2:315,26): *in spirituali matrimonio.* Cf. SC 61.1 (SBO 2:148,19): *faciet spirituale coniugium.*

8. SC 83.6 (SBO 2:302,11–12): *sic amare nupsisse est.* Cf. SC 83.3 (SBO 2:299,23): *si perfecte diligit, nupsit.*

9. SC 7.2 (SBO 1:32,5–6).

10. SC 12.11 (SBO 1:67,26–30).

He begins with the splendid passage already quoted in the last chapter, affirming the affinity of the soul with the Word and the universal possibility of attaining this degree of union. All that is necessary for spiritual progress is that the soul 'take care to preserve its natural quality, the heavenly beauty which was given to it originally, and to be zealous in enhancing it and adorning it with the bright garments of good behaviour and love'.[11] By God's gift three streams flow toward the sea: nature, the practice of virtue, and the self-forgetfulness of love. But it is especially through love that the soul makes it way back to the Word and becomes one with him.[12]

Such conformity marries the soul to the Word. The one who is like him by nature now shows itself like him by an act of the will, loving in the same way that it is itself loved. Therefore, if it perfectly loves it has been married.

What can be a source of greater pleasure than such a close union of wills? What can be more desirable than the love by which you, O soul, are not satisfied with human teaching, but go directly to the Word, remaining joined to the Word, familiarly relating and discussing whatever falls within the mind's grasp and the range of bold desire.

Such a soul has really entered into a spiritual and holy contract of marriage. Perhaps, instead of 'contract', I should say 'contact', since there is here, without doubt, question of an embrace. This is because when two will the same things and reject the same things, they become one spirit.[13]

Bernard then points out that the love between the soul and the Word is of the most intimate kind, in which are

11. SC 83.1 (SBO 2:299,2–5).
12. SC 83.2 (SBO 2:299,19).
13. SC 83.3 (SBO 2:299,21–29).

equally excluded the hope of external profit and every kind of fear.

Love is its own merit and reward. It seeks no justification beyond itself nor any fruit external to itself, for the act of love is, of itself, fruition. I love because I love. I love in order to receive love.[14]

In the case of the relationship of the soul and the Word, a special factor is introduced: 'the bridegroom is not only a lover; he is Love itself'.[15] To love Love is the ultimate act of uprightness, the purest expression of human being, the definitive conformity with the *ordo* established by God. Not to love Love, but to love other things instead, is fundamental and total disorder. The theme of *ordinatio caritatis* is never far from the forefront of Bernard's awareness. He was not a romantic; he knew that love's delights yield themselves only to those who take steps in the practical order to enhance the relationship. The fullest expression of love presupposes a whole complex of humbler manifestations of disinterested good-will and care. This means, in the case of the relationship of the soul to the Word, subordinating all alternative loves to love of Love itself.

Love is a great thing—so long as it flows back to its own beginnings, returns to its origins, and draws from its sources the means by which it may permanently flow.[16]

The love which the soul experiences is not its own, it is but the reflection and effect of God's love for it. It takes courage to love, because love involves such complete self-giving that it can appear as a form of death. It is only when one has experienced the life-restoring love of

14. SC 83.4 (SBO 2:300,24–26).
15. SC 83.4 (SBO 2:300,12).
16. SC 83.4 (SBO 2:300,26–28).

another and felt its effects inwardly that it becomes possible
to loosen one's hold and renounce narrow self-possession.
To love God plausibly, one must have first experienced his
love for oneself. It is in this sense that divine charity is the
cause of human love.

> When God loves, he wishes for nothing more than
> to be loved in return. He loves for no other purpose
> than to be loved, knowing that those who love him
> will be made happy by their very experience of such
> love.[17]

The soul's return of love is marked by the same
gratuity which characterises God's initial movement of
love. It seeks for nothing in recompense for its love and
labours willingly without a thought of reward.

> Rightly does the bride renounce all other affections
> in order to give herself entirely to loving. It is in
> returning love that she responds to love, and even if
> she totally poured herself forth in love, this would
> be little in comparison with that ever-flowing tor-
> rent which is its source. For there is no comparison
> in the volume of flow of lover and Love, of soul and
> Word, of bride and bridegroom, of Creator and
> creature, no more than there is a comparison be-
> tween one who is thirsty and the running streams.[18]

Even though the soul's love cannot match that of the
Word, Bernard continues, it can still be whole-hearted.
'Even though the creature loves less because it is less,
nothing can be lacking to completeness if it loves with all
that it has.'[19] Spiritual marriage takes place when the soul,
undeterred by its limited capacity to love, gives itself totally
to responding to its experience of the love of God. This is the
source of the soul's most complete happiness.

17. SC 83.4 (SBO 2:301,9–11).
18. SC 83.6 (SBO 2:302,1–5).
19. SC 83.6 (SBO 2:302,10–11).

For who can doubt that the soul is loved first by the Word, and to a greater extent. He both anticipates the soul in loving and excels it. Happy is the one who is thus anticipated by the blessing of such sweetness! Happy is the one to whom it is given to experience the great pleasure of this embrace! This is nothing else than a love which is holy and chaste, a love which is sweet and pleasant, a love characterised as much by its serenity as by its sincerity, a reciprocal love which is both strong and intimate, which joins two not into one flesh, but into one spirit, so that they are no longer two, but one. This is what Paul says in the text, 'He who adheres to God becomes one spirit with him'.[20]

Several interesting features of this sermon and its doctrine may be noted. Firstly, Bernard's teaching on spiritual marriage is the logical extension of his conviction that the human being was created with an affinity and tendency toward the Word. Spiritual marriage is the culmination of the movement of human being to its goal. The nuptials about which Bernard speaks are not rarefied mystical phenomena,[21] but universal possibilities. Union with the Word in the fullest possible sense is no more than the grace-generated realisation of universal human capability for divine union. It is no more than the embrace with which the Father welcomes the prodigal on his return, the experiential confirmation of the gift of divine adoption, the realisation of baptismal implications, the act of becoming a sharer in the divine nature. There is nothing arcane about spiritual marriage in Bernard's view; if the experience is rare it is not because it is

20. SC 83.6 (SBO 2:302,13–20).
21. Such as are described as 'tokens of espousal' in Herbert Thurston's *The Physical Phenomena of Mysticism* (London: Burns and Oates, 1952) pp.130–140.

restricted to a chosen few, but because few have the confidence to take seriously the unconditioned love which God has for all. When the soul assents to the potentialities with which God has freely endowed it, and, under grace, allows the whole of its life to respond totally to his love, then a spiritual oneness results. It is interesting to note that, in describing this state, Bernard opted to make most use of Cicero's treatise *On Friendship* which is, to say the least, a supremely 'unmystical' source.[22]

In describing spiritual marriage, Bernard speaking, not about states of fervent elevation or about experiences as much as about the concord of wills which can be achieved only when the human being subjugates his will to that of his Creator. It is really a very humble event, with little of the spectacular about it. It is simply a matter of a little human being saying 'Yes' to the mysterious power of divine love and allowing it to carry him beyond the narrowness of human perspectives into the boundlessness of God.

Hence, it must be said, the embrace of the Word is fundamentally the experience of the full implications of living in harmony with the will of God. This is not to be understood in the sense of mere objective conformity with positive prescriptions and legitimate commands, but rather as having all one's sensitivities and instincts suffused with spiritual light so that God's gift of himself is not so much 'out there', as within, moulding subjectivity. The text which most readily sprang to Bernard's mind in this respect was 1 Cor 6:17: 'The one who adheres to God is one spirit with him'. The goal of desire for God and the culmination both of nature and of human striving is this *unitas spiritus*.

22. Cf. R. Gelsomino, 'S. Bernardo di Chiravalle e il "De Amicitia" di Cicerone', *Analecta 5*, pp. 180–186. These dependencies are noted by J. Leclercq in *Recueil 1*: 294 and E. Gilson, *Mystical Theology*, pp. 136–137.

UNITY OF SPIRIT

1 Cor 6:17 is one of the most significant texts in Bernard's spirituality and, in some way, it summarises his whole approach. The one who achieves spiritual union with God, whether this be understood as the contemplative experience during the course of this present life or the final felicity of the next, is the one who makes the effort to remain close to him in the practical details of living. Such a view of spiritual progress is proper not only to Bernard. It is strongly characteristic of western mysticism in general and of benedictine monachism in particular.

The text from Corinthians is often used yoked with Ps 72:8: *mihi adhaerere Deo bonum est,* and occasionally with that of Ps 62:9, *adhaesit anima mea post te,* with the idea of adhesion as the joining point.[23] *Adhaerere* is said to connote a voluntary, even moral, adhesion to God which is effectively expressed as much in everyday conduct as in affective desire.[24] 'Union with God can never be anything but the accord of two distinct wills, and *therefore* this union with God can be effected in no other way than by and through love.'[25] *Unior cum conformor:* 'I am united when I am conformed'.[26]

Bernard used 1 Cor 6:17 with various nuances. When he wished to exploit the motivational potential of the text, 'unity of spirit' became a term for the contemplative

23. It may be under the influence of Ps 72:8 that Bernard often substitutes *Deo* for *Domino* in citing 1 Cor 6:17. On Ps 72:8, cf. SC 32.2 (SBO 1:227,6), SC 71.6 (SBO 2:218,2), SC 71.10 (SBO 2:221,12), SC 79.4 (SBO 2:274,23–24), SC 85.12 (SBO 2:315, 14–17), Div 4.3 (SBO 6a:95,15–16), QH 8.11 (SBO 4:434,14).

24. Cf. J.-M. Struyven, 'La notion d'amour pur d'après saint Bernard', COCR 8 (1946) 69–90, especially p. 82.

25. E. Gilson, *Mystical Theology,* p. 126.

26. SC 71.5 (SBO 2:217,15).

experience, possible even within the confines of earthly
life.[27] At other times, he manifests an awareness that such
experience must necessarily be incomplete this side of eternity and so applies the phrase *unitas spiritus* to the future
life,[28] and even to the resurrection of the body when it, also,
will be spiritualised and thus capable of being absorbed into
the unity.[29] In a completely different context, he applies the
text to the life of the Holy Spirit within the Trinity.[30]

Unity was a theme which engaged Bernard's attention
more than once. The appreciation of it is central to his personal philosophy of life, as it was to his efforts in the practical
world of problems and politics. Unity will, of course, be
perfect only in the future life, but here below an imperfect
unity is achieved when love binds together the variety and
plurality of human existence.[31] Although there is some fluctuation in his terminology,[32] it is clear from the long
development in SC 71 that unity is a divine quality, bond-
ing together with the *gluten amoris* whatever is disparate.

On the contrary, the human being and God, because
they are not of the one substance or of the one nature,
cannot be said to constitute 'one thing'. They are,
however, said to be — with absolute and certain
truth — 'one spirit'. This is on condition that they are
mutually joined with the glue of love. Such a unity is
not so much a matter of coincidence of essence as of
convergence of wills (*non tam essentiarum cohæren-
tia, quam conniventia voluntatum.*[33]

27. Dil 27–28 (SBO 3:142–143).
28. SC 26.5 (SBO 1:173,14).
29. Div 92.1 (SBO 6a:347,7–8).
30. O Pasc 1.8 (SBO 5:117,20).
31. This theme is developed in Apo 5–9 (SBO 3:84–87).
32. Cf. M. Standaert, 'Le principe', p. 212, note 153, where he
compares the terminology of Div 80.1 Div 33.8, and Csi 5.18.
33. SC 71.8 (SBO 1:220,5–9). On *gluten,* cf. Div 4.3 (SBO 6a:
96,3–4) and SC 8.2 (SBO 1:37,17).

The unity of which Bernard speaks is accomplished at a spiritual level, far excelling the physical (*carnalis* or *coniugativa*) union of the married state and certainly have nothing to do with the sentimental union imagined by romantic piety, and erroneously attributed to Bernard by Pourrat and others.[34]

It cannot be stated too often that the relationship between the soul and the Word is one that has its origins in the tendency of the soul toward the Word as a result of being created *ad Imaginem*. When one first becomes aware of this movement, a 'carnal' love for Christ, a sentimental attachment to the person of Jesus through an imaginative dwelling on his mysteries is not unusual. It is a beginning, in many cases, a necessary beginning, but it is transcended in the process of spiritual growth.[35] The phenomenology of such a development has not always been understood.[36] Gilson, in particular, strove hard to correct the widespread misconception about this aspect of Bernard's teaching.

> Charity, of course, is essentially spiritual, and a love of this kind can be no more than its first moment. It is too much bound up with the senses unless we know how to make use of it with prudence, and to lean on it only as something to be surpassed. . . .
>
> This sensitive affection for Christ was always presented by St. Bernard as a love of a relatively inferior order. It is so precisely on account of its sensitive character, for charity is of purely spiritual essence. . . .

34. Pierre Pourrat, *La spiritualité chrétienne*, vol. 2: *Le moyen âge* (Paris: Gabalda, 1928) pp. 29–116. Cf. J.-C. Didier, 'La dévotion a l'humanité du Christ dans la spiritualité de saint Bernard', *La Vie Spirituelle: Supplement* (August-September 1930) pp. [1]–[19].

35. Cf. Pasc 4.2 (SBO 5:111,5–8).

36. A good note on this is found in Stiegman's *Language of Asceticism*, p. 183, note 119.

We should, therefore, misapprehend the place it occupies in St. Bernard's conception of the spiritual life if we thought that on this score it might be neglected. To pass beyond it is not to destroy it, but rather to preserve it by completing it with another . . . The spiritual outweighs the carnal, and the latter is no more than a beginning; but we shall see that even from this beginning, the soul already attains a summit.[37]

Just as there are degrees of love, so there are degrees in union. Bernard was clearly of the opinion that the sensual or sensitive aspect of human nature is an obstacle to complete union with the Word, since it continually draws the human being in the direction of self-gratification. The closer and more complete the union achieved, the more removed it is from the claims of the flesh and from those of worldly existence and, hence, the more spiritual it becomes.[38]

In this regard, Bernard often quotes the text of 2 Cor 5:16: 'If we had once known Christ according to the flesh, then we know him no longer in that way'.[39] The fundamental bond between the Christian living in faith and the God whom he serves is accomplished on a spiritual level. Conformity with Christ begins with sentiment, grows through imitation, and reaches its culmination in spiritualisation—a progressive union with the Christ who has ascended to the place in which he was before. The soul

37. E. Gilson, *Mystical Theology*, pp. 79–80.
38. Cf. K. Knotzinger, 'Hoheslied und bräutliche Christusliebe bei Bernhard von Clairvaux', *Jahrbuch für mystiche Theologie* 7 (1961) 7–88. Cf. various articles on Bernard's Christology by A. van den Bosch in COCR 21–23 (1959–1961).
39. Cf. SC 20.7 (SBO 1:119,6), SC 33.6 (SBO 1:237,12), p Epi 2.1 (SBO 4:319,15), Tpl 12 (SBO 3:225,4). The text is also quoted, in the sense we are discussing, by John Cassian, *Conf.* 10.6 (SChr 54:80). Following, as it does, on Cassian's discussion of the anthropomorphite heresy, it becomes an even stronger statement.

is rising, with Christ, above the level of the earth in order to encounter him as the Word beyond all time, one in being with the Father. 'The spiritual man must finally transcend the flesh and penetrate to the *Christus-Spiritus*.'[40] There is a clear distinction between the *amore spiritus* and the *carnis affectus;*[41] only those who allow themselves to be made spiritual will experience a close union with the Word.[42]

The theme of *Christus-Spiritus* is particularly associated with Bernard's emphasis on and devotion to the mystery of Christ's ascension.[43] In the rebuke addressed to Mary Magdalen, *noli me tangere,* Bernard saw an invitation addressed to all believers to look above fleshly realities in approaching Christ.[44] In his ascended state he cannot be approached through bodily means but only spiritually.[45] This is not the leaving aside of his humanity, but its glorification. Through being assumed fully into the non-material being of the Word, the glorified humanity of Christ loses every trace of spatio-temporal limitation, and thus becomes a more potent means of furthering the divine economy of salvation.[46]

Another text of particular importance in this respect is Bernard's frequently-used variant reading of Lam 4:20: *Spiritus ante faciem nostram Christus Dominus, sub*

40. P. Delfgaauw, 'An Approach to St Bernard's Sermons on the Song of Songs', COCR 23 (1961) 148–161, p. 153.

41. SC 33.2 (SBO 1:234,14–15).

42. SC 75.2 (SBO 2:248,16). Cf. SC 69.7 (SBO 2:201,8–9).

43. This will be treated later in the chapter. Cf. A. Altermatt, 'Christus pro nobis: Die Christologie Bernhards von Clairvaux in den "Sermones per Annum"', ASOC 33 (1977) 1–176, especially pp. 138–141.

44. SC 28.8–10 (SBO 1:196–199), QH 9.9 (SBO 4:441,30).

45. SC 28.10 (SBO 1:199,8). Bernard's expression is un-translatable: *talem talis taliterque tange.*

46. SC 76.1 (SBO 2:255,3–4), Hum 12 (SBO 3:26,3).

umbra illius vivimus inter gentes, 'The spirit before our face is Christ the Lord, in his shadow we [shall] live among the peoples'.[47] Daniélou traces the quotation in this form to Origen's commentary on the Song of Songs, with reference to the text of Song 2:3, *Sub umbra eius quem desideraveram sedi.*[48]

The way in which Bernard used the text makes it possible for us to affirm, with a reasonable degree of assurance, that he regarded all spiritual experience in this present life as a foretaste of the final, definitive spiritual union which is realised in glory. It is, in some way, situated between the dark and unyielding experience of pure faith and the full light of the eternal day, it is the experience of the shadow, caused by the overlap of darkness and light.[49]

In the future life, shadows will flee and the soul will enter into a state of complete spiritual unity with the Word. In the meantime, the soul has to recognise the non-carnal character of its relationship with the Word, even though it continues to live in the flesh. And so there is a need for continual effort to keep locating faith at the level of the intangible.[50]

47. Following is a preliminary listing of passages in Bernard's works which cite Lam 4:20 either wholly or in part. Note that he fluctuates between *vivimus* and *vivemus* according to the extent of the eschatological colouring in the context. SC 3.5 (SBO 1:17,11), SC 20.3 (SBO 1.115,22), SC 20.7 (SBO 1:119,8–9), SC 31.8 (SBO 1:224,6), SC 40.4 (SBO 2:27,6), SC 45.4 (SBO 2:52,23–24), SC 48.7 (SBO 2:71,25–26), SC 72.5 (SBO 2:228,13), SC 75.2 (SBO 2:248,17), Adv 1.10 (SBO 4:168,17–19), Asc 3.3 (SBO 5:132,25), Asc 6.11 (SBO 5:156, 8), Pent 3.3 (SBO 5:172,14), Nat BVM 1 (SBO 5:275,14). A total of sixteen.

48. Origen, *In Cant* 3 (PG 13:153bc).

49. SC 45.5 (SBO 2:52–53).

50. Cf. Denis Farkasfalvy, 'The Role of the Bible in St Bernard's Spirituality', ASOC 25 (1969) 3–13. Jean Daniélou, 'S. Bernard et les Pères grecs', *Théologien*, pp. 48–51. *Id.,* 'Christos Kyrios', *Rech SR* 39 (1952) 328–352. John Morson, 'The Shadow Symbol: From Origen to Bernard', *Hallel* 5 (1977) 5–10.

This teaching on the spiritual Christ is not a denial of present and universal access to the Word, but a statement of its rudimentary nature. It is not to be thought that the denial of temporal and spatial limitation to the glorified Lord is, in some way, a loss to him or a diminishment in his availability. On the contrary, Christ is more present to the human race than ever. Any constraint on the relationship comes from the fact that human beings are not able to perceive this presence, so long as they remain on the level of the carnal. Hence they must look to a future phase of existence in which such obstacles to union will have been removed.

The theme of *Christus-Spiritus* also serves as a reminder that relationship with the incarnated Word transcends the human categories of sex, nationality, culture and time. There is no anomaly, for instance, in a male speaking of 'spiritual marriage' with the Word, since neither the Word nor the soul, as far as Bernard was concerned, is of a determinate gender. Notwithstanding the fact that it is always the soul who is described as the bride, Bernard uses *animus* and *anima* much more loosely than, for example, William of St Thierry. His choice is largely dictated by the inner logic of the passage, the biblical texts used or by considerations of style. It is only with reference to the image of the *sponsa Verbi* that, following the established tradition in this matter, Bernard emphasises the feminine character of both the soul and the Church.

Spiritual marriage is desired by the human being because it is the means by which he is elevated to partake in the divine life of the Word through his incarnated and glorified humanity.

For if marriage in the flesh makes two into one flesh, how much more does a spiritual joining (*copula*) bond together two in one spirit. For he who adheres to the Lord is one spirit with him[51]

51. SC 8.9 (SBO 1:41,24–28).

Since this perfect union in spirit is achieved, not in this life, but in the next, it is now necessary to examine what Bernard has to say about the final glorification of the human being in Christ, which takes place in heaven.

DESIRE FOR HEAVEN

Desire for heaven is firmly embedded in the Catholic tradition of doctrine and spirituality.[52] It has been stoutly defended whenever its legitimacy or utility has been challenged. Thus the *magisterium* responded negatively to certain opinions of Meister Eckhart,[53] Luther,[54] Molinos,[55] the followers of Jansen,[56] and Fenélon.[57] Heaven is not viewed, in this tradition, as the ultimate inducement or reward as much as a theological corollary to the doctrine of a God determined to do good for the human race. He whose love was diffused in creating and who gave himself in the Incarnation and in the sending of the Holy Spirit, carries this gratuitous self-giving to its ultimate realisation. This is the fundamental content of Catholic belief about heaven.

Theologians and pastors, like St Bernard, who were very much engaged in asserting the inferiority of merely mercenary love, had no difficulty in reconciling unselfishness with an ardent desire for the blessings of the future age. They regarded the doctrine of heaven as a logical consequence of God's love for humankind and

52. Cf. François Cuttaz, art. 'Ciel', DSp 2: cols 890–897.
53. Cf. A. Schönmetzer (ed.) *Enchiridion Symbolorum, definitionum et declarationum de rebus fidei et morum*, (Freiburg Br: Herder, 35th edn., 1973), [= DzS], #959.
54. Cf. DzS #1581.
55. Cf. DzS #2207, #2212.
56. Cf. DzS #2310, #2313.
57. Cf. DzS #2356.

accepted his promise of good with simplicity and delight. Not to desire what God had promised to bestow was understood by them as a sign of defective hope and of inward crippling, not as virtue.[58] No matter how insistent they were on purity of intention, they were not Stoics.

From the earliest times, the monastic tradition took the scriptural texts about heaven at their face value, understanding them as an affirmation and sometimes a description of the future benefits which God had in store for those who lived their love for him. Simply and gratefully they accepted that all would be very well, and in this faith they persevered in their struggling and endured many hardships. We often find the text of 1 Cor 15:19 quoted: 'If for this life only we have hope in Christ, then of all human beings are we the most to be pitied'.

Cassian affirmed, in his first and fundamental conference, that, over and above immediate goals, the ultimate object of all monastic striving is obtaining access to the Kingdom of God.[59] St Benedict, although more subdued than his immediate source, the *Rule of the Master,* nevertheless often places heaven as a goal which must be kept constantly before the monk's eyes. He refers to this ultimate objective as heaven,[60] the Kingdom,[61] heavenly exaltation,[62] eternal life,[63] and the heavenly homeland.[64] The whole purpose of monastic living is, in Benedict's view, to allow the divine charity so

58. *Pace* A. Nygren, *Eros and Agape,* pp. 646–650, and *passim.*
59. Cassian, *Conf* 1.4. (SChr 42.81).
60. RB 7.8.
61. RB prol 50.
62. RB 7.5.
63. RB 4.46, etc.
64. RB 73.8.

to permeate the monk's life that his heart is ever expanded in its capacity to receive the gift of God.[65] Monastic life, since the sixth century, is referred to simply as *conversatio* and the specific monastic vow is *conversatio morum*, both terms owing at least something to the influence of Phil 3:20: *Conversatio nostra in coelis est:* 'Our citizenship is in heaven'.[66]

The theme of heaven, already strong in Augustine, was taken up and enthusiastically expanded by Gregory the Great, who constantly returned to the subject of heaven both in his sermons to the people and in his more technical works, presumably destined for a mainly monastic readership.[67] Devotion to heaven is one of the characteristics of medieval monastic culture, as Jean Leclercq established.[68] The vitality and universal appeal of the theme is evident in a variety of ways. It appears continually in liturgical texts and in works of hagiography. It receives important treatments at the hands of such individual writers as John of Fécamp and Peter Damian. It even finds expression in the art of the Gothic era,[69] and reaches some sort of apogée in Dante's *Paradiso.*[70]

Bernard often mentions heaven. His teaching on this is, to some extent, the counterpart to his anthropology

65. RB prol 49.
66. Cf. M. Casey, 'The Benedictine Promises', *Tjurunga* 24 (1983) 17–34.
67. On this, see J. B. McClain, *The Doctrine of Heaven in the Writings of St Gregory the Great* (Washington: Catholic University of America Press, 1956) with ample bibliographical and textual information, up till that date.
68. *Love of Learning*, pp. 57–75.
69. Cf. Emile Mâle, *The Gothic Image: Religious Art in France in the 13th Century* (London: Collins/Fontana, 1961).
70. Cf. R. Guardini, 'Bernhard von Clairvaux in Dantes Göttlicher Komödie', in *Die Chimaere*, pp. 54–70.

and together both areas of reflection contribute to the understanding of the present life of the human being, lived, as it is,
in the overlap. Heaven is viewed by Bernard as the ultimate
restoration of the conditions of the primeval paradise, the
gratuitous and super-abundant repletion of all the potential-
ites inherent in that original situation. It seems that Bernard
was one of those who recognised in the account of human
origins a first delineation of the shape of things to come.

Bernard, in common with most latin tradition, made a
great deal of use of the notion of the heavenly homeland,
patria. Feeding on such texts as Heb 11:13 ('. . . seeing
them from afar and greeting them and confessing that we
are but visitors and travellers on the earth')[71] and Heb 13:14
('Here we have no abiding city, but we seek one in the
future'),[72] this tradition proposed an interpretation of human life as a journey away from home, a *peregrinatio*. During this time of absence, the true human being yearns only
for his homeland; to return there is the ultimate object of all
his wandering. It is undeniable that this theme was enriched
by the language and images generated by thought under
the influence of Neo-platonism, but its basis was biblical.[73]

71. Heb 11:13 appears in SC 33.2 (SBO 1:235,1), SC 50.8 (SBO
2:83,10) both nuances not noted in the critical apparatus of SBO;
Ded 4.6 (SBO 5:387,16), Mart 5 (SBO 5:403,15–16).

72. Humb 2 (SBO 5:442,5), Ep 204 (SBO 8:63,15), Ep 374.1
(SBO 8:335,9), etc.

73. To understand the notion of *peregrinatio*, one should remind oneself of the considerable inconvenience involved in travelling in the ancient world. Bernard, no doubt, knew this by personal
experience. 'We can translate *peregrinus* by "pilgrim"; but only if
we realise that Augustine detested travelling . . ." (Peter Brown,
Augustine of Hippo [London: Faber and Faber, 1967] p. 324).
Some typical occurences of the theme in Augustines *In Ioan* are 5.1
(CChr 36:40), 6.2 (53), 10.13 (109), 17.9 (175), 27.2 (270), 28.9
(282–283), 30.7 (293), 32.5 (302), 32.9 (305), 34.10 (316), 35.9
(322).

For the bride, things will be different in the homeland. What is ugly now, *in loco peregrinationis suae*, will be made beautiful, without stain or wrinkle. Instead of having to make her way laboriously as she does *in via*, she will reign and the future will yield a comfortable existence.[74] Death was viewed, in such a context, not as an unhappy event signalling the termination of a life. It was a return home,[75] the end of an exile.[76] 'This will be a repatriation: to go forth from the bodily homeland into the region of spirits.'[77] In SC 26, Bernard has a long consideration of the 'tents of Kedar', which he interprets as our bodies, being but portable dwelling-places for the time of exile. It is corporeity which is the deciding factor in the pilgrim status of the human being.

> What are these 'tents' if not our bodies, in which we make our pilgrim way? 'For we have here no abiding city, but we seek one in the future.' And while we are in these bodies, we fight as [soldiers living] under canvas, dedicated to violence for the sake of attaining the Kingdom. For the life of the human being on earth is a warfare, and while we yet fight in this body we are far away from the Lord, that is, from the light. For the Lord is light, and in so far as anyone is not with him, he must be reckoned to be in the darkness, that is, in Kedar.
>
> In this way, he is able to identify with the lament, 'Alas for me that my sojourning is prolonged. For I have dwelt with the inhabitants of Kedar and my soul has been too long a sojourner'.
>
> The dwelling-place, which is our body, is not a citizen's residence or the home of one belonging to

74. SC 25.3 (SBO 1:164–165). Cf. Pre 59 (SBO 3:292,19), Sept 1.3 (SBO 4:346,20), Asspt 1.1 (SBO 5:229,2). For the phrase *in via*, see SC 53.5 (SBO 2:98,23), Palm 1.2 (SBO 5:44,1).

75. SC 27.1 (SBO 1:181,26).

76. SC 50.8 (SBO 2:83,11).

77. Csi 5.2 (SBO 3:468,10–11).

this country. It is, rather, a tent for a soldier or a shelter for a traveller. This bodily tent is, I say, a tent of Kedar, in so far as it cheats the soul of the sight of boundless light which is its object, for the time that it remains here below. It permits the soul to see the light only indirectly and obscurely, and never face to face.

Bernard then goes on to explain that it is the fact that the soul is forced to live outside its native ambience which causes it to lose some of its natural charm and grace, and take on some of the unattractive qualities of the region through which it is forced to pass.

Do you not now see the source of the Church's dark hue and of the blemishes which cling even to souls most endowed with beauty? They are due to [their having to dwell in] the tents of Kedar, to their being laboriously engaged in warfare, to the length of their unhappy sojourn, to the troublesome restraints of exile and, finally, to the fact of the body itself, so fragile and yet so heavy to bear. 'For this corruptible body weighs down the soul, and living on earth inhibits one's power of thought.' Because of all this, they long to be dissolved so that, having put aside the body, they may fly to the embrace of Christ. So we hear the lament of one so unhappy, 'Unlucky man that I am, who shall liberate me from this body of death!' Such a one knows that there is no possibility, whilst dwelling in tents of Kedar, of preventing the sullying, wrinkling and staining of purity. Hence, he longs to leave and have done with the body.[78]

78. SC 26.1–2 (SBO 1:169,–170). Bernard is probably following Jerome in taking Kedar to mean 'darkness or sorrow', and has thus interpreted 'the tents of Kedar' as 'the tents of darkness'. Cf. Jerome's *Liber interpretationis hebraicorum nominum* under *Cedar* (CChr 72:63).

One text which is formative of Bernard's view that it is corporeity which keeps the human being at a distance from God is 2 Cor 5:6: 'Knowing that for as long as we are in the body we are far from (*peregrinamur*) the Lord.'[79] Bernard qualified his balder statements of the view in his treatise *On Precept and Dispensation*, showing that he understood the body in a moral rather than a purely physical or ontological sense. 'It is not the body which is the cause of our pilgrim-status, but the importunaties of the body (*corporis molestiae*).'[80] It is because we turn to our bodies and away from God that they become a barrier which blocks our view of him, *intentio praepediatur*. 'As for concern with the body, what is it if not a certain state of being absent from God? And what is this state if not that of the pilgrim?'[81]

As a pilgrim, the soul or the Church, as the case may be, has to endure all the hardships associated with journeying in a foreign land, as well as the feeling of nostalgia for its own home and the desire to rest forever in a harmonious ambience.

> For during the time of my mortality and whilst I am in the place of my pilgrimage . . . I have eaten the bread of sorrow and I have drunk the wine of compunction . . . My soul is often cast down and groans within me, unless I receive from your table some gift of your mercy from which I may draw relief.[82]

It happens, however, that the very experience of catching some crumbs of consolation from the heavenly table has the effect of increasing the sense of homesickness

79. SC 59.5 (SBO 2:138,7–8), Pre 59 (SBO 3:291,23–26) where it is joined with Phil 3.20; Ep 18.2 (SBO 7:67,7–8), Ep 144.1 (SBO 7:344,13).
80. Pre 59 (SBO 3:292,12–13).
81. Pre 60 (SBO 3:293,6–8).
82. SC 33.7 (SBO 1:238,23–239,5).

and thus causes the soul's desire to grow. Desire for the future life of heaven is nurtured by an appreciation that this present life is temporary and transient. It is but a preparation for what is permanent.

Two things bring consolation to the Church in the time and place of its pilgrimage. One comes from the past: it is the memory of the Passion of Christ. The second is from the future: when the soul reflects that its destiny is with the saints and that it will, indeed, share in it. These two elements, representing, as it were, both the forward and the rear view, fill the Church's gaze with unquenchable longing.[83]

In commenting on the text of Song 2:12: 'The voice of the turtle-dove is heard in our land', Bernard offers a long meditation on the relationship of the present life to what will be experienced in the homeland.

'The voice of the turtle-dove is heard in our land.' While human beings look only to the earth for a recompense for their service of God, even though the earth be flowing with milk and honey, they will never come to an understanding of the truth that they will remain pilgrims for as long as they are on earth. Nor will they grieve, like turtle-doves, when they remember their homeland. On the contrary, they misuse the land of their exile, thinking it to be their homeland, allowing themselves to eat rich foods and to drink honeyed wine. Because of their conduct, the voice of the turtle-dove has not been heard in our land for a long while.

Bernard's fundamental premise is that desire for heaven exists only in the context of a certain detachment from the delights of earth. Here he states the theoretical basis of his condemnation of rich foods and mulse which also appears in the *Apologia* and in his Advent sermons.

83. SC 62.1 (SBO 2:154,21–24).

If the present life is too comfortable, it extinguishes all desire for the future. Desire for heaven, Bernard thought, began in earnest only with Christ's proclamation of the Kingdom. Thus, he continues:

> When the promise of the Kingdom of heaven was made, human beings understood that they no longer had, here below, a permanent dwelling-place, and so they began to seek one that was in the future. It was at that time, clearly, that the voice of the turtle-dove first sounded in our land. For, even now, the holy soul longs for the presence of Christ. It bears the delay of the Kingdom with poor grace and, from afar, salutes that desired homeland with groans and sighs.
>
> Now can you see how the soul which acts thus, while on earth, is fulfilling the role of the chaste and grieving turtle-dove? Why should the absence of Christ not move me to many tears and daily groaning? 'O Lord, all my desire is before you, and my groans are not hidden from you.' You know that I have been exhausted with my groaning, but happy is the one who can also say, 'Every night I drench my pillow with tears, I bedew my bed with weeping'.
>
> Such grieving is to be found, not only in me, but in all those who await his coming in love. For did not he, himself, say, 'Can the wedding guests mourn while the bridegroom is with them? But the days are coming in which the bridegroom will be taken from them and then they will mourn'. This is as though he were saying, 'Then will the voice of the turtle-dove be heard'.
>
> So it is, O good Jesus. The days have indeed come. For creation has been groaning in travail until this time, awaiting the manifestation of the children of God. And not only creation. We also groan inwardly, as we wait for the adoption of sons, the redemption of our bodies, We recognise, therefore, from

this that for as long as we are in the body we are pilgrims, far from your presence.[84]

Such inward groaning and lamentation is a positive effect of grace, a fact which it is hard to convey in English translation. It is aroused through the operation of the Holy Spirit whose function it is to alert the soul to its pilgrim-status and to the temporary and insubstantial character of present satisfactions. By loosening the bonds which attach us to sensual gratifications, he creates an affective void from which emerges a desire for the things of heaven.

We have been transferred from death to life by the life-giving Spirit, and according to our daily experiences, it is by his illumination that our desires are made worthy and our groanings, which come from him, make their way to God to find mercy in his sight.[85]

The theme of pilgrimate and journeying, which has strong biblical precedents, gained a great depth and richness in the course of its transmission. Sometimes it generated a practice of actual pilgrimage, on the part of the faithful, or, in the monastic circles, legitimated the appearance of various species of wandering monks. By the twelfth century, it was generally recognised that a life lived according to this spirituality need not involve movement in a physical sense. In fact, monks were usually discouraged from participating in pilgrimages. The theme had been spiritualised; at its core was not physical mobility, but detachment from earthly rootedness and comfort.[86]

84. SC 59.4 (SBO 2:137,11–138,3).
85. SC 59.6 (SBO 2:139,6–9).
86. On the theme of pilgrimage see also, A. Ballano, 'La peregrinación en San Bernardo', Cist 22 (1970) 106–116 and 196–204. Stiegmann, *The Language of Asceticism*, pp. 99–103. P. Brown,

In the course of comparing this present life with the realities of the world to come, Bernard often designated the present stage of existence by the word *interim:* for the time being, meanwhile.[87] This term refers to the period during which the human being lives in the flesh,[88] subject to multiplicity,[89] and constrained in his choice of courses of action.[90] In this age, one is prevented from seeking God because of external tasks,[91] so that one can make contact with him only indirectly and obscurely,[92] through the 'eye of faith',[93] and by the hearing of the Word.[94] While on earth, the soul can do no more than desire the presence of God,[95] and find a degree of restedness in calling to mind the heavenly dwelling-places.[96]

Even though the primary thrust of the comparison

Augustine of Hippo, pp. 313–329. J. Keenan, 'The Cistercian Pilgrimage to Jerusalem in Guillaume de Deguiville's "Pélerinage de la vie humaine"', in *History 2,* pp. 166–183, especially pp. 172–178. J. Leclercq, *Sources,* pp.35–90. U. Engelmann, 'Monachi Peregrini', *Regulae Benedicti Studia* 3/4 (1975) 121–124. G. Constable, 'Monachisme et pélerinage au Moyen Age' and 'Opposition to Pilgrimage in the Middle Ages,' both reprinted (without re-pagination) in *Religious Life and Thought (11th-12th Centuries)* (London: Variorum Reprints, 1979). F. C. Gardner, *The Pilgrimage of Desire: A Study of Theme and Genre in Medieval Literature* (Lieden: Brill, 1971).

87. Cf. Christine Mohrmann, 'La langue et le style de S. Bernard', in SBO 2: p. xvii. We find the same usage occasionally in Augustine, for instance, *In Ioan* 35.5 (CChr 36:302).

88. QH 7.2 (SBO 4:413.14). Cf. SC 20.7 (SBO 1:119,14–15).

89. Sept 2.3 (SBO 4:352.2).

90. SC 23.10 (SBO 1:145,21).

91. SC 22.3 (SBO 1:131,1–3).

92. SC 26.1 (SBO 1:170,13).

93. SC 76.2 (SBO 2:255,20–27).

94. SC 28.6 (SBO 1:196,3).

95. QH 8.3 (SBO 4:427,24). Cf. Ep 18.2 (SBO 7:67,25–26).

96. SC 62.1 (SBO 2:155,7–9).

centered on the use of *interim* is habitually restrictive, there is a recognition of the positive aspects of this intervening period. Some anticipation of future happiness is possible. 'The time will come when he will show his face and we will be saved. For the time being, however, he goes before us with the blessings of sweetness.'[97] It is possible, even in this age, for the human being to reap the harvest of celebration with the first fruits of the Spirit,[98] to have already the fruit of holiness which will be brought to completion in eternal life.[99]

Interim is often used in an ordinary, banal sense, without giving any indication of eschatological content or comparison. It remains, however, one of Bernard's ordinary terms for distinguishing earthly existence from final fulfilment in the age to come. Its presence in a text is often a signal that some comparison between this age and the hereafter is intended.

The tension between the present and the future is also illustrated by the traditionally accepted antinomy of Jerusalem and Babylon. Building on biblical foundations, african Christians elaborated a theory covering the relationship of the elect to the reprobate in terms of alternate citizenship. God's friends belong to the Jerusalem which is above, his enemies are denizens of Babylon. This image was erected into a system by Augustine, and the ringing categorisations of *The City of God* imposed themselves on christian reflection far beyond the boundaries of actual readership.[100]

In a rolling sentence, made interesting by the inclusion of a vernacular neologism, Bernard enunciated a principle of utter hostility between the two cities. *Inter*

97. SC 61.6 (SBO 2:152,9–10).
98. SC 37.2 (SBO 2:10,16–17).
99. SC 37.4 (SBO 2:11,13–14).
100. Cf. Peter Brown, *Augustine*, pp. 313–315.

Babylonem et Ierusalem nulla est pax sed guerra continua: 'Between Babylon and Jerusalem there is no peace, but continuing warfare'.[101] This present life relates to Babylon,[102] whereas the goal of our striving is the Jerusalem which is above, our mother,[103] the city of the great King.[104] Heaven is, accordingly, not only the place in which all individual tendencies find their satisfaction; it is also a cosmic climax, the culmination of the collective strivings of all human history. Its primary character is theological; it is not deduced from reflection on the human condition. It follows, rather, from the nature of God. Heaven is blissful because God is there. About the city of the great King, Bernard had this to say:

. . . With regard to spiritual food, I must also sigh before I eat. And as I sigh and weep, I wish that the smallest particle from that heavenly banquet might be mine, so that I, like a pup, might eat from the crumbs which fall from the masters' table. O Jerusalem, the city of the great King! He fills you with the finest corn and rejoices you with the waters of a river. There is no weighing out for you, only supreme supply and satiety. There is no limitation for those whose lot has been cast with you.

But I am one subject to change and limitation. How long will it be before I arrive at this one goal of all my striving? How long will it be before I am satisfied with the sight of your glory, O Lord? How long before I am made drunk with the richness of your house? How long before you give me to drink

101. Par 2.1 (SBO 6b:267,4).

102. Asspt 1.1 (SBO 5:229,10), Apo 10 (SBO 3:90,9), O Pasc 2.3 (SBO 5:119,21). Cf Gal 4:26.

103. Div 19.6 (SBO 6a:164,18), SC 27.7 (SBO 1:186,20). Cf. Ps 47:3.

104. SC 53.4 (SBO 2:98,12), Sept 1.3 (SBO 4:347,6), Asc 6.4 (SBO 5:152,9).

from the river of your delight? For very little of its dew
ever falls on this earth, and there is not enough for me
even to swallow my spittle.[105]

As usual, Bernard's description is moulded by combining
several distinct strands of scriptural imagery. He is lyrical,
but his thought is always under control. The prevailing
tone of his reflections is habitually theological. The
language he employs comes from the same biblical,
patristic, and liturgical bed-rock where he usually quar-
ried, but there seems to be a sense of heightened excite-
ment in its flow. These passages describing heaven always
have a particularly personal note about them. The interesting thing, however, is that far from becoming more
imaginative or innovative, Bernard seems, in these lyrical
outbursts, to rely more heavily on traditional themes and
images, though these are intimated and combined with
supreme artistry and great originality. In such descriptions of heaven, Bernard does not verge on the bizarre,
which is a danger when authors are carried away into im-
agining the culminating fulfilment of merely individual
needs and fancies.[106] Bernard, on the contrary, never gave
priority to imaginative projections. He remained firmly
within the sphere of traditional theological symbolism.
His prose owes more to his skill with words than to the
wild rampages of uncontrolled imagination.

Bernard's basic picture of the heavenly Jerusalem,
the object of all human desire, is that of latin Fathers,
especially as this was mediated by the liturgy. The squares

---

105. Sept 1.3 (SBO 4:347,2–14). This is a pastiche of quotations of
verses from different Psalms, for instance, Pss 79:6, 47:3, 80:17,
147:14, 45:5, 121:3, 16:15, 71:6.

106. Thus in John of Fécamp's evocation of the heavenly state in
the *Confessio theologica* (ed. J. Leclercq, lines 396–444) he speaks of
heaven being free from the noise of hammering (lines 423–433) and
from anything which is black in colour (line 441).

of Jerusalem will be paved with pure gold, and all its streets will cry out "Alleluia!" '107 It cannot be stressed too much that heaven is rarely, for Bernard, merely the projected satisfaction of human needs and aspirations. It is primarily the region of the divine. Knowledge about this sphere of existence is merely an extension of what we know from revelation about the nature of God.

Bernard used all his poetic craftmanship to convey his ardent vision of blessed life with God.

> O true noon-day
> when warmth and light are at their peak
> and the sun at its zenith
> and no shadows fall,
> when stagnant waters dry up
> and their fetid odours disperse.
>
> O never-ending solstice
> when dayling lasts forever.
>
> O noon-day light,
> marked with the mildness of spring,
> stamped with summer's bold beauty,
> enriched with autumn's fruit,
> —and lest I seem to forget—
> calm with winter's rest from toil.108

One of the most sustained descriptions of heaven occurs in the context of a comparison with other regions where human beings may find themselves.

> O blessed region of the angel hosts, in which the Blessed Trinity is seen by the blessed face to face, and where those lofty armies never cease to cry out with lofty applause, 'Holy, holy, holy, Lord God of power and might!'

107. SC 76.5 (SBO 2:252,11–12). This unknown version of Tob 13:22 is also used in Apo 8 (SBO 3:89,3–4); it may derive from the Easter responsory *Plateae tuae*. Cf. J. Leclercq, *Recueil 1:* p. 306.
108. SC 33.6 (SBO 1:237,21–25).

A place of delights where the just are given to drink from the river of delights. A place of splendour, where the just shine forth with all the brilliance of the night-sky. A place of happiness, where eternal joy is on their heads. A place of plenty, where nothing is wanting to those who see him. A place of sweetness, where the Lord sweetly makes his presence known to all. A place of peace, where the marvels of his deeds are evident. A place of satiety, where we are satisfied when his glory is revealed. A place of vision, where a great sight is seen.

O sublime and richly endowed region! From this valley of tears do we send up our sighs to you, where there is wisdom with no trace of unknowing, where there is mindfulness without forgetting, where there is understanding without error and where the power of insight shines unfettered.

This is the region where the Lord himself goes around ministering to his elect, manifesting himself to them as he really is. It is here that God will be all in all, and where the whole created universe, in wondrous array, will give glory to the Creator and joy to the creature.

Therefore, O spiritual soul, run through this region with the eyes of desire and see the King of Glory in his glorious attire, attended by the legions of the angels and adorned by the armies of the saints. See him putting down the proud and exalting the lowly, see him condemning demons and redeeming human beings. And then say to him, 'Happy are they who dwell in your house, O Lord, forever singing your praise.'[109]

Following St Benedict, Bernard often quoted 1 Cor 2:9: 'Eye has not seen nor has ear heard and it has not

109. Div 42.7 (SBO 6a:260,9–261,4).

entered into the human heart to conceive what God has prepared for those who love him.'[110] From this text he drew the idea of the incomprehensibility of heaven. 'It is absolutely impossible for us to know what we shall be in the future.'[111]

> The deep happiness of the heavenly homeland, for which our earthly pilgrimage continues to sigh, transcends not only every human sense, but also goes beyond the understanding of the heart. Let no one doubt this, even though he is a believer in name alone.[112]

This is an extremely important point in coming to an understanding of Bernard's notion of desire as pre-existing any conscious act. The human being is never able to comprehend, at the level of consciousness, even at the peak of his poetic powers, exactly what it is he desires. He knows that he desires and he also knows the correct name for what he desires, but he has no firsthand comprehension of the object of his yearning. That heaven transcends human understanding confirms that desire for heaven is more an instinct of being rather than the result of a known and consciously chosen goal.

One of the designations given to heaven since New Testament times and found within the monastic tradition is 'the Kingdom', and this phrase occurs regularly in Bernard's writings.[113] Thus, speaking with reference to the Lord's Prayer, he says,

110. SC 11.9 (SBO 1:57,6–7), SC 28.9 (SBO 1:198,23–25), V Nat 4.8 (SBO 4:225,14–15), QH 10.1 (SBO 4:443,6–7), Ded 4.6 (SBO 5:387,12–13), Div 41.3 (SBO 6a:154,9–10). Cf. RB 4.77.

111. Sept 1.1 (SBO 4:345,15–17). 1 Jn 3:2 is often used in this context. The deployment of this text will be discussed in a later section of this chapter.

112. Div 111.1 (SBO 6a:385,8–11).

113. Cf. QH 2.1 (SBO 4:389,15–16): *regnum;* Dil 10 (SBO 3:127,12): *regnum coelorum;* Div 1.1 (SBO 6a:73,19): *regnum Dei.*

For the soul desires and demands that the Lord make himself like those particular wild beasts who seem to have a capacity for running faster. In particular, it gives testimony to its great longing. This is what it asks each day when it says in the prayer, 'Thy Kingdom come'.[114]

In that Kingdom, it is the idea of *glory* which figures most prominently in Bernard's thinking. The splendour and brilliance of the Godhead saturates everything and is, in turn, relfected by all whom it touches. The phrase from 2 Cor 4:7: 'an eternal weight of glory' is apt.[115] The text from Rom 8:18 was also important for Bernard since it contrasts the puniness of the sufferings experienced in this present life with the glory to be revealed *in nobis*.[116] In pursuance of the theme of the restoration of the image, 2 Cor 3:18 is often cited in various forms: 'Then, with unveiled face, we shall look upon the glory of God, and we shall be transformed into his image, from brightness to brightness, as by the Lord, the Spirit.'[117]

The glory of heaven comes from the presence of the Word, the bridegroom of the soul.[118] 'He is the culmination to which we shall come. Then the soul shall thirst no more.'[119] It is because union with the Word is achieved ultimately only in heaven that Bernard gives him the title of the 'heavenly bridegroom'.[120]

114. SC 73.3 (SBO 2:235,13–16).

115. QH 3.3 (SBO 4:395,5–7), Ded 4.6 (SBO 5:388,6–7).

116. Div 1.4 (SBO 6a:76,14–15): 'We will not be standing by as uninvolved and empty-handed spectators, nor will the glory to be revealed be outside us; it will be in us.'

117. SC 31.2 (SBO 1:220,26–28).

118. SC 33.1 (SBO 1:234,10): *de desiderio praesentiae seu gloriae sponsi.*

119. Div 41.3 (SBO 6a:254,14–15).

120. For instance, SC 29.3 (SBO 1:204,29), SC 76.7 (SBO 2:258,13).

Glory will permeate all the inhabitants of heaven. Reaching out from the glorified humanity of Christ,[121] it will touch everyone,[122] bringing unity and communion to all who share its radiance.[123] 'That will be the time when what is now a little bundle of myrrh will become a huge mass of glory.'[124] The mystery of the heavenly glory is not, however, accessible to the gaze of human scrutiny; the human being had better attend to his own affairs and to make sure that he is not led astray through curiosity.[125] Bernard often made the point that the content of the eternal life offered to human beings is God's gracious gift of unlimited happiness.[126] He speaks of 'the happy life . . . which knows only joys',[127] and cites Ps 64:5 'In your house we are filled with good things'.[128] He did not hesitate to use the word *voluptas,* pleasure, in this connection,[129] possibly on the basis of Ps 35:9: 'They are made drunk by the richness of your house and you give them to drink of a torrent of pleasure'.[130] We find regular references to the eschatological banquet,[131] and to the state of inebriation which characterises it.[132] Some foretaste of this joy is possible in the present life, but its culmination awaits the next.[133] The

121. SC 28.9 (SBO 1:198,14–15).
122. SC 28.11 (SBO 1:200,7).
123. SC 27.6 (SBO 1:186,10–11).
124. SC 43.1 (SBO 2:41,20–21): *ingens cumulus gloriae.*
125. SC 38.5 (SBO 2:17,7–8).
126. QH 4.1 (SBO 4:398,5–7), Nat BVM 3 (SBO 5:276,24).
127. Div 41.3 (SBO 6a:254,7).
128. SC 11.9 (SBO 1:57,8), Div 1.4 (SBO 6a:76,17–18).
129. Div 33.1 (SBO 6a:222,11): *mons voluptatis aeternae.*
130. Cf. Dil 33 (SBO 3:147,14).
131. Sept 1.3 (SBO 4:347,4–5), Nat BVM 3 (SBO 5:276,13–14).
132. SC 7.3 (SBO 1:32,18), SC 76.2 (SBO 2:255,20–27). The theme of *inebriatio* occurs in Augustine's *In Ioan,* for instance: 8.3 (CChr 36:83), 9.3 (92), 9.4 (93), 15.16 (156).
133. Dil 32 (SBO 3:146,23), Sept 1.3 (SBO 4:347,11, Nat BVM 3 (SBO 5:276,25), Ep 11.8 (SBO 7:59,3).

source of this sober intoxication is love, its effect is ultimate self-transcendence, the complete loss of reflexive self-consciousness and total transformation into a movement toward the Other, forgetfulness of self and absorption in God. 'When the soul experiences this sort of affect, it becomes intoxicated with love of God and quite oblivious of itself. It experiences the self as a pottery shard. It is wholly engaged in moving toward God and in adhering to him, and thus it becomes one spirit with him.'[134]

The soul, lost in wonder and in the cessation of independent selfhood, discovers its real personality in the context of a relationship. We are here in the realm of properly mystical experience, characterized by such words as *excessus*,[135] *stupor*,[136] and *raptus*. This will be discussed more fully in the following chapter. What is merely a beginning in this life comes to completion in heaven.

Sometimes Bernard speaks about heaven as the desired haven of shelter and rest after the toil and dangers of this earthly pilgrimage. We yearn for heaven under the impulsion of present hardship, knowing that we were made for more than misery. 'Let us hasten, therefore, to a safer place.'[137] For in heaven is to be found true *securitas*[138] and eternal *requies*.[139]

134. Dil 27 (SBO 3:142,9–12). Cf. Ep 11.8 (SBO 7:59,4–5).

135. The phrase probably has its roots in 2 Cor 5:13: *mente excedimus*, supported by Ps 67:23, Acts 10:10 and 11:5. This means that the views of Gilson in *Mystical Theology*, pp. 25–28, are to be taken with some reserve, as we will later explain.

136. SC 33.2 (SBO 1:234,30), SC 35.3 (SBO 1:250,21).

137. SC 33.4 (SBO 1:235,26–28).

138. SC 33.2 (SBO 1:234,27), Div 33.1 (SBO 6a:222,8), Ep 374.1 (SBO 8:336,4). *Securitas* is used with a pejorative sense in QH 1.1 (SBO 4:385,18–19), QH 3.4 (SBO 4:396,6), etc.

139. OS 3.3 (SBO 5:351–352), Ded 4.6 (SBO 5:388,5).

Rightly, then, does the bride sigh for that place of pasture which is also characterised by peace and quiet, by safety and celebration, by wonderment and amazement. . . . Who would not desire vehemently to be pastured in such a place, for the sake of that peace and that abundance and that fullness. There is nothing in that place of which to be afraid, nothing of which to grow tired and nothing is lacking. For Paradise is a safe place of habitation, the Word is a food which is sweet to the taste, and the richness of eternity is very great indeed.[140]

Bernard's acceptance of the idea that desire continues even in heaven has already been mentioned. There are several texts which clearly attest to his belief that one's appetite for God increases in the state of blessedness.

In this place we find satiety without the sense of having indulged too much. Here we find a desire to penetrate deeper which is never quenched, yet which has no sense of unrest about it. Here we experience that eternal and incomprehensible desire which knows no lack. Here, finally, is that state of sober intoxication which does not come from drinking wine. This state does not result from being drenched with wine but from being set afire for God.[141]

In heaven, both the supply and the demand are increased indefinitely, *copia pariter et voluntas.*[142] In one sense, the hunger,[143] the thirst,[144] and the search,[145] which are the realities of our present life with God remain in heaven. We continue to penetrate further into the heart

140. SC 33.2 (SBO 1:234,28–30 and 235,6–9).
141. Dil 33 (SBO 3:147,19–22).
142. SC 31.1 (SBO 1:220,2–4).
143. Div 15.3 (SBO 6a:141,20), Dil 11 (SBO 3:127,23–25).
144. SC 3.1 (SBO 1:14,15): *solus qui bibit adhuc sitiet.*
145. Div 4.5 (SBO 6a:97,16).

of the divinity, totally satisfied, yet mysteriously driven forward.[146]

> For it is a fact that this happy discovery does not extinguish desire but extends it. How can the consummation of joy be also its consumption? It is more like oil to its flame. And so it is. Happiness is complete, but there is no end to desiring, and because of this the search goes on.[147]

According to Bernard, heaven is the homeland of every human being, but it is the Christian, and expecially the monk, who can, in the words of Phil 3:20, claim citizenship in that country.[148] Earthly existence is a temporary journey, rendered supportable only by the hope of attaining the goal. Such a hope is kept alive by a serious effort to keep the future happy prospects in mind. It is through the 'memory' of heaven that present trials are tolerated,[149] hope is kindled,[150] courage is confirmed,[151] and a sense of perspective is given to one's thinking.[152] 'When the memory of heaven recedes, one makes one's way with diminished desire.'[153] This being so, Bernard encouraged his readers to be thoroughly familiar with what God has in store for them, to reach out and 'to touch the gate of heaven with the hand of holy desire'.[154]

---

146. Cf. Jacques Hourlier, CF 3:28 (Introduction to William of St Thierry's *On Contemplating God*).

147. SC 84.1 (SBO 2:303,12–16). Cf. Augustine, *In Ioan* 3.21 (CChr 36:30), but perhaps *In Ioan* 63.1 (CChr 36:485–486) restricts the former text to this present life.

148. SC 61.3 (SBO 2:150,5), etc.

149. SC 11.7 (SBO 1:154–155).

150. QH 7.1 (SBO 4:412,4–5).

151. QH 7.1 (SBO 4:413,10–11).

152. QH 6.2 (SBO 4:405,12).

153. Quad 6.1 (SBO 4:378,7).

154. SC 49.3 (SBO 2:74,21).

By your devotion penetrate the heavens and mentally walk around the supernal dwelling-places.
Salute the patriarchs and the apostles, the choirs of
the prophets and martyrs. Be filled with admiration
at their exploits and allow yourself to be overwhelmed by the great beauty of the angelic ranks.[155]

It was to the memory of heaven that Bernard looked for a
cure to sadness and the overcoming of an unproductive
heaviness in the spiritual pursuit. By dwelling on the
prospect of future happiness, he hoped to rekindle interest and warmth in wan and woeful spirits.

There are people who grow tired in their zeal for
spiritual things and, as a result, they gradually
become lukewarm. Defective in spirituality, they
walk sadly along the ways of the Lord. With a heart
that is dry and uninterested, they do what they are
told, but they often grumble. They complain that
the days are too long, and so are the nights, saying
with holy Job, 'When I go to bed I say "When can I
get up?" and when I get up, I will already be eagerly
awaiting the fall of night.'
    When it happens that one is subject to such a
state, the Lord may draw near to us as we are walking. It may happen that he who is from heaven may
begin to speak to us about heaven, singing the dear
songs of Zion and telling us about the city of God
and the peace of that city and about the per-
manence of that peace and about eternity itself.
Then, I tell you, such a happy account will carry the
sluggish and sleepy soul along with it. The result
will be that it will remove all disgust from the soul
of the hearer, and all tiredness from his body.[156]

The preaching of heaven is, in Bernard's practice, not an
exotic doctrine for the advanced, but a standard means of

155. SC 35.2 (SBO 1:250,19–22).
156. SC 32.4 (SBO 1:228,16–20).

motivation at every level of spiritual growth. This is, perhaps, one reason why Bernard's teaching is not eccentric. It is too closely linked with the main lines of his thought to be aberrant. Furthermore, to be able to serve as a stimulus for others, this eschatological vision had to be communicable, clearly located within the accepted symbolic universe in which they operated.

THE VISION OF GOD

The heavenly city of Jerusalem was interpreted by Bernard as meaning 'the vision of peace'.[157] The object of desire is thus the reversal of the disturbing blindness and the resultant confusion which, together, constitute the condition of life on earth. Heaven is, above all, a place where the elect are able to see. Because they look upon God face to face, nothing is excluded from their sight. Speaking of the details of the spiritual unity which will exist between the soul and the Word, Bernard stated:

> With regard to each other, there will be a love which is both chaste and consummated, full knowledge, clear vision, a strong bond of union, a relationship which cannot be broken apart and perfect likeness.[158]

On the day of the Lord, all those who have sought him in this life will catch sight of God.[159] Then 'all their work will be turned into leisure and all that they will have to do will be to look and to love'.[160] From that experience will flow both

157. This is the traditional interpretation, guaranteed by Jerome's *Liber interpretationis hebraicorum nominum*, (CChr 72: 121, 146, 152, 154, 155). Cf. V Nat 2.1 (SBO 4:204, 12–13), Epi 3.3 (SBO 4:305,23–24), Par 3.4 (SBO 6b:276,22).

158. SC 82.8 (SBO 2:297,28–29).

159. Ep 204 (SBO 8:63,18). Bernard's use of the phrase *in visione corporali* is loose and does not represent his habitual approach to what would become, in later theology, a controverted issue.

160. SC 72.2 (SBO 2:226,15–16).

the fulfilment of desire and the fullness of joy.[161] The texts used by Bernard in advancing his teaching are familiar ones: the comparison between the indirect and obscure vision of this life with the face to face encounter of the next as in 1 Cor 13:12,[162] 2 Cor 3:18 on seeing the glory of God with unveiled faces,[163] and especially 1 Jn 3:2: 'When he appears we shall be like him, because we shall see him face to face'.[164] In many of Bernard's employments of these texts, he made specific mention of the fact that such a face to face vision of God necessarily involves a certain likeness. 'I do not know with what likeness of nature the soul will be enabled to look upon God, once its face is unveiled, but it is necessary that it be conformed to him and transformed into his very image.'[165] 'It will happen that when I appear you will be totally beautiful, just as I myself am totally beautiful. Because you will be very like me, you will see me as I am.'[166]

There is a great difference between our partial and incomplete vision of God in this life and the final and total vision which is proper to the next.

Now he appears to whom he wills and as he wills, not as he is. It is a fact that no one, be he a sage or saint or prophet, is able to see God for as long as he remains in this mortal body. But whoever is worthy will be able to see him thus in eternity.[167]

The God who dwells in inaccessible light is not visible to crude mortal sight,[168] and the human being can no

161. SC 41.2 (SBO 2:30,1-3), SC 31.8 (SBO 1:224,26-28).
162. Csi 5.27 (SBO 3:490,16), etc.
163. SC 62.7 (SBO 2:160,3), etc.
164. SC 31.2 (SBO 1:220,6-7), etc.
165. SC 69.7 (SBO 2:206,23-25).
166. SC 38.5 (SBO 2:17,23-25). Cf. Div 123 (SBO 6a:401,2-3).
167. SC 31.2 (SBO 1:220,11-12).
168. SC 70.5 (SBO 2:211,1-2).

more see God while on earth than he can look directly into the face of the sun.[169] To be able to perceive God the
soul must be transfigured from brightness to brightness.
'The brighter it is, the closer it is to God.'[170] The soul
thus perceives God, not as something outside itself, but
in the very act of reflecting, with all the intensity of its
being, the glory God radiates on it.[171] The soul
transcends all that bespeaks limitation, even the
humanity of Christ, *qua* limited,[172] to become majesty
of the divinity.

Whatever foretaste the human being may receive of
this heavenly vision, it remains vastly inferior to the complete experience, reserved to the future.[173] Even the little
that is given during the time of pilgrimage is liable to be
lost, eroded by his pursuit of lower gratifications.[174] Bernard declares that it is the next life which is the time of
vision; this present life is, rather, characterised by hearing, since it is by hearing that the Word of God is accepted in faith.[175]

'Thus we live in the shadow of Christ, when we are
walking by faith and are being nourished by his flesh so
that we can find life.'[176] Here below, our sight is weak;
we are constantly bedevilled by doubt and uncertainty,
and our eyes are darkened.

We are in shadow for as long as we walk by faith and
not through direct vision. Therefore, the just one is in
the shadow since he lives by faith. One who lives by
understanding is to be counted among the blessed,

169. SC 31.2 (SBO 1:220,11–21).
170. SC 31.1 (SBO 1:221,4–7). Cf. SC 28.5 (SBO 1:195,20).
171. Div 1.4 (SBO 6a:76,15–16).
172. OS 4.2 (SBO 5:357,2–5).
173. SC 45.6 (SBO 2:53,3–4).
174. SC 24.6 (SBO 1:158,1–2).
175. SC 41.2 (SBO 2:29,28–29).
176. SC 31.10 (SBO 1:225,25–26).

since he no longer lives in the shadow but dwells in light.[177]

But a time will come when shadows flee and light grows strong. At that time, the shadows will completely disappear. That will be a time of clear daylight, where vision will be unlimited. Then there will be not only sweetness for the throat, but fullness for the stomach, without there being any sense of cloying.[178]

And at that time we shall be seen, even as we see, since we shall live 'in the sight of God, not in the shadow', *in conspectu Dei, non in umbra*.[179]

The image of face to face vision, which Bernard drew from tradition and adapted to suit his own theological perspective, is one which indicates something of the transparency of being characteristic of the future life when all that is will be purified of whatever occludes the splendour of the divine glory. When the soul looks upon the face of God it lives, for it is totally saturated with light and is enabled to mirror this radiance without any trace of darkness or shadow. In the heavenly state human being is transformed. Just as sin deforms human nature and causes it to degenerate so that, during his earthly life, the human person is blocked from the vision of God, so in the final consummation, the sight of God is granted, human nature is restored, and the whole wide world of human concern is brought to fulfilment.

THE RESURRECTION OF THE BODY

When Bernard affirmed the traditional faith in the future life, he did so with the clear understanding that

177. SC 48.6 (SBO 2:71,3–6).
178. SC 48.8 (SBO 2:72–73).
179. Nat BVM 3 (SBO 5:279,14–15).

the ultimate stage in the process was the resurrection of the body. He did mention the independent immortality of the soul, almost in passing,[180] but his main theological interest was elsewhere.

Bernard was no enemy of the flesh, except in so far as it refuses to cede priority to the spirit. The predominantly negative tone of his references to the body and the flesh derives from the fact that, in the historical order, the carnal aspects of the human being are mostly in rebellion.[181] Bernard sees heaven as the transformation and glorification of the whole human being. This includes the rehabilitation and elevation of the body and the *animae passiones;* it is not their anihilation.[182] 'The blessed hope is placed within our breasts by the very promise of Christ that not a single hair of our heads will perish.'[183] 'Not only our hearts will rise, but also our bodies, each according to its kind.'[184]

Bernard's view of human being is not, be it said, substantially indebted to the findings of independent philosophy, since he manifests far more interest in the resurrection of the body, which is a tenet of faith, than in the immortality of the soul which is said to be a conclusion accessible to reason alone. Aelred Squire notes that this approach has been lost for centuries.

The fact is that while orthodox Christians have gone on saying in their creeds that they "believe in the

---

180. QH 8.2 (SBO 4:427,8–9). In general, see QH 8.6 (SBO 4:431,3), Div 87.4 (SBO 6a:332,4).

181. Cf. QH 10.3 (SBO 4:444,26).

182. Div 34.4 (SBO 6a:231,13–15).

183. QH 8.2 (SBO 4:427,20–27).

184. SC 72.6 (SBO 2:229,20–22). By comparison, for a presentation on Augustine's views on the resurrection of the body, see Margaret R. Miles, *Augustine on the Body* (Missoula: Scholars Press, 1979) pp. 99–126.

resurrection of the body", St Bernard in the first half of the twelfth century is the last Western spiritual writer of undoubtedly major status to give the doctrine a clear and definite place in his vision of the meaning of Christian life.[185]

The resurrection of Christ and its consequences in the lives of his followers were important themes in the doctrine and devotion of all the early Cistercians.[186] Christ's rising from the dead was viewed in terms of a great victory over the powers of evil and the means by which the heavenly glory could be made manifest on earth.[187] This mighty act was, however, only a beginning. It represents the first-fruits of what is going to be an immense harvest.[188] For 'where the Head goes, there the members must follow'.[189]

But note that, in the season following the resurrection, new flowers appear as its signs. Under grace there is a new summer with a budding forth. The fruit from such a birth will be the future general resurrection at the end of time, the effects of which will remain forever.[190]

It is often within this context that the words of Phil 3:21 are quoted: 'He will reform our bodies and make them like his own radiant body'.[191] 'Happy is this expectation and blessed this hope, since the future resurrection

185. *Asking the Fathers* (London: S.P.C.K., 1973) p. 57.

186. M.-N. Bouchard, 'Le résurrection dans la spiritualité des premiers auteurs cisterciens', COCR 37 (1975) 114–129. A Altermatt, 'Christus pro nobis', pp. 129–135. B. McGinn, 'Resurrection and Ascension in the Christology of the Early Cistercians', CN 30 (1979) 5–29.

187. Dil 8 (SBO 3:125,20–21).

188. SC 58.8 (SBO 2:132,18–21).

189. Pasc 1.8 (SBO 5:83,5–6).

190. Dil 8 (SBO 3:125–126).

191. SC 47.7 (SBO 2:66,2–3).

will be far more glorious than the human being's first estate.'[192] In an eminent way, humanity will shrug off the image of earthly existence and come to be impressed, instead, with the image of heavenly existence.[193] It will be clearly seen to walk in newness of life, no longer subject to the forces of corruption and decay.[194]

It is this new life which is, properly, the object of desire.[195] In it, God satisfies every desire of the soul,[196] and human life is renewed from day to day.[197] As the terminus willed by God for every human life, it is, in Bernard's view, a worthy focus for hope, aspiration and desire.

Bernard's specific theological interest in the theme of the resurrection of the body was particularly the effect of his devotion to the mystery of Christ's ascension into heaven. This single event seemed, in Bernard's eyes, not only to convey a programme for life on earth, but also to proclaim the form of what was prepared in the future.

THE THEME OF THE ASCENSION

Bernard had great personal devotion to the mystery of the Lord's ascension, a fact that may be deduced from the number of sermons which he preached on this theme,[198] and from his determined efforts to influence the General Chapter of the Cistercian Order to legislate

192. QH 10.5 (SBO 4:446,26–27).
193. SC 25.4 (SBO 1:165,4–6).
194. SC 43.3 (SBO 2:42,30–43,1).
195. Pasc 1.8 (SBO 5:93,13–14). Cf. Palm 3.5 (SBO 5:55,15–16).
196. SC 11.5 (SBO 1:57,24–25), on the basis of Ps 102:5.
197. SC 72.11 (SBO 2:232,27), on the basis of 2 Cor 4:16.
198. Six sermons for the ascension plus Div 60 and 61, to which may, perhaps, be added six sermons for the assumption of the Virgin Mary.

for a procession on the occasion of this feast.[199] For him, the ascension was the crowning feature of the life of Christ, evoking not only the ultimate victory of God's love over sin and the powers of evil, but also grounding the hopes and aspirations of humanity.

It is on this basis that monastic spirituality has often been viewed as 'ascensionist'. 'Reference to Christ's Ascension is not incidental; it is typical of mediaeval mysticism. It is, perhaps, clearest in Bernard of Clairvaux.'[200] 'The Jerusalem above is the end the monk strives for. He will rise toward it through everything which calls to mind — and gives reality to — an ascension.'[201]

For Bernard, the ascension was 'the fulfilment and the consummation of all the other solemnities and the felicitous conclusion of the whole journeying of the Son of God'.[202] But it was not merely the glorious culmination of the earthly career of the Word which moved him. The ascension is also important because of what it does for us. 'He ascended for *our* glorification.'[203] This is noted in several passages.

If the birth and resurrection of the Lord are appropriately celebrated with devout solemnity, then it is right that today's feast of the ascension should be kept with no less devotion. This is not to detract from the other feasts, but it is appropriate because this feast is their end and completion.

Surely it is an occasion for solemn joy when the heavenly Sun, the Sun of Justice, adapts himself to

199. This was in 1151.Cf. J. Leclercq, *Études*, p.154.

200. A. Nygren, *Eros and Agape*, p. 635.

201. J. Leclercq, *Love of Learning*, p. 61.

202. Asc 2.1 (SBO 5:126,8–9). Cf. J. Leclercq, 'Le mystère de l'Ascension dans les sermons de saint Bernard', COCR 15 (1953) 81–88.

203. Ann BVM 1.4 (SBO 5:15,14–15). Cf. A. Altermatt, 'Christus pro nobis', pp. 140–141: 'Die Himmelfahrt Christi "pro nobis"'.

our benighted conditions and tempers the splendour
of his unapproachable light with the cloud of flesh and
the sack-cloth of mortality. And it is certainly a cause
for much gladness and rejoicing when he breaks out of
the sack-cloth and girds himself with joy . . . Do you
not see that the solemnity which we are celebrating today is the crowning glory of all the other feasts, communicating their fruit and increasing their grace.[204]

In SC 79 Bernard is commenting on Song 3:4:
paululum cum pertransissem eos, and he draws a fine
distinction between *transire* and *pertransire,* probably
best translated by Luddy's 'to pass' and 'to pass beyond'.[205] The soul passes from death to life through its
hope in the resurrection; if it wishes to pass-beyond this
world to share in the glory of Christ, it needs to have a
lively faith in his ascension. 'Therefore to believe the
resurrection is *transire;* to believe the ascension also is
pertransire.'[206]

If I may put matters more clearly: If the Lord Jesus
had been raised from the dead but had not yet
ascended, it could not be said of him that he passed-
beyond but only that he passed [from death to life].
If this were the case, it would also suffice for the
bride seeking him simply to pass, without passing-
beyond. But since Christ has not only passed in his

204. Asc 4.1 (SBO 5:137–138). McGinn points to the importance
of the ascent-descent motif in Bernard's view of the work of Christ. He
descends to the human level so that the natural desire of human beings
to ascend may be given effect. This happens by association with the
return of Christ to glory. The descent of Christ would thus appear as the
condition of salvation, whereas the ascent together with redeemed
humanity is the accomplishment of that act.
205. Ailbe Luddy (trans.), *St. Bernard's Sermons on the Canticle
of Canticles* (2 vols, Dublin: Browne and Nolan, 1920) vol 2: p. 435,
note.
206. SC 79.3 (SBO 2:273,26–27).

resurrection, but also passed-beyond in his ascension, therefore the bride appropriately not only passes, but also passes-beyond, since she has followed him into heaven by her faith and devotion.[207] The doctrine of the ascension thus becomes an element in spirituality; the soul has to pass-beyond, to seek the things that are above, as Bernard often reminds his readers in the text of Col 3:1-2 used in the liturgy, where Christ sits at the right of the Father.[208] Just as Christ's whole career was a matter of 'seeking heaven', so it is desire to follow him in his ascension which should principally characterise his disciples.[209] Using the words of 1 Pet 2:21, Bernard reminds his readers that Christ's ascent was left as an example. 'The way of ascension, he himself demonstrated to us.'[210] 'He himself is the way by which we ascend, just as he is also the homeland for those who have arrived.'[211] The force of the ascension is not limited to the level of moral suasion. Its mystery is permanently impressed on the hearts of Christians and re-enacted in their lives. 'Christ himself once ascended in bodily form unto the heights of heaven, but now he continues spiritually to ascend, every day, in the hearts of the elect.'[212]

Happy is the one who ascends that blessed mountain with desire and perseverance, so that he may receive a place to dwell in that sanctuary and be seen by God the Father and by his saints, and at the same

207. SC 79.3 (SBO 2:273,20-26).
208. SC 59.5 (SBO 2:138,16), SC 75.2 (SBO 2:248,13), SC 75.12 (SBO 2:253,30), V Nat 2.3 (SBO 4:206,6-7), Asc 2.2 (SBO 5:127,16-17), Asc 6.4 (SBO 5:152,7-8), Asc 6.5 (SBO 5:152,22), etc.
209. SC 23.1 (SBO 1:139,8), Asc 4.6 (SBO 5:143,2).
210. Asc 4.6 (SBO 5:142,10).
211. Div 60.1 (SBO 6a:291,6-7).
212. Div 61.1 (SBO 6a:293,14-16).

time be granted the sight of God's power and glory. The blessed mountain is none other than the greatest of all mountains, the high-ridged mountain, Jesus Christ the Lord.[213]

The twelfth century witnessed the flowering of a strong emphasis on eschatology. Although the tendency was relatively universal, it assumed different meanings and forms of expression according to the variety of contexts in which it fourished. On the one hand, there was eschatology present in the categories chosen to express the realities of christian life. We might term this a 'spiritual eschatology'. On the other hand, as Bernard McGinn's book *Visions of the End* amply demonstrates, there was a strong current of another sort of eschatological thinking which might be termed 'apocalyptic'. Perhaps this had its origins in the millenarianism which burgeoned as the year 1000 drew close. Nurtured by the climate of urgent reform and the various crusades against the powers of evil, and reinforced by the bizarre movements which seemed to be the work of anti-christs, this tendency reached its culmination in the works of Joachim of Fiore (1135–1202).[214]

Elsewhere, McGinn emphasises the difference between the *subjective* purposes of spiritualising eschatology, i.e. motivation and encouragement, and the information-generating objectivism of the apocalyptic approach.[215] The spiritual eschatology was aimed at helping

213. Div 33.9 (SBO 6a:227–228).

214. B. McGinn, *Visions of the End: Apocalyptic Traditions in the Middle Ages* (New York: Columbia University Press, 1979).

215. *Id.*, 'Saint Bernard and Eschatology', in *Leclercq Studies*, pp. 162–163.

people cope by reminding them of the good things to come; apocalyptic claimed to provide signs and information which would help people predict what would happen and when. McGinn also notes that the spiritual eschatologist often referred more to *prefigurations* of final things rather than to the actual realities themselves.[216]

Taking the texts of Bernard which speak about the Day of the Lord, the reader is impressed first with the conclusion that Bernard was more interested in the qualitative difference between the present and the future than in measuring the quantitative distance between them.[217] 'Bernard, unlike his fellow Cistercian, Otto of Freising, did not accept the widespread belief that eschatological times were present.'[218]

Bernard's approach to most subjects was governed by his spiritual and monastic priorities. Politics, war, ecclesiastical appointments, and theological controversies were all assayed according to the same standards — sometimes disastrously. So it may be concluded of his dabbling in eschatology. Whatever borrowing Bernard made from currents of eschatological thought, even from apocalyptic, would have followed the same pattern. It would have been adapted to serve Bernard's purposes rather than permitted to pursue its own intrinsic logic. He would espouse such views to the extent that they could be exploited to serve his purposes, but in so doing he would adapt them to suit his own perspective.

216. *Ibid.*, pp. 164–165.
217. Cf. SC 13.6 (SBO 1:73,12, based on 1 Tim 1:12: SC 72.6 (SBO 2:229,20–22), Ep 204 (SBO 8:63,18). In SC 36.2 (SBO 2: 2,5–6), Bernard quotes 1 Cor 7:29: *Tempus enim breve est.* Cf. SC 68.6 (SBO 2:200,11).
218. Bernard Flood, 'St Bernard's View of Crusade', in *Australasian Catholic Record* 47 (1970) 133.

We have seen in this chapter that Bernard's thinking about the future life is of a piece with the whole
fabric of his thought. It is the logical extension of his anthropology. It is also interesting that as this theme
developed, his teaching became more constrained, in the
sense that he clung more closely to Catholic tradition,
and more overtly than almost anywhere else, sought to
construct his presentation on a chain of biblical texts. His
eschatology, also, is an integral component of his
philosophy and doctrine.

There is, however, one major area that remains
unexplored, although it has surfaced repeatedly in the
discussion thus far. It is time now to examine the practical or behavioural implications of Bernard's teaching on
desire for God.

CHAPTER SIX

DESIRE AS DIALECTIC

WE HAVE SEEN in the preceding chapters that Bernard gives evidence at having arrived at a coherent synthesis of the anthropological and eschatological aspects of the life of grace. It is important to realise, however, that this theological position is formulated primarily with a view to supporting and explaining his teaching on the experiential and behavioural aspects of the human being's movement toward God.

Bernard expounded the Scriptures with a view to exploiting their moral or practical potential. He was not primarily an exegete or a theologian or an ethician. He was a pastor of souls, interested in communicating to those in his charge something which might help them to continue their struggling. He speaks of the spiritual process not with a view to furthering 'science' but to keep others informed of the likely pattern their own lives with God would follow.

In this chapter, accordingly, we shall examine the relationship of Bernard's teaching on desire for God with everyday behaviour and experience. We hope to demonstrate that it is in this area of practical, pastoral concern that Bernard's teaching comes together.

THE PRICIPLE OF INTERMEDIACY

Bernard's primary concern with present practical response to grace is illustrated by his Advent sermons.[1] To the traditional dichotomy between the first coming of Christ in history and his return at the end of time, Bernard added a third element, an intermediate coming, his entry through grace into everyday lives. This is one of Bernard's few theological innovations, and it certainly indicates that his area of special expertise was the practical workings of grace in ordinary human experience.

In the augustinian triad *sin : grace : glory,* which was used widely in medieval times, it was the middle term which most attracted Bernard's attention. His work, like Augustine's abounds in ternary systems, but with Bernard the interest generally lies with the central phase. In fact, one of his normal techniques of expounding a particular theme is to sandwich it between its antecedents and its consequences. Instead of looking analytically at some reality, he prefers to see it as part of a process.[2]

1. I have tried to demonstrate this in my introduction to M. Casey (trans.) *The Advent Sermons of Bernard of Clairvaux* (Belgrave: Australian Benedictine Studies Series, 1979). His sixth sermon for Advent is entitled, *De medio adventu et triplici innovatione* (SBO 4:188–190). It deals explicitly with this theme, though the perspective of the intermediate coming is characteristic throughout the entire series.

2. The triads which abound in Bernard's writings are different from those found in Augustine's, where a strong Trinitarian nuancing

Bernard's triads are not fixed sequences. He allowed
his focus to expand and contract according to the precise
point he was seeking to communicate. Sometimes he followed the logic of the text or feast which was the occasion
of his remarks, sometimes it was a practical issue that
decided his point of entry, at other times it was simply a
personal attraction or interest. The content varies but the
form used, that of a presentation of a series of three, remains remarkably consistent. Thus he divided history into three segments, *creation : reconciliation : restoration*
'which is at the end of time, in the future'.[3] Between the
baseness which is from the earth and the exaltation which
is proper to heaven, there is a middle time, in which the
new life begins to appear.[4] This is the time of the
Church, in which the future life, although not fully
realised, begins to manifest itself against the backdrop of
unbelief.[5] It is inferior relative to the final culmination,
but is certainly more excellent than what went before.[6]

---

is often in evidence. Nor do all Bernard's triple listings represent a
deliberate emphasis on the intermediate term. Often there is question merely of a rhetorical ploy: three items being considered as
many as most audiences can handle without losing the thread of
argument. In the *Sententiae,* Bernard has a wide variety of
numerical sequences. Sometimes these represent a theological viewpoint, but more often they are simple points listed schematically as
the skeleton of an oral presentation. Notwithstanding these reservations, in the items to be discussed below, it is suggested that, in
many cases, Bernard's triple listings are not random enumerations
which ran out of material before reaching the fourth item. It is, on
the contrary, Bernard's regular way of presenting material with a
view to highlighting the middle term. On some of the triads found
in Bernard's work, see M. Basil Pennington, 'Three Stages of
Spiritual Growth according to St Bernard', StM 11 (1969) 315–326.
    3. SC 23.4 (SBO 1:141,3–4).
    4. SC 25.4 (SBO 1:165,6).
    5. SC 68.5 (SBO 2:199,19).
    6. SC 45.6 (SBO 2:53,3–4).

The life of the Church in the present sphere of existence is one which is itself marked by stages of growth in grace.[7] These will find their full realisation only in the future.[8] It is a state similar to that of those who have newly entered monastic life, who have renounced the world without having yet progressed far beyond it, who have the blossom, but not the fruit, only the hope of the fruit.[9] The middle phase is, expecially, a time for hope[10] — hope fed by what has already been accomplished, hope directed toward what is yet to be.

There are three levels to be distinguished: that of beginners, that of proficients, and that of those who are perfect. The beginning of wisdom is the fear of the Lord, the middle stage is one of hope, and the completion is charity, as the Apostle says, 'The fullness of the law is charity'. The one who begins in fear, bears the cross of Christ with patience; one that advances carries it willingly, but whoever has reached the consummation of charity embraces it ardently.[11]

The middle time is also marked by faith. There is more ample access to light than either the heathen or the Patriarchs of the Old Testament enjoyed, yet this is not to be compared with the fulness of light expected in the future. We live neither in darkness nor in daylight, but in the shadow of faith.

Just as we affirm that there was, among the ancients, a shadow and symbol of the truth which shines forth directly for us in the grace of Christ present in the flesh, so it cannot be denied that we ourselves live, for the time being, in a shadow of truth, compared with what will be in the future. Otherwise the words

7. SC 51.9 (SBO 2:89,4–6): *per incrementum gratiae.*
8. SC 50.2 (SBO 2:79,8–10).
9. SC 63.6 (SBO 2:165,6–8).
10. SC 51.9 (SBO 2:89,4–6).
11. And 1.5 (SBO 5:430,9–13).

of the Apostle are rejected, 'Our knowledge is partial and our prophecy is partial', and 'I do not judge myself to have grasped it'.
There must be a distinction between one who walks by faith and another who walks by sight. Therefore, the one who is just walks by faith, whereas he who has attained blessedness rejoices in sight. For the time being the human person lives in the shadow of Christ, whereas the holy angel glories in the splendour of the face of glory.[12]

The shadow is, accordingly, a middle phase of light, an adaptation of the brilliance of eternal light to the darkened power of human vision, done with the intention of educating and preparing the human being for the stronger light of the eternal day.[13] Even the shadow itself is, however, divided into three phases, when Bernard wishes to emphasise a finer point.

We are not yet in paradise, nor do we yet desire to be drawn up into the third heaven. For the time being, we are nourished by the flesh of Christ, we venerate his mysteries, we are influenced by his example. We keep faith, and thus we truly live by his shadow.[14]

A different schema is proposed in the same context: we *are* in the shadow through faith, we *live* in the shadow through works, we *rest* in the shadow through contemplation. 'It is as much more to rest in the shadow than to live in it, as it is to live in it rather than merely to be in it.'[15] Faith, it would seem, is presupposed in his hearers and contemplation is a gift or consequence that does not yield itself to attempts at acquisition; the only fruitful

12. SC 31.8 (SBO 1:225,3–11).
13. SC 31.9 (SBO 1:225,13–14).
14. SC 48.7 (SBO 2:72,10–13).
15. SC 48.8 (SBO 2:72,16–17).

field in which to invest energies is that of good works, understood as flowing from faith, and, in some way, preparing the heart for contemplation. Thus the work of faith interposes itself between sin and final salvation; it transforms the consciousness through the agency of the *memoria*, funnelling both past and future into the present.[16] Faith itself will be complete only when the believer physically follows his Head and Exemplar into glory.[17]

Many other triads attest to Bernard's awareness that the active christian life has both a past and a future and that its progress tends to be influenced at one time by one pole, and at others by the opposite. Love of God can be carnal, rational, or spiritual, following the standard anthropological trichotomy of St Paul.[18] We pass from reconciliation through adoption to glorification.[19] This is symbolised by the imagery of the three kisses.[20] The same progression can alternatively be expressed as confession, piety, and love,[21] or as fear, love, and contemplation.[22]

A word should be said concerning the chronology of

16. SC 61.3 (SBO 2:150,13–14).

17. SC 72.11 (SBO 2:233,5).

18. SC 20.9 (SBO 1:120,23–24). Cf. SC 50.4 (SBO 2:80,11–12), where the key word is *affectio*. This schema differs from that proposed in Ep 11 to Guigo and later developed in *De diligendo deo*, though in the latter he eliminates the fourth and final stage from this life's possibilities.

19. Sent 2.65 (SBO 6b:38,12–17).

20. The first kiss is reconciliation and the remission of sin, symbolised by kissing Christ's feet. The *medius osculus* is the kiss of the hand, which refers to the practice of virtue. The kiss of the mouth is the prerogative of the bride, it refers to personal intimacy, knowledge of secrets, and contemplation. Cf. SC 3.5 (SBO 1:17, 6–11), Sent 1.8 (SBO 6b:9,10–13), and Sent 2.164 (SBO 6b:55,5–8).

21. Epi 3.8 (SBO 4:309,10–20); cf. SC 7.8 (SBO 1:34,21–22): *confitentes : continentes : contemplantes*.

22. Hum 5 (SBO 3:19,22–24).

triadic progressions. Bernard often seems to speak as though one phase has to be complete before the next one begins, so that, for as long as spiritual development continues, there is no going back on what has been left behind. It is evident, however, from a closer reading that he regards all three components as being present and operative all the time; what changes is the relative importance of a particular element at a particular time. Often, the special circumstances of an individual will mean that the classical progression is not observed, that his beginning will not, for instance, be marked by contrition and compunction. What usually happens in such cases is that the compunction aspect of spiritual growth remains latent until such time as there is plausible opportunity for its emergence.

One of Bernard's more important triads concerns the degree to which grace is internalised. This sequence is described as *disciplina : natura : gratia*.[23] In a first stage the human being responds to grace by acting on the basis of willpower and self-contraint and so forces himself to do what he believes to be right. After a period of practice he finds, however, that less coercion is necessary. He has been formed by good habit and prolonged self-exercise and so is able to perform acts of virtue freely, from an inner basis. Finally, he may find that he is progressively able to act without much struggle. On the contrary, good behaviour appears pleasurable and its opposite unattractive. Hence he does what he has to do not from discipline nor from good habit, but from delight. *Gratia* in this context means, not God's grace, but the pleasure or gratification experienced by the doer.[24] This schema is also embodied in Bernard's teaching on the triple freedom in

23. SC 23.6 (SBO 1:141–142).
24. This is a strong emphasis in Augustine's thought. Cf. P. Brown, *Augustine of Hippo*, pp. 154–155.

the treatise *On Grace and Free Choice,* where the qualification is added that to act from delight is a perfect possibility only in the next life.

Understanding present experience was for Bernard a matter of appreciating it in terms of the opposing forces which he conceived as co-operating in bringing it about. Because there are two diametrically different principles involved there is a fluctuation in experience according to which has the greater influence at any given moment. Sometimes one is firmly impressed with an awareness of sin, an absence of strength, and the frailty of foundations with the corresponding conviction of the need for drudgery, application, and effort. At other times, on the contrary, experience seems to be dominated by such a degree of rest and comfort, and such a clear experience of the kindly providence of God that it already evokes the future life of the blessed. Thus, as far as Bernard was concerned, the primary character of human spiritual life is not its static stability and samelessness, but its alternation—its tendency to wobble from one extreme to the other.

THE THEME OF ALTERNATION

Desire for God and the movement of the soul toward him present themselves to reflexive self-awareness under different forms. Spiritual growth takes place within the context of a dialectic in which the predominantly negative experience of the destructive power of sin is pitted against an affective, faith-inspired involvement with heavenly realities. The first demands a response of discipline and effort from the human being, whereas the second calls him to cease from toil and to devote himself wholly to rest and trust. It becomes vitally important, therefore, that one appreciate at which phase of the dialectic one presently is. Yesterday's response may no longer be appropriate.

It is important to recognise that both sorts of experience are integral to spiritual development. To wish to eliminate either is to risk disaster. Fear and hope are the two complementary means by which the soul makes progress, the one inspired by the prospect of judgment, the other by a recognition of the power and extent of the mercy of God.[25] Desire for God is, accordingly, as much sustained by the sobering experience of fear and apprehension in the face of condemnation, as it is by the progressive initiation into the satisfactions and joys of heavenly life.

This substantial variation in experience was termed by Bernard, *alternatio* and *vicissitudo*. He recognised that such subjection to change was an inherent necessity in spiritual growth. It is derived not from external forces accidental to the person, or from subjective dispositions or defects. It is Bernard's firm teaching that alternation between positive and negative experience is a universal law of spiritual growth. More than this; the absence of such variation he viewed with suspicion — it gives ground for the presumption that such a life is inauthentic and subject to delusion.[26]

25. SC 6.8 (SBO 1:29,23–26).

26. Cf. Jean Mouroux, 'Sur les critères de l'expérience spirituelle d'après les Sermons sur les Cantiques des Cantiques', *Théologien*, pp. 253–267. 'For the soul in progress, vicissitude is the drama of life. And, paradoxically, it is the drama which itself becomes a criterion of authenticity. For as long as one remains subject to this drama, one remains in the truth, because the drama of vicissitude is the necessary expression of temporal existence and the pilgrim state and, as such, is an authentic criterion of a real experience of God.' (Translated from p. 262). The term *alternatio* occurs in a similar vein in one of the conferences of Odo of Cluny: 'We have already pointed out that, by a secret judgment, there is, in the lives of both the good and the wicked,

The dialectic of presence and absence is, of course, a constant theme in the Song of Songs itself. It is not surprising, therefore, that Bernard often took advantage of its suggestions to expatiate on the subject. In a gloss on SC 32.2 found in a Merton College manuscript, *vicissitudo* is explained as meaning *temporis interruptio,* a break in continuity. It was, perhaps, more than that for Bernard. Negative experience is not merely an interruption of the normal, anticipated course; it has as much validity in the process as a whole as does its opposite.

There is no doubt that Bernard's understanding of the underlying cause of this alternation is built on an appreciation of the intrinisic changeableness of everything human. He saw clearly that sin and its effects were just as much part of the historical condition of the human being after the Fall as desire for God and the experience of grace. In this he demonstrated himself to be firmly in the life of Augustine, who clearly stated that anyone who thinks that spiritual life is a simple, painless proceeding has no knowledge either of human nature or of the height of the aspirations with which it is afflicted.

---

a constant variation between good times and hard times. This secret judgment brings it about that the good are confronted with the effects of their negligences so that, in this way they are more completely liberated from the prospect of eternal condemnation. On the other hand, the wicked expericence fully all the good which they do, so that their torments might be greater in the after-life. . . . The saints fear good times even more than they fear times of suffering. They know that adversities in this life cause the desire for heaven to grow. They drive a person to keep going forward to that place where there is perfect rest. On the other hand, they meet times of prosperity with fear and suspicion. . . . God has so arranged matters, by a secret judgment, that the good shall not, in this life, receive their reward by unbroken prosperity and the wicked shall be led to amend their lives through the experience of tribulation. . . . This is why our affairs change so much' (PL 133:617c–618c).

Whoever thinks that in this mortal life a man may so disperse the mists of bodily and carnal imaginings as to possess the unclouded light of changeless truth, and cleave to it with the unswerving constancy of a spirit wholly estranged from the common ways of life—he understands neither what he seeks nor who it is who seeks it.[27]

Before beginning our reading of the texts in the *Sermons on the Song of Songs*, it may be useful to recall seven points which we will meet constantly. Alternation in spiritual experience is due to

1. the unpredictable and unsearchable interventions of God,
2. the contingency and changeableness of human nature,
3. the need for effective tactics to negate the effects of sin and concupiscence,
4. the special character of each individual vocation and destiny,
5. the balance of acts required within the context of a single life,
6. the variety of vocations within the Church, and
7. the seasons of human life in which different elements feature; i.e. the dictates of developmental change.

The opening passages demonstrate Bernard's awareness that development takes place in spiritual life and that not everything which is valuable at one stage is suitable for all other levels. In the very process of growth, the soul's attention is progressively drawn from elementary to more subtle nuances.[28]

It is this sensitivity which is at the heart of many of the numerical sequences enunciated by Bernard. The first of these occurs in SC 3, where he discusses the three kisses,

27. *De consensu evangelistarum* 4.10.20, quoted and translated in P. Brown, *Augustine of Hippo*, p. 147.
28. SC 1.1–2 (SBO 1:3–8).

insisting that the kiss of the mouth about which the Song speaks, and which signifies personal intimacy with the Word, is only possible after preparation.

I do not wish to be at the top immediately. I wish to go forward gradually. Just as brashness in a sinner is displeasing to God, so he delights in a sinner's modesty. You will please him more speedily if you keep to your own level and do not seek things which are above you.[29]

The order dictated by the nature of things cannot be subverted.[30] At different stages of development, the same movement toward God is concretely embodied in a variety of dispositions and practices.

These stages of development are accompanied by different subjective experiences. 'They are, therefore, three affects of soul, or three levels. . .'.[31] The grace of God is equally active throughout, even though it seems to the individual that he rarely reaches his objective.[32] Forgiveness of sins, the enablement of virtue and contemplative experience are equally effects of the graciousness of God, even though they are refracted differently and thus experienced by the human being.[33]

In Sermons five and six, Bernard reminds the reader that human beings occupy a middle place in creation, lower than the angels.[34] They should not be dismayed at their slowness of understanding, nor that they make progress only 'gradually and, as it were, little by little'.[35]

---

29. SC 3.4 (SBO 1:16,14–17).
30. SC 3.5 (SBO 1:17,6).
31. SC 4.1 (SBO 1:19,1): *Sunt ergo tres animarum affectus sive profectus*. The same view is found in greater detail in Div 8.1 (SBO 6a:111,8–11) and Div 73 (SBO 6a:311,9–11).
32. SC 4.1 (SBO 1:18,11 and 19,4).
33. SC 4.1 (SBO 1:19,2–4).
34. SC 5.5 (SBO 1:23,22–23).
35. SC 5.4 (SBO 1:23,6–8).

God's role in the restoration of humanity is recalled
in Sermon six. But, it is pointed out, he acts both
through his mercy and through his judgement. These are
the two feet by which he walks around in the minds of
those devoted to him.[36] The result of this action is also
dual; the human being experiences both fear and
hope.[37]

It has sometimes been granted to a poor man like
myself to sit at the feet of the Lord Jesus and, according to the condescension of his kindness, I have
embraced now one foot and now the other.

And if it happened that I became forgetful of his
mercy and, driven on by conscience, I clung too
long to the foot of judgment then, at once, I was
cast down by an unbelievable fear and by misery
and confusion. I was surrounded on all sides by a
terrifying darkness and was able only to cry out in
fear from the abyss, 'Who understands the power of
your anger, and fears the strength of your fury?'

But if I leave the foot of justice and cling more tenaciously to the foot of mercy, I become slack, negligent, uncaring, tepid in prayer, slothful in action,
ready to laugh, and not circumspect in conversation.

The result is that both states are more lacking in
stability than they should be. But since I have been
instructed by the experience of my master [the
Psalmist], it is not judgment alone or mercy alone
but both together that will be my song. I will not
forget your just decrees, and both mercy and judgment will be my song in this place of pilgrimage,
until the time comes when mercy is lifted above
judgment. Then unhappiness will be silent and my
glory will sing to you without regret.[38]

36. SC 6.6 (SBO 1:29,4–5), SC 6.7 (SBO 1:29,16–17).
37. SC 6.8 (SBO 1:29,25–26).
38. SC 6.9 (SBO 1:30,9–24).

Fear and hope are complementary experiences, equally necessary; they are not alternatives.

One of the most significant expositions of the theme of alternation occurs in Sermon seventeen. Previously Bernard had been speaking of the necessity of grace and of the role of the Holy Spirit. Now he goes on to speak of deeper mysteries: the Holy Spirit can be as active through his experienced absences as he is when he is perceived by the soul to be present.

Do you think that, having penetrated so far into God's holy place and having examined something of that wondrous mystery, we might dare to go still further and investigate realities which are even deeper? For this Spirit has access not only to the hearts and bowels of human beings, but also to the very depths of God. Hence we are always safe when we follow him both to our own hearts and to the higher realities above us.

One thing is, however, necessary. We must keep guard over our hearts and over our understandings, lest we think him present when he is not and, so, go astray through following our own instincts instead of his.

This is really the major concern of Bernard's development of the theme, that his readers might learn to discern what comes from the Holy Spirit and what is from themselves. Unless they appreciate the fluctuation inherent in the action of the Spirit, they may be led astray.

For the Spirit comes and goes as he wills, and nobody knows readily where he comes from or where he goes to. Now it is possible not to know *where* he comes and goes without endangering our salvation. To be ignorant of *when* he comes and goes is, however, clearly very dangerous.

The Spirit comes and goes according to his own

dispensation; if we do not remain very vigilant and so fail to observe this, then we will never experience desire for him in his absence, nor will we render due reverence to him and obey him when he is present. It is a fact that the Spirit leaves us from time to time, in order that we may seek him more instantly. How will this happen if we do not even notice his departure? And, again, how can his majesty be worthily received when he comes to console, if his presence is not detected. The mind which is ignorant of his departure is liable to be misled, and being unmindful of his return, will not give thanks for the visitation.

Bernard then alludes to the narrative in the Elijah cycle in which the younger prophet, Elisha, begs his mentor not to depart without leaving some token behind him. He continues:

We are thus taught and admonished by the prophet's example to be vigilant and careful with regard to the work which the Holy Spirit is ceaselessly accomplishing, with all the remarkable subtlety and sweetness of his divine skill, in the depth of our being. Let it never be that his masterly anointing, by which he instructs us about everything, is taken away from us without our being aware of the fact. If this is so, we shall never be led astray regarding this adorable gift and, on his return, he will not find us unprepared. On the contrary, we shall wait for him with uplifted gaze and with breasts swelled, ready to receive the Lord's ample benediction.

Whom does the Lord seek? Surely it is those who are waiting for their Master when he returns from the wedding-feast. And it is a fact the he never returns from those abundant delights of the heavenly banquet with empty hands.

Bernard now goes to the heart of the matter. Discernment of the different movements of the Spirit is important because he acts in the soul differently with a view to accomplishing different objectives. This means that the soul's efforts to co-operate with the actions of the Holy Spirit are necessarily varied. Furthermore, no particular experience can ever be singled out as the effect of the Spirit's action, since he proposes himself for human acceptance in different forms.

Therefore we must remain alert, alert at all times, since we can never know in advance when the Spirit comes and when he goes. For it is a fact that the Spirit does come and go and that the human being who stands with his support must fall when this support is withdrawn. He does not, however, collapse entirely, since the Lord, once again, stretches out to him a helping hand.

For people who are spiritual, or rather for those whom the Lord intends to make spiritual, this process of alternation goes on all the time. God visits by morning and subjects to trial. The just one falls seven times and seven times gets up again. What is important is that he falls during the day, so that he sees himself falling and knows when he has fallen and wants to get up again and calls out for a helping hand, saying: 'O Lord, at your will you made me splendid in virtue, but then you turned away your face and I was overcome'.[39]

Bernard recognised that this is arcane teaching: the action of God in the experience of absence is not generally recognised. Bernard here sketched out an extraordinary view of the workings of grace that is both solidly founded and very encouraging. He affirms that the Lord allows the human being to sin so that, having experienced what life-without-God is like, he might return to

---

39. SC 17.1-2 (SBO 1:98-99). Some parts of the sermon quoted are similar to a section in Hilary of Poitiers' *De Trinitate* 12.56 (PL 10:470ab).

his Father with greater commitment than ever. When
God seems to withdraw from someone, it is inevitable
that sin will result, *necesse est*. The removal of the divine
support confronts the human being with his overwhelming frailty, and this happens repeatedly. Those whom
the Lord intends to advance in union with him do so
through the experience of the dialectic of sin and salvation in their own lives; there is no short way.

In Sermon eighteen, Bernard describes the positive
side of spiritual experience, the feeling of love and desire
aflame in contemplation. He notes, however, that the
experience is sudden and unexpected and then passes
quickly. It cannot be prolonged.[40]

The theme of the changeableness of the spiritual life
returns in Sermon twenty-one, where Bernard again affirms that such changes are due to the Spirit's dispositions.

> Do you not see that those who walk in the Spirit
> can, in no way, remain for long in one state? One
> does not always make progess with the same facility.
> This is because one's ways are not one's own. They
> are moderated by the Spirit according to his plans.
> Sometimes progress is slower and, at other times, it
> is fast.[41]

Following on from this theme, he returns to discuss the
dual effect of divine action in the soul

> Learn from this expression that a twofold help can
> be expected from above in the spiritual task, namely
> correction and consolation. One of these works on
> the outside, the other interiorly. Correction
> punishes brashness, consolation raises one up and
> gives confidence. The former produces humility,
> the latter gives comfort to timid hearts; one makes

40. SC 18.6 (SBO 1:107,15–20).
41. SC 21.4 (SBO 1:124,20–23).

us circumspect, the other dedicated. Correction
teaches fear of the Lord, consolation tempers that fear
with an infusion of kindly joy. Thus it is written, 'Let
my heart rejoice to fear your name', and 'Serve the Lord
in fear and trembling, rejoice before him'.
Thus 'we are drawn' when we are exercised by
trials and temptations. 'We run' when we are visited
by interior consolations and inspirations, as if we
were breathing in sweet-smelling ointments.[42]

In the following sermon, Bernard speaks about the
variety of Christ's gifts to the Church and the wide range
of possible response to grace, according to the particular
gift and vocation which each has.

We do not all run in the same way. . . . You will
see some who burn vehemently in the pursuit of
wisdom, others who are more animated in the direction of repentance and the hope of pardon, others
again who are led by good example toward the practice of virtue, and others still who are inflamed to
piety by the memory of the passion.[43]

This passage heralds Bernard's strong conviction that,
even within the unity of monastic observance, there is
scope for variety among individuals and, it is to be
presumed, for change within the lives of each. The
theme is often stated in the *Sententiae* and a beautiful
description of monastic variety occurs in Div 42.[44] 'We do

42. SC 21.10–11. One is tempted to stretch the translation
somewhat to render 'challenge' instead of 'correction'.
43. SC 22.8 (SBO 1:135,9–13). There are many statements of the
variety of forms assumed by the monastic vocation, for instance,
John Cassian, *Institutes* 5.4.3 (SChr 109:196) with the consequence
stated in *Conf* 9.8 (SChr 54:48): 'There are as many forms of prayer
as there are states of soul, or rather, there are as many as the totality
of states experienced by all souls together'.
44. Div 42.4 (SBO 6a:258,16–23). 'The monastery is truly a
paradise, a region fortified with the rampart of discipline. It is a

not all run in the same way.' 'Each individual finds his
own secret with the bridegroom.'[45] Many changes take
place in the recesses of conscience. In SC 23, Bernard
refers to a more visible aspect of alternation, that of the
transition from action to contemplation. He compares
the restedness and sense of wonder which the bride experiences in the act of contemplation with the labour and
fatigue which characterises other activities.[46] Then, in a
word drawn from or shared with John of Fécamp, he
laments the rarity and brevity of spiritual exaltation:
Rara hora et parva mora![47] The joy which is needed to
counterbalance dread cannot be gained or maintained
through one's own efforts; one must await the unpredictable visitation of the Lord.[48]

In SC 31, Bernard speaks about the various forms in
which the Word presents himself in this present life,
alternating from one visitation to the next.

------

glorious thing to have men living together in the same house,
following the same way of life. How good and how pleasant it is
when brothers live in unity! You will see one of them weeping for
his sins, another rejoicing in the praise of God, another tending the
needs of all and another giving instruction to the rest. Here is one
who is at prayer and another at reading, here is one who is compas-
sionate and another who inflicts penalties for sins. This one is aflame
with love and that one is valiant in humility. This one remains humble when everything goes well and the other one does not lose his
nerve in difficulties. This one works very hard in active tasks, the
other one finds quiet in the practice of contemplation.'
    45. SC 23.9 (SBO 1:144,6–9): *unaquaque invenit secretum sibi
cum sponso.*
    46. SC 23.11 (SBO 1:146,6–9). Cf. Thomas Merton, 'Action and
Contemplation in St Bernard', in *Thomas Merton on St Bernard*, CS
9 (Kalamazoo: Cistercian Publications, 1980) 23–104.
    47. SC 23.15 (SBO 1:148,20). Cf. John of Fécamp, *Lettre à une
moniale*, line 78, in *Fécamp*, p. 208.
    48. SC 23.15 (SBO 1:149,11–14).

The Word, who is the bridegroom, appears frequently to zealous minds, but not always in one form (*non sub una specie*). Why is this? It is because he is not yet seen as he is. That vision will be permanent because the form under which he will be seen will be permanent. It simply is; it is subject to no alteration of past, present and future. Once you remove past and future, there is no basis for alteration, nor for any shadow of change.[49]

Hence there is a distinction to be made between the Word as he *is*, and the Word as he *appears*. The first is attainable only in the next life, the second— involving a multiplicity of forms—is all that is possible now.[50] So the Word appears in different forms to evoke different responses in the heart of the recipients, according to their states and needs.

I am not saying that he appears as he is, even though the way in which he presents himself is not totally alien from the reality. Nor is he continually at hand, no matter how dedicated the minds are that await him. Nor is he equally present to all. It is fitting that the taste of the divine presence vary, according to the various desires of the soul. In this way, the infusion of the taste of the heavenly sweetness is adapted one way and another to suit the different longings of the soul which seeks him.[51]

The same sermon points out that the presence of the object of the soul's desire is infrequent and that this rarity is a source both of suffering and of the increase in the intensity of the desire itself.[52] The following sermon takes up this theme, reiterating that the visitations of God are swift and sudden.[53]

49. SC 31.1 (SBO 1:219,7–12).
50. SC 31.2 (SBO 1:220,5–11).
51. SC 31.7 (SBO 1:223,19–24).
52. SC 31.5 (SBO 1:222,3–5 and 23–24).
53. SC 32.2 (SBO 1:227,6–21).

It is only after this mortal life that such an interplay of presence and absence will terminate. Meanwhile, desire is increased by the experience of absence and with each subsequent return the union between the soul and the Word becomes a little stronger and more intense. As the soul grows in the recognition of its own resourcelessness, its dependence on God increases and it becomes progressively detached from other sources of support. But it is only through the experience of bitter desolation that this comes about.[54]

Sermon thirty-seven speaks of the way in which sadness and pain give way to the perception of God's presence on occasion, and how it is possible, even now, to have a sense of drawing in the harvest.

> Any one of us who, after bitter and tearful beginnings in monastic life, has rejoiced to be lifted up on the wings of grace and to have been able to breathe easily in the hope of consolation, has surely gathered in the harvest already. He has reaped the fruit of his tears. For he has perceived God and it is from him that he hears it said, 'Give him a share in the fruit of his hands'.[55]

Yet life does not always yield such a meed of pleasure. In Sermon thirty-eight, the bridegroom is transformed into a dire master, angrily reproaching the bride for her defective self-knowledge and consequent complacency.

> He says, 'If you do not know yourself, then go out!' How fearfully the bridegroom thunders at his bride! He is no longer a bridegroom but a master. But he speaks not from anger but with a view to purifying the bride through fear so that, once purified, she will be worthy of the vision for which she longs, which is reserved for the pure in heart.[56]

54. SC 36.6 (SBO 2:7,24–8,5).
55. SC 37.4 (SBO 2:11,5–9).
56. SC 38.3 (SBO 2:16,13–16).

This *dura et austera increpatio* was aimed at eliminating presumption. It was really a sign of love rather than a token of dislike or annoyance, even though it brought suffering and sadness in its train.[57] As always, Bernard wanted his readers to veer away from extremes, 'lest joys lift one too high, or sadness cast one down too low'.[58]

Yet, to many, it seems that the negative phase of development is too dominant. To this Bernard brings his teaching about the breathing-space, *respiratio*, which God always grants, even when pain persists. *Respiratio* was a term much used by Gregory the Great and it appears often in the *Sacramentarium* which bears his name. It signified a breathing-spell in the midst of toil and fatigue.[59] In spirituality it came to have the sense of occasional moments of relief given to the soul in the midst of phases marked by predominantly negative experiences. Here, Bernard is contrasting the soft experience of wine with the hard and bitter taste of myrrh.

> If you have put aside your sins, then you have drunk what is bitter, but if you have been refreshed by a holier life in the hope of life, then the bitterness of myrrh has been changed for you into the wine which gladdens the human heart.[60]

Both experiences are, however, used by the spiritual physician, Christ, for the welfare of souls.[61]

In Sermon fifty-one, Bernard is speaking of the way in which contemplation overflows into action. Since contemplative experience cannot be prolonged whilst the

---

57. SC 39.1 (SBO 2:191,1–10).
58. SC 43.2 (SBO 2:42,12).
59. SC 44.1 (SBO 2:44,24). Cf. L. Brou, *Les oraisons dominicales de l'Avent à la Trinité* (Bruges: Ed. de l'apostolat liturgique, 1960) p. 92.
60. SC 44.1 (SBO 2:44,22–45,1).
61. SC 44.3 (SBO 2:46,1–3).

human being remains in the body, it must be supplemented by compatible activity. There is, he concludes, reciprocal support between action and contemplation. Mary and Martha were, after all, sisters.[62] This brings Bernard to an aspect of the idea of alternation which was commonly emphasised among the Cistercians of that era, expecially Aelred of Rievaulx. The fact of change in spiritual experience means that there should be a parallel flexibility in spiritual exercises. A monk's life ought to be balanced by an interchange of activities so that it is wholesome on a long-term basis at every level of being: physical, emotional, intellectual, creative, and spiritual. It was thought that cisterican life, with its alternation of activities, responded realistically to the substantial changeableness of all human existence.[63]

Later in the same sermon, Bernard refers to the soul which fluctuates between fear and hope,[64] and suggests that each person has eventually to find his own mean between the fear of punishment, on the one hand, and confident assurance, on the other.[65]

Sermon Fifty-four raises the topic of alternation in connection with the contrast experienced within a single life between the sense of being graced and the opposite feeling, that of reprobation.

> Happy are those who are found worthy occasionally, even if it be rarely, to drink from this torrent of delight. Even though it does not flow all the time, at least sometimes the water of wisdom and the fountain of life spring up so that they may be in

62. SC 51.2 (SBO 2:85,9–10).
63. Cf. Charles Dumont, 'St Aelred: The Balanced Life of the Monk', *Monastic Studies* 1 (1963) 25–38, especially pp. 31–33. See also Aelred's *Inst Incl* 9 (SChr 76:64–66).
64. SC 51.9 (SBO 2:88,29–89,1).
65. SC 51.10 (SBO 2:89,10–11).

such ones a source of water leaping up into eternal life. This onrush of water brings joy to God's city all the time and in abundance. I wish that occasionally it would flood our earthly mountains, and that he would not disdain to visit some of them, so that once they are adequately watered, some few rare drops might filter down to us, who are valleys, so that we need remain dry and sterile no longer. In a region which is never thus watered, which is bypassed by the streams of wisdom, there can be only unhappiness, neediness, and a great famine.[66]

In the following sermon the mercy-judgment antithesis reappears. 'Therefore there are two good things which are proper to the bridegroom, mercy and judgement.'[67] 'As for you who desire the coming of a Saviour, make sure that you also fear the examination of the judge.'[68]

The following sermon again gives the cause of the human being's lack of stability as his bodily status. Because this is a source of so many sins, it results in a barrier being erected between God and the soul.[69]

Sermon Fifty-seven begins with a statement about variety within the life of grace. 'See how grace develops and mark the different levels of the divine condescension.'[70] From this Bernard derives the lesson of vigilance, so that the bride is able to recognise the bridegroom beneath the different guises he assumes in visiting her.

[The upright person] will be visited frequently and he will never be ignorant of the time of his visitation, even though the One who visits spiritually

66. SC 54.6 (SBO 2:106,11–21).
67. SC 55.2 (SBO 2:112,4).
68. SC 55.2 (SBO 2:112,14–15).
69. SC 56.3 (SBO 2:116,3–9).
70. SC 57.1 (SBO 2:119,10–11).

comes in secret and with stealth, like a bashful lover. The soul of sober mind, however, who keeps a close watch sees his coming from a long way off.[71]

Such sobriety is buttressed by three qualities. One who possesses it will be circumspect with regard to himself, regretfully recognising his failures; he will strive always to be pleasing to God; and finally, with regard to his neighbours, he will aim to serve and to prove himself useful.[72] In other words, vigilance for the coming of the bridegroom is not a passive matter of looking down the road with longing, but it is expressed through attention to the details of evangelical living. No single activity exhausts its potential nor is any one course of action able to impose itself to the exclusion of alternatives. Bernard is not speaking of instability or capriciousness, but of a realistic and flexible response to life's concrete exigencies. Speaking with reference to Song 2:10: 'Rise up and hasten . . . and come', he explains:

In this text take note of the things I have spoken to you about more than once. I am speaking of the interchange between holy quiet and necessary action and the fact that there is, in this life, never enough scope for contemplation, nor is our time of holy leisure of sufficient length, since the more pressing usefulness of duties and tasks keeps us on the move.[73]

It is important to understand that Bernard recognised that there are practical tasks to be done in daily life which exclude contemplation. That he laments the paucity of opportunities for holy leisure is not to be taken as an indication that, ideally, external works are to be eliminated. He recognises their necessity. He blames not the

71. SC 57.4 (SBO 2:121,27–122,1).
72. SC 57.11 (SBO 2:125–126).
73. SC 58.1 (SBO 2:127,18–20).

tasks themselves but the situation which imposes them, the fact that we are still in the body. Bernard is not saying that the way of contemplation involves the refusal to become involved in those activities which are dictated by inner and outward circumstances.

From this fundamental principle follows the important discussion of the seasonal variation in spiritual growth and in personal endeavour. 'As with everything under heaven, not every time is suitable and appropriate for this work.'[74] There needs to be a sensitivity to the requirements of each moment. Winter, for example, is no time for pruning the vines; instead they are left in their disordered state until the season of change and intervention arrives.

> He knew that the time of pruning had not yet come and that there would be no response from the vines for his hard work. Why was this? Because in the hearts of those without faith it was still winter. The winter squalls of malice still covered the earth and were more likely to wash away the seeds of the Word than to nurture their growth, and thus bring to nothing the cultivation of the vines.[57]

Spring is the mid-point between winter and summer, between unbelief and charity. This is the right time for pruning to facilitate future growth. The principle which Bernard enunciates here is of paramount importance: temptations and opportunities are always present, but they vary in intensity from season to season. They are best attacked when they are weakest, since at that stage one's limited resources are most likely to be victorious. Brashly to rush in without preparation and without knowledge may result in squandering energy with no

---

74. SC 58.4 (SBO 2:129,4).
75. SC 58.6 (SBO 2:130,25–131,2).

improvement. Bernard's conclusion is that our response to grace needs to be discerning, since it must take account of seasonal variation, both with regard to ourselves and also in connection with our pastoral efforts for others.[76] Bernard now goes on to examine how it is possible for the Word to absent himself from his bride.[77] Having referred to the different sentiments aroused by such coming and going,[78] he speaks of the brevity of the experience of the Word's presence. 'On that day, or perhaps it would be better to say, in that hour—or even half an hour— . . . my mouth will be filled with joy and my tongue with celebration.'[79] The experience of being visited by the Word he describes thus:

> I have no doubt that the bridegroom is present whenever I receive some insight into the Scriptures, whenever a word of wisdom wells up within me, whenever light pours down on me from above, unveiling mysteries, whenever heaven's most ample lap overflows to fill my soul with an abundant shower of lofty thoughts. These ample measures belong to the Word and it is from his fullness that we have received them. And if it should happen, at the same time, that he pours into my heart a rich but humble devotion by which the love of perceived truth generates in me a necesary hatred and contempt of vanity, lest knowledge inflate me and I am lifted up by the frequency of his visits, then I recognise that he is acting toward me in a fatherly manner. I am then sure that the Father also is present.[80]

76. SC 64.1 (SBO 2:166,21): *pro temporum diversitate.*
77. SC 67.2 (SBO 2:189,14). The theme is resumed in SC 74.
78. SC 67.3 (SBO 2:190,8–10).
79. SC 67.1 (SBO 2:193,8–11). The allusion to the half-hour depends on a reference to Rev 8:1: 'There was a great silence in heaven for half an hour.'
80. SC 69.6 (SBO 2:205,27–206,6).

In Sermon seventy-two, Bernard indulges himself by making an arcane distinction between spiration and aspiration, under the influence of the text of Song 2:17: *Donec adspiret dies et inclinentur umbrae*. Returning to the idea of *respiratio*, he makes the point that relief is granted to us only on condition that some effort is made to correspond with the Spirit's workings against the power of the flesh. His negative operation will continue for as long as we resist it. It is in recognising its necessity and accepting the purification that a breathing-spell is found. The suffering continues but it no longer causes confusion and desperation by its perceived unprofitability. The Spirit's action necessarily causes pain to the flesh-dominated will; if the will allows itself to be deflected from concupiscence, then relief will follow.[81]

The most prolonged and beautiful presentation of alternation is found in SC 74, which discusses the idea of the Word's return after an absence. Since the Word cannot return unless he first depart, it follows that the joy experienced in such a reunion is prepared for by the experience of absence and by the 'departure' of the Word from the soul. 'The Word of God, who is himself God and the bridegroom of the soul, comes to the soul and leaves it, just as he wishes.'[82] Such coming and going is, however, qualified by the word *aliquantisper*, for a time, and by the observation that there is question more of a change in the soul's affects than of any movement on the part of the Word.[83] The Word 'withdraws' so that the soul, in its desolation, may experience a more intense and explicit desire. 'Perhaps this is the reason for his withdrawal, that he may be sought with greater eagerness and held with even greater strength.'[84]

81. Cf. SC 72.9 (SBO 2:231,10–11).
82. SC 74.2 (SBO 2:240,23–24).
83. SC 74.1 (SBO 2:240,2–3) and SC 74.2 (SBO 2:240,25).
84. SC 74.3 (SBO 2:241,13–14).

You might ask, therefore how it is that I know that
the Word has arrived, since all his ways are beyond
scrutiny. I know because he is living and active. As
soon as he arrives within, he shakes my sleepy soul
into life. He moves and softens and pierces my heart
which previously had been hard, stony, and twisted
out of shape. The Word begins to root up and to
destroy, to build and to plant. He waters the arid
soil and enlightens the gloom; he opens up what
was closed and sets fire to what was frigid. At the
same time he makes the twisted roads straight and
the rough pathways smooth. And all this is done so
that my soul may bless the Lord and all that is
within me give thanks to his holy name.

The 'coming' of the Word is signalled through its effects; experience alone, however, is not a good indicator, since the
movements of the Word often elude human sensibility.

So it is that, when the bridegroom comes to me, as he
sometimes does, he never signals his presence by any
token, neither by voice nor by vision nor by the sound
of his step. By no such movement do I become aware of
him, nor does he penetrate my being through the
senses. Only by the movement of the heart, as I have
already said, do I come to realise that he is with me. It is
by the expulsion of my vices and the repression of carnal affects that I become aware of the might of his
power. I am lost in wonderment at the depth of his
wisdom when he subjects my inner life to scrutiny and
correction. It is from a slight improvement in my
behaviour that I experience his goodness. It is from the
reformation and the renovation of the spirit of my
mind, that is of my inner self, that I perceive his
beauty and attractiveness. From the consideration of
all these together, I come to be overwhelmed by his
great kindness.[85]

85. SC 74.6 (SBO 2:243,9–27).

Thus Bernard describes the return of the Word. His presence is experienced by the inflamed sensitivity of the spirit and confirmed reflexively through its effect in forging new values and in reforming behaviour. When someone comes to his senses and 'returns to himself' and 'finds his heart', then the Word must be inferred to have come — though in what form, only the recipient knows. He comes when he is found. In a brilliant passage which builds upon themes in the tenth book of Augustine's *Confessions,* Bernard goes on to describe the coming of the Word in greater breadth.

He does not come in through the eyes, for he has no colour; nor through the ears, since he makes no sound. It is not through the nose that he comes, since he does not mingle with the air but with the mind; to the atmosphere he gives being, not odour. He does not gain entry through the mouth, since he is not food or drink. He cannot be contacted through touch, since he is impalpable. How, then, does he find entrance?

Perhaps he does not 'come' at all, since he does not enter from the outside, nor is he an external object. But, on the other hand, neither does he come from inside me, since he is good and I know that inside me there is nothing good.

I ascended to what was highest in my soul and, lo, the Word loomed loftier. I descended to the depths, and he was found to be yet deeper. If I looked out, I saw him beyond my outer limits. If I gazed within, more inward yet was he. It was then that I realised the truth of what I read, 'In him we live and move and have our being'. Happy is he in whom dwells the One by whom he lives; happy is he who lives for and is moved by such a One.[86]

86. SC 74.5 (SBO 2:242,24–243,5).

Whoever penetrates to the heart of his being is confronted by the indwelling Word, larger than any aspect of himself. When the Word is thus discovered, the latent powers of the soul flare into life, producing not only a changed awareness but, gradually having an effect on understanding, affectivity and behaviour. To be visited by the Word is to confront One greater and more powerful than oneself.

Conversely, as was noted also in Sermon seventeen, the departure of the Word causes the human being to fall back into his habitual state of weakness.

> And when it happens that the Word departs, it is as though you were to remove the fire from beneath a boiling pot. Immediately it turns lifeless and stops boiling and beings to get cold. For me, this is the sign of his departure. My soul necessarily feels sad until his return, when he again, as usual, reheats my heart within me. For this is the sign of his coming back.[87]

Again he stresses the automatic counter-effect of the Word's departure, *necesse est*. The soul is necessarily dispirited and appears to itself to have degenerated and declined to its former state. But this is not the case. Taking up a teaching often stated by Gregory the Great, Bernard noted that each time the soul finds itself thrown back to the level of the unspiritual, it finds progressively less joy than before. It is no longer able to be fully absorbed by pursuits which previously brought it utter satisfaction. 'While he is absent, who is the only source of my enjoyment, nothing else can bring me pleasure.'[88]

87. SC 74.7 (SBO 2:243,28–244,2). Cf. Gregory the Great, *Moralia* 23.43 (PL 76:277–278).

88. SC 74.7 (SBO 2:244,9–10). Cf. Gregory the Great, *In Ev* 11.2 (PL 76:1118a), *In Ev* 25.2 (PL 76:1191a), *In Ev* 37.1 (PL 76:1275a).

The presence of the Word gradually causes alternative sources of gratification to lose their savour. Even though the soul continues to feel a counter-attraction downwards, progressively it gains less delight from its falls. Sin becomes boring and is significant more as a sign of despair or rebellion or as a tacit appeal for help than as a positive pursuit of pleasure. The very *ennui* experienced in the return to the unspiritual has the effect of reinforcing the soul's growing conviction that only in God is true happiness to be found. The very unsatisfactoriness of sin is more effective than a thousand sermons. The jaded after-taste of self-indulgence eventually causes the soul to hunger for a complete, uncompromised relationship with the Word.

At the end of this sermon, Bernard added an important qualification: the Word's visitation yields both grace and truth. It embodies both positive and negative features, the former to draw the soul closer to the Word, the latter progressively to detach it from material and carnal pre-occupations. Unless both forces operate, growth is unthinkable.[89]

There is a reminder in Sermon seventy-five, that the successful quest is always a protracted business; it can never be brought to its conclusion in a single night's efforts.[90] The difficulty of finding the Word is partly of his making. It is a trick in the game of love, a device intended to increase and bring out into the open the soul's desire to find him.[91] Such a search, therefore cannot be dull; it is required that the seeker also be somewhat devious, adapting his efforts to the concrete conditions of life.[92]

Though every time is not suitable for the search, we can be assured that the present is always apt; the danger

89. SC 74.8 (SBO 2:244,14–24).
90. SC 75.1 (SBO 2:247,18).
91. SC 75.2 (SBO 2:248,3–7).
92. SC 75.3 (SBO 2:249,1–3).

comes from trying to accomplish today's search tomorrow.[93] Furthermore, the search must be carried out diligently, tirelessly, and with a heart aflame; merely a routine effort is not enough.[94] It is the precise purpose of the alternation of presence and absence to keep the seeker alert, always mindful that what is sought is beyond the level of human comfort. To demonstrate this, Bernard evokes the image of the holy women seeking the Lord after the resurrection.[95]

Where he is you cannot enter now, but you will come afterwards. But keep working, keep following and seeking him and do not allow yourself to be frightened off your search by that inaccessible brightness and sublimity. Never despair of finding him. . . . Seek him by desire, follow him through action, and in faith you will find him.[96]

After raising briefly the idea of different levels in love,[97] Bernard continued the theme of the search in Sermons eighty-four and five, making the point that the conscious motives for seeking the Lord vary from individual to individual and, perhaps, from one stage of life to the next.[98] On the other hand, the Word also adapts himself to suit the condition of the soul.

All that is within the Word is one, with a simplicity which derives from the divine nature. But the effect of this on the soul is not single but plural. This is due to the soul's manifold necessities which require varied treatments.[99]

93. SC 75.3 (SBO 2:249,3–4) and SC 75.5 (SBO 2:250,12–13).
94. SC 75.5 (SBO 2:250,16–18).
95. SC 75.8 (SBO 2:251,19–252,10).
96. SC 75.6 (SBO 2:257,28–258,6).
97. SC 83.5 (SBO 2:301,12).
98. SC 85.1 (SBO 2:307,14–17).
99. SC 85.7 (SBO 2:312,3–4).

Thus it is that though the Word constantly acts for the soul's welfare, its moments of spiritual exaltation are rare and of short duration: *dulce commercium sed breve momentum et experimentum rarum!*[100]

After a brief observation about the choice of suitable times and places for prayer,[101] Bernard concluded his treatment of the theme of alternation by enumerating a number of different but overlapping effects of contact with the Word through prayer.

He is the remedy for our wounds. He is help in time of trouble. He is the source of repair for those who are falling back and he is the source of abundance for those who advance. Finally, he is the means by which human beings have or receive whatever is good and appropriate for them.[102]

Our survey of the passages in the *Sermons on the Song of Songs* which impinge on the theme of alternation has been somewhat prolonged. It has been worthwhile, however, because of its practical application and also because of the prudence and wisdom it demonstrates in Bernard. Perhaps, at this point, the several strands of his thought can be brought together.

In the movement of the soul toward God it is possible to anticipate a dual stream of experience. On the one hand, there are moments of pleasure and relief in which God seems very close and progress assured. But such moments of spiritual exalation are comparatively rare, and they do not last long. For the bulk of his life with God, the human being experiences nothing but the heaviness of his own nature and the labour and toil of spiritual endeavour. He is conscious of being urged

100. SC 85.3 (SBO 2:316,8).
101. SC 86.3 (SBO 2:319,1–3).
102. SC 86.3 (SBO 2:319,4–8).

onward by reason and faith, by fear of the consequences of acting otherwise and even by a certain acceptance of external constraints. Joy in doing good is not the norm. The great cause of troubleness is the changeableness of life's demands.[103] This unsettles one's projections about the future and relativises one's assessments of personal identity. At times it becomes very difficult for the struggling wayfarer to continue and yet he does not really believe that life without God could be pleasurable or even tolerable. Once he has been exposed to the attractiveness of God, he is unable fully to forget it. Yet, through weakness, this memory often slips his mind and so he fails and falls.

The test is not, however, *whether* he falls; it is how he handles the inevitable fall. One who is just may fall seven times a day without giving cause for undue alarm, so long as he is aware of the difference between falling and standing upright and is prepared to look for support to God's love.[104]

This ultimate temptation to which the human being is subjected is one that comes by God's deliberate design. It is not accidental to spiritual progress or the result of human failure. He has to cope with the fact that God cannot be contained within human programmes and that his action is not accessible to human understanding. The alternation of affects and experiences is due to the working out of the divine plan for progress. Some change is caused by the intrinsic weakness of the flesh — a fragility of body and frailty of resolution — some is caused by developmental dynamics, but it is the action of the Word which presides over all.

If it is true that the whole of human life is impressed with the pattern of alternation, then desire for God must pass through the same confusing mixture of positive and

103. SC 32.2 (SBO 1:227,21): *sed molestat vicissitudo.*
104. SC 17.2 (SBO 1:99,16–21).

negative extremes. It is induced forward by hope and, at the same time, kept from falling back through fear.[105] Hence the progress of desire for God is marked, on the one hand, by an accelerating immersion in the things of God. On the other, it is also characterised by the experience of the absence of God, by a sense of personal failure, by frustration at the extent of compromise on one's life and by the impossibility of making stable, irreversible and visibly certifiable progress.

Desire is charmed by the anticipatory moments of grace; the appetite for God is sharpened in them and one's confidence in one's capacity to enjoy God is strengthened. Yet desire's true substance is fuelled more by the experience of absence than by any sense of achievement. It is during periods of lying fallow that the soil of the heart begins to yearn for seed and fruit and thus to become receptive. Without negative experience desire would soon degenerate into a sentimental self-sufficiency.

The human being experiences the saving grace of the Lord as manifold. The desire for God is simultaneously fidelity to nature, attainment of self, submission to creation's order, acceptance of revelation, following of the Gospel, dedication to Christ, flight from sin, reformation unto virtue, pursuit of wisdom, seeking contemplation, a yearning for heaven, conformity to the risen Lord, spiritual union with the Word. At times one or other aspect will predominate. But desire for God is, in Bernard's view, all of these things. To seek to remove it from this integrated vision and to restrict it to the sphere of mere affective longing is to miss Bernard's characteristic viewpoint. Desire for God is the motive-force of a whole range of grace-inspired pursuits; it also alternates.

The intrinsic changeableness of the christian experience

---

105. Cf. Par 1.5 (SBO 6b:264,9).

of grace means that no single experience can be isolated as normative of human response to God, nor any particular mode of behaviour specified as universally expressive of such response. There is flexibility both in experience and in obligation which calls for a sustained sensitivity on the part of the subject and a determined detachment from personal expectations and projections.

If sadness were our continual state, who could bear it? If, on the other hand, things always went well, then who would not think little of them? Wisdom, the careful controller of all things, alternates the course of the temporal life of his chosen ones with a necessary changing between good things and bad. By such a regimen they will neither be crushed by adversity nor lose discipline through too much joy. Also, it is by this means that joys are more appreciated and difficulties more readily endured. Blessed be God forever![106]

THE LAST THINGS IN THE PROCESS OF REALISATION

As the soul grows in grace, it becomes progressively more able to receive God and be transformed into his dwelling-place. 'Grace confers on it what nature denied and so it grows, not in substance, but in strength. It grows in glory.'[107] This is to say that the soul *already* manifests something of the fruits of eternal life.[108]

The positive pole in the dialectic of salvation is evident in the fact that the realities of eternal life are, even now, being achieved. In Bernard's teaching, the final things are already in the process of being realised.[109]

106. Ep 136 (SBO 7:332,4–8). This letter was addressed to Pope Innocent II in 1134.
107. SC 27.10 (SBO 1:189,8–13).
108. SC 37.4 (SBO 2:11,7–8).
109. C. H. Dodd first used the term 'realised eschatology' in his 1935 book, *The Parables of Jesus* (London: Collins/Fontana, 1961)

Thus, the moments which the soul experiences itself moved spiritually by love, joy, and consolation were viewed by Bernard as foretastes of heavenly beatitude, given with a view to stimulating a more intense desire for the final realities.

There are four specific areas in which Bernard asserted that aspects of heavenly life are manifested in the present. Firstly, the practice of virtue and the reformation of morals can be regarded as radical steps in permitting full scope for grace to act. As such they have a liberating effect on awareness, which Bernard referred to as the 'paradise of a good conscience'. Secondly, monastic *conversatio* with its renunciation of the world, the flesh, and the devil was, to him, an eminent example of heavenly life lived here below. He thought that such a life was comparable to that lived by the angels and that the monastery itself was a sort of paradise, *paradisus claustralis*. Thirdly, contemplative experience, referred to by St Paul as entry into the third heaven, seemed to Bernard to be an initiation into that total self-transcendence and involvement with God which will characterise future existence. Finally, growth in grace is

---

p. 161. The expression was modified privately by Ernst Haenchen into *sich realisierende Eschatologie,* and communicated to Joachim Jeremias who made use of it in his study, *The Parables of Jesus* (London: S.C.M., 3rd edn, 1972) p. 250. Dodd had already signified his acceptance of the improved phrasing, together with that of 'inaugurated eschatology' (cf. *The Interpretation of the Fourth Gospel,* [Cambridge University Press, 1968] p. 447, note 1). I have tried to convey Bernard's version of this New Testament emphasis with the phrase 'the last things in the process of realisation', which I offer as an interpretation of *sich realisierende Eschatologie.* I believe that it is important to stress that, for Bernard, it was a matter of eternal realities being progressively realised and manifested within space and time through the free assent of the recipient of grace. It was not an automatic cosmic process.

growth in likeness to the Word, and this means growth in wisdom. Wisdom itself is viewed as the 'outshining of eternal light',[110] the manifestation of the heavenly radiance within the sphere of earth. Each of these areas will now be examined.

The Paradise of a Good Conscience

Consonant with his overriding practical interest, Bernard easily affirmed that the practice of virtue is the natural outcome of desire for God. 'God is sought by good works.'[111] 'God is unable to please the one who is not pleasing to God.'[112] There is, accordingly, scope for effort. About those unwilling so to exert themselves, Bernard said, 'They do not bother to seek the one whom they desire to find; they long to catch up with him, but they do not follow his steps.'[113] Here we have an emphasis which is consistent and firm throughout western monastic tradition. God is not experienced in isolation from daily living. The experience of the divine reality is a part and an effect of the transformation of the entire life. Submission to the Word in everyday living is the best means of nurturing personal growth in the dimension of prayerfulness. It is by the diligent practice of virtue that the Church prepares itself to become 'worthy and capable of the fullness of grace'.[114]

110. SC 17.3 (SBO 1:100,1), SC 25.6 (SBO 1:166,17–18), SC 28.2 (SBO 1:193,11), SC 70.5 (SBO 2:210,11). The expression is based on the Vulgate Wis 7:26, although Bernard usually replaces *vitae* with *lucis,* so that his description of wisdom is *candor lucis aeternae.*
111. SC 75.4 (SBO 2:249,18).
112. SC 24.8 (SBO 1:162,5–6).
113. SC 21.2 (SBO 1:123,15–17).
114. SC 27.3 (SBO 1:184,6–9). On the perspective described in this paragraph, cf. M. Casey, 'St Benedict's Approach to Prayer', CSt 15 (1980) 327–343.

Such conformity marries the soul to the Word. It is similar to him by nature, but it needs to show itself similar to him through the assent of the will, loving as it is itself loved.[115]

There is a strong ethical perspective in Bernard's mystical stance.[116] The grace of God is impeded by human refusal to accept its implications in the sphere of the practical. Everything depends on assent: experience of God, growth in spirituality, the practice of virtue, the attainment of contemplation, the realisation of ultimate potential.

To meditate on and to desire what is above is uprightness. In its completeness it can be defined by experience and by the act of the will. In my view, you are upright if you have a correct sense of things and if your actions are in harmony with this experience. The state of the mind is beyond sight; it can only be known through faith and action.[117]

It is through efforts in the behavioural sphere that the human being principally strives to please God. In making this his goal he is animated by the same burning zeal as the angels and demonstrates that 'he is a citizen of the saints and a member of God's household'.[118] For, 'a holy soul is, itself, a heaven'.[119]

The working of grace is manifested through the *ordinatio caritatis,* the re-insertion of the human being into the order of reality willed by God.

---

115. SC 83.3 (SBO 2:299,21–23).

116. Cf. W. Williams, 'L'aspect éthique du mysticisme de saint Bernard', in *Son Temps 2,* pp. 308–318. William O. Paulsell, 'Ethical Theory [*sic:* the table of contents has 'ethical theology'] in the Sermons on the Song of Songs,' in *Chimaera,* pp. 12–22.

117. SC 24.7 (SBO 1:159,8–12). Cf. A. Forest, 'L'expérience du consentement selon S. Bernard', COCR 18 (1956), 269–275.

118. SC 27.7 (SBO 1:187,8–11).

119. SC 27.8 (SBO 1:187,18).

> Love is a great thing, so long as it runs back to its
> own beginning, returns to its origin and flows back
> toward its source, since this is where it continually
> draws the content of its own flow.[120]

In Bernard's mind there was no doubt that such an establishment of priorities and the subjection of all loves to
Love was absolutely necessary for growth.[121] The result of
such regulation of affections is an increased sensitivity to
the presence of God and a heightened ability to discern
his will. The person develops a sort of homing instict, an
ability to decide, among plural possibilities, which leads
directly to heaven. One who is wise follows his own
heart, knowing that it has a feeling for what is of God.[122]

The *ordinatio caritatis* is possible only if the human being experiences a conversion, a turning toward the hope of
future glory. The two actions are complementary. It is impossible to be filled with zeal for heaven without renouncing alternative affections,[123] and leaving unfulfilled the
desires of the flesh.[124] 'If you eliminate what is superfluous,
an awareness of what leads to salvation will emerge.'[125]
Observance of the precepts of God may seem like a very
humble and external task, but it causes a sensitivity to
spiritual realities to blossom in the soul, restoring it to the
insight which sin had caused to recede.[126] When a human

120. SC 83.4 (SBO 2:300,26–29).

121. SC 49.5 (SBO 2:75,27). On this theme, see M. Standaert, 'Le
principe de l'ordination dans la theologie spirituelle de s. Bernard',
COCR 8 (1946) 176–216.

122. SC 85.9 (SBO 2:313,12–14), Bernard notes that those who
follow their hearts are either rogues or sages. On the difficulties of
discernment, cf. SC 32.5 (SBO 1:229,13–25).

123. SC 83.6 (SBO 2:302,1): *cunctis renuntians affectionibus.*

124. SC 31.6 (SBO 1:223,6–8).

125. SC 58.10 (SBO 2:134,12–13).

126. SC 28.7 (SBO 1:197,1–2).

being orders his life, he resumes his proper rank in the *ordo* of creation and thus, once again, is in contact with heaven and thus able to be influenced and renewed thereby. Heaven is not only a future. As far as Bernard was concerned, it is also another region which co-exists with the present, which is able to infuse spirituality into human affairs whenever the relationship between them is right.

Bernard emphasised the role of self-awareness in human spiritual growth. A life lived in accordance with a healthy conscience is supremely happy. It is a paradise: *paradisus bonae conscientiae.*[127] Virtue is its own reward since to act in accordance with conscience brings with it a sense of belonging to God, irrespective of the pain and suffering externally occasioned.

Conscience was understood by Bernard as the dwelling-place of God, where God comes into contact with the human being. He described it in terms of the bridal chamber,[128] and of the marriage bed itself.[129] It is, above all, the area in which the Holy Spirit is active, watering human sterility so that it bear fruit,[130] reminding the human being of the divine adoption and all that this entails.[131] Conscience speaks with all the authority of God; it is not subject to the individual's control.[132] The degree of strength with which it utters sentence is an indication of the extent to which heavenly

127. Par 1.1 (SBO 6b:261,9–10).
128. SC 46.9 (SBO 2:61,13). On Bernard's teaching on this matter see, P. Delhaye, 'La conscience morale dans la doctrine de saint Bernard', *Théologien*, pp. 209–222. This was later expanded into a short monograph, *Le Problème de la conscience morale chez S. Bernard*, Analecta Mediaevalia (Namur, 1957).
129. SC 47.2 (SBO 2:63,1).
130. SC 18.5 (SBO 1:107,8–11).
131. SC 8.9 (SBO 1:41,17–18), OS 2.3 (SBO 5:344,13–19).
132. Ep 7.11 (SBO 7:39,5–23).

life flourishes within. The voice of conscience becomes stronger in proportion as a will is fundamentally turned to God. Conscience always takes God's side in any question and does not hesitate to chastise those who act against his will,[133] intervening with a severity sufficient to 'terrify even a seasoned warrior'.[134]

A good conscience is a foretaste of paradise, a conscience not followed is a sort of hell,[135] a prison where the soul is tortured by reason and memory.[136] It is the task of conscience so to 'gnaw' at the sinner as to make his life unbearable with the end in view that, as his tolerance diminishes, he might consider repentance.[137]

A darkened conscience will yearn for any sight in heaven or on earth, but this is impossible. Darkness cannot hide one's own self. Such ones still see themselves even though they can see nothing else. The works of darkness follow them, and not even darkness itself can sufficiently envelop them. Once such works of darkness have found entry into a human being (though, in one sense, they are also innate), they remain and nothing can eliminate them and, so, conscience will never cease its nibbling.[138]

The paradise of a good conscience belongs only to those who have complied with the precepts of God's law with a right intention. It is only to the extent that the actions performed flow from the inner centre of the human being and express his fundamental love for God that

133. Ep 7.9 (SBO 7:37,14).
134. Tpl 3 (SBO 3:216,19).
135. Asspt 4.4 (SBO 5:247,9): *infernus quidam et carcer animae rea conscientia est.*
136. Asspt 2.4 (SBO 5:234,10–11).
137. The verb used is *remordere*. Thus Ep 7.3 (SBO 7:37,14), Ep 253.3 (SBO 8:151,16), Pre 49 (SBO 3:287,7–8).
138. Csi 5.25 (SBO 3:488,11–17).

they produce in the subject an anticipation of heavenly bliss. The search for God both in its immediate and ultimate forms demands an act of assent from the seeker. This conscious and deliberate act of the will is further reinforced by actions expressive of this consent. The search for God and the desire to be united with him can be regarded as being pursued in good faith only to the extent that the human being strives to live conformably to that endeavour. Those who live thus already experience something of heaven.

The Monastic Paradise

Monastic life was also understood by Bernard as a means by which future beatitude was gradually realised in the course of temporal existence. The monastery was, for him, a *paradisus claustralis,* an expression which Gilson insists means 'a paradise not *the* paradise'.[139]

The basis of this idea was the conception that it was the monk, *par excellence,* who was called upon to live a heavenly life. It was to him, above all, that Phil 3:20 could be applied. Bernard describes himself as 'a monk and a citizen of Jerusalem',[140] and it was because monks were attached to the true Jerusalem that they were not permitted to leave their monasteries in order to visit the earthly city.[141]

I think that the Prophet is designating by the name 'Jerusalem' those who, in this world, live the religious life, imitating as best they can the manner of life which is characteristic of the Jerusalem which is above.[142]

139. Cf Div 42.4 (SBO 6a:256,16). See also Gilson, *Mystical Theology,* p. 91.
140. SC 55.2 (SBO 2:112,25). Cf. SC 27.7 (SBO 1:186,28).
141. Ep 459 (SBO 8:437,14–15). Cf. Ep 544 (SBO 8:511–512).
142. SC 55.2 (SBO 2:112,19–21).

A series of antitheses in another context makes the point even clearer: 'From the throne to the sewer, from heaven to the manger, from the monastery to the world, from paradise to hell. . .'.[143] Monastic life, expecially in it cistercian form, lay always at the centre of Bernard's thinking. He was, perhaps unconsciously, something of an elitist: he believed that there was no surer way to heaven. Monastic profession was like a second baptism which restored the tarnished divine likeness to tis pristine brilliance.[144] Monks are able to live their lives under constant instruction in heavenly discipline.[145] 'The bed of rest typifies cloisters and monasteries, where it is possible to live quietly away from the cares of the world and the worries of human life.'[146] It is this lack of turmoil and anxiety which seemed to him to be the specific characteristic of the cloister, evoking as it does, the very atmosphere of heaven.[17] The image of Mary as against Martha and Lazarus,[158] and that of Rachel as against Leah,[149] come readily to Bernard's mind as scriptural confirmations of his point of view—notwithstanding the fact that he himself seems to have experienced precious little of such carefree quiet.

At the heart of this theme is the idea that since the monk has refused to live at the level of the world and the

143. SC 63.6 (SBO 2:165,22–28).
144. Cf. Pre 54 (SBO 3:388–389). See also, J. Leclercq, 'Tradition, Baptism and Profession: The Genesis and Evolution of the Consecrated Life', Aspects pp. 71–98.
145. SC 27.7 (SBO 1:186,19).
146. SC 46.1 (SBO 2:56,18–19).
147. SC 46.4 (SBO 2:57,28).
148. E.g. SC 57.10–11 (SBO 2:125–126). Cf. Daniel Csanyí, 'Optima Pars: Die Auslegungsgeschichte von Lk 10.38–42 bei den Kirchenvaetern der ersten vier Jahrhunderte', StMon 2 (1960) 5–78.
149. For instance, SC 46.5 (SBO 2:58,21).

flesh, he has, in some sense, permitted himself to be freed and so lifted up to the level of heaven.[150] Bernard uses the fact that some people can live such a life to demonstrate the possibility of liberation from necessity and to ground his assertion that all human beings ultimately aspire for lofty things.[151]

Monastic life is aimed at a certain purity of heart which is the means of access to the vision of God.[152] As such it strives to be an 'angelic life',[153] not in the sense of being inhumanly or impractically spiritualist, but in the sense of being totally alive with the divine, just as Mary, the mother of Jesus, was.[154] Human destiny is placed between that of the angels and that of the beasts; each person has to decide in which category he will cast his lot.[155] Bernard believed that the monk was, above all, someone who willingly and energetically gave himself to living on the side of the angels.[156]

The Third Heaven

Another area which reveals heavenly life unfolding in time is that of mystical experience, occasionally referred

150. Cf. Dil 11 (SBO 3:127,19–20).
151. SC 27.6 (SBO 1:185,22–26).
152. SC 28.5 (SBO 1:95,28).
153. Apo 24 (SBO 3:101,7–8).
154. Asspt 4.6 (SBO 5:249,1).
155. SC 5.5 (SBO 1:23,22–24).
156. Cf. Garcia M. Colombas, *Paradise et vie angélique: Le sens eschatologique de la vocation chrétienne* (Paris: Cerf, 1961) especially the section running pp. 231–252. A. Lamy, 'Bios angelikos', *Dieu Vivant* 7 (1946) 59–77. J. Leclercq, 'Monasticism and Angelism', *Aspects*, pp. 151–162. This article gives references to other contributions to the discussion from the same author. Louis Bouyer, *The Meaning of Monastic Life* (trans. Kathleen Pond) (London: Burns & Oates, 1955) pp. 23–40. V. Ranke-Heinemann, 'Zum

to by Bernard in terms of St Paul's reference to his being rapt to the third heaven (2 Cor 12:2). As far as Bernard was concerned, contemplation is a matter of being lifted up beyond the confinement of earthly existence into the unrestrained freedom of heavenly life. It is an *excessus*, a state of self-transcendence, the experiental foretaste of the *unitas spiritus* realised through the kiss of the Word. The experience of *excessus* is proper to the next life, since it is not there undermined by the exigencies of bodily existence. In this life, however, some rudimentary form of *excessus* is possible, limited according to the degree of spiritual freedom enjoyed.

Gilson was of the opinion that the term came from Erigena's translation of the *Ambigua* of Maximus the Confessor. This seems hardly demonstrable since the expression has a perfectly ordinary background in Old and New Testaments, in John Cassian and Gregory the Great.[157]

Ideal der *vita angelica* im frühen Mönchtum', GuL 29 (1956) 347–357. E. von Severus, '*Bios Angelikos*. Zum Verständnis des Mönchslebens als "Engelleben" in der christliches Ueberlieferung', in *Die Engel in der Welt von heute*, Liturgie und Mönchtim, 21 (Maria Laach, 1957) pp. 56–70.

157. Cf. Gilson, *Mystical Theology*, p. 26. The key texts in the history of *excessus mentis* as far as Bernard is concerned seem to be Ps 67:28 (*Ibi Beniamin adolescentulus, in mentis excessu*) and 2 Cor 5:13 (*mente excedimus*). The term occurs regularly in Cassian. *Inst* 2.10.1 (SChr 109:74: *per excessum mentis*), *Inst* 2.10.2 (SChr 109:76: *interrumpat nostrae orationis excessum*), *Inst* 3.3.4 (SChr 109:96: *in excessu mentis*), *Inst* 3.3.7 (SChr 109:100: *in excessu mentis*), *Conf* 9.14 (SChr 54:51: *per ineffabiles excessus domino refert*), *Conf* 9.31 (SChr 54:66: *in excessu mentis* — said of the prayer of St Antony), *Conf* 19.5 (SChr 64:42: *ad caelestes illos rapiebamur excessus*). The phrase also occurs in Gregory the Great, for instance, *In Ezek* 1.5.12 (PL 76:826c), and in the Middle English mystical tradition. Cf. Wolfgang Riehle, *The Middle English Mystics* (London: Routledge & Kegan Paul, 1981) pp. 92–94. The whole of chapter 7, 'Technical terms for the mystical union and for ecstasy', is worth reading.

Bernard views 'theoric contemplation'[158] as something which seizes the human mind and carries it off (*rapitur*).[159] During this state, the mind is suspended or held aloft.[160] It is introduced into an unaccustomed spaciousness.[161] There is an interruption of the activities of the senses and a movement away from the priorities of sensual life.[162] This can be described as a sort of death in which the soul is snatched away from itself and the mind soars upward, going beyond all ordinary mental processes.[163]

The effect of this state of self-transcendence is not produced by an exercise of the will or by employment of special skills on the part of the individual. It is not the ultimate moment of performance. It is achieved only by love. It is really quite simple. For a time the person so loves the Word that he forgets himself.

In this latter kind [of spiritual marriage] there is, now and then, an experience of *excessus* and a recession from bodily senses so that *the soul is so aware of the Word that it is no longer aware of itself.* This happens when the mind, enticed by the unimaginable sweetness of the Word is, somehow, stolen from itself. It is seized and snatched away from itself so that it may find pleasure in the Word.[164]

Bernard noted that this experience finds expression in two ways. It is, at once, the experience of the inpouring of light into the understanding and the infusion of devotion. The former gives comprehension to the mind so that it is able to understand the Scriptures and know all mysteries. The

158. SC 23.3 (SBO 1:140,19–20), SC 23.9 (SBO 1:144,25).
159. SC 62.4 (SBO 2:158,4), SC 85.13 (SBO 2:315,25).
160. SC 27.12 (SBO 1:190,26).
161. SC 57.8 (SBO 2:124,9).
162. SC 52.4 (SBO 2:92,17).
163. SC 52.4 (SBO 2:92,9–15). This is, as far as I can presently determine, Bernard's only use of *exstasis*.
164. SC 85.13 (SBO 2:315–316,3).

latter brings affective warmth, the sense of being devoured by a burning fire with the consequent consumption of vice and purification from its effects.[165]

Contemplation was viewed by Bernard as a means by which wayfarers to paradise are fed.[166] It corresponds to the vision of God which, in heaven, sustains the life of the blessed. It is the means by which the human being while on earth, obtains some access to the things of heaven,[167] even to the highest realities,[168] and to something of the mystery of the deity itself.[169]

The heavenly character of contemplation is, in Bernard's view, illustrated by a second distinction which he made between contemplation which has the 'state and the happiness and the glory of the heavenly city' for its object, and that which is concentrated more directly on the 'majesty, eternity or divinity of the King himself'.[170] What he seems to be saying is that in our present condition we cannot have God as the direct object of our contemplative intuition. What we are looking at is, rather, the cloudier and more diffuse object, which is heaven itself. In this life it is not possible to look directly upon God.

There is a forthright passage in the treatise *On Grace and Free Choice* which gives Bernard's view that contemplation is a real, though fleeting, participation in heavenly blessedness.

THAT THE LIBERTY OF BLISS IS EXPERIENCED BY THOSE
WHO ARE LIFTED UP IN THE ACT OF CONTEMPLATION

What is to be said of those who are sometimes

165. SC 49.4 (SBO 2:75,19–21). SC 57.8 (SBO 2:124,6–10) seems to suggest that the intellective stage is later.
166. SC 48.7 (SBO 2:72,10–13), SC 33.6 (SBO 1:238,8–9).
167. SC 35.2 (SBO 1:250,30–251,1).
168. SC 22.1 (SBO 1:122,10).
169. SC 49.4 (SBO 2:75,14–15): *ad id divini arcani.*
170. SC 62.4 (SBO 2:157,13–16).

snatched away in the Spirit through the self-transcendence of contemplation, and who are, thus, able
to experience something of the sweetness of heavenly joy? Do they experience this freedom from
unhappiness as often as this takes place? It is not to
be denied that these, though they are still in the
flesh, do enjoy the liberty of bliss, even though the
experience is rare and very brief. They, like Mary,
have chosen the better part, and it shall not be
taken away from them. Those who, in the present,
hold on to what is not to be taken from them, certainly experience what is future. And what is future
is happiness, and since happiness and unhappiness
cannot co-exist, therefore, when the Spirit allows
them to share such happiness, then they enjoy the
liberty of bliss, even though this is partial experience, very deficient relative to the full experience, and also exceeding rare.[171]

Contemplation is a foretaste of the delights of
heaven. Many of the images discussed in the previous
chapter are, accordingly, applied by Bernard to the contemplative experience. In some texts it can be difficult to
decide whether, in fact, he is talking about one to the exclusion of the other.

The primary effect of growth in love for the Word
and a deepening prayerfulness is an increase in quiet,
stillness, and calm, both during prayer and generally.
The soul firmly attached to the Word gradually becomes
immune to disturbance from passion, external events,
ambition, and diabolical incitements to despair. Thus in
its love for him, the soul grows quiet, wrapped about

171. Gra 15 (SBO 3:177,4–15). 'Liberty of bliss' renders *libertas
complaciti* and 'freedom from unhappiness' its synonym *libertas a
miseria*. 'The self-transcendence of contemplation' translates *excessus contemplationis*.

with gentleness and freedom from upset.'[172]

In his shadow I sit. To sit means to be quiet. It is a greater thing to rest in the shadow than simply to live in it, just as it is a greater thing to live in it than merely to exist in it.[173]

To qualify the state of contemplation, Bernard employed a range of words commonly found in the monastic tradition with reference to such matters.[174] This includes, *quies* (quiet),[175] *sedere* (to sit),[176] *securitas* (safety),[177] *dormire* (to sleep),[178] *vacare* (to be disengaged),[179] and *otium* (leisure).[180] What Bernard was describing when he spoke of 'rest' is not mere pious somnolence, nor is it vague oceanic feeling of non-identity. It is not a state of blankness characterised by mental void and lack of feeling. It is inactivity only in the sense that it is an intense state of being acted upon. The soul is not doing anything because all its resources are involved in responding to what is acting upon it. It is true that, in this state, the soul has stopped responding to lower stimuli, and this produces measurable changes on the physiological level. It is important to note that this desensitisation is not an end in itself; it is the automatic effect

172. SC 77.5 (SBO 2:264,29).
173. SC 48.8 (SBO 2:72,16–17).
174. Cf. J. Leclercq, *Otia* and *Vocabulaire*.
175. SC 18.6 (SBO 1:107,15), SC 23.11 (SBO 1:146,13), SC 23.15 (SBO 1:148,16), SC 23.16 (SBO 1:149,16–20), SC 33.6 (SBO 1:238,8–9), SC 41.5 (SBO 2:31,17), SB 48.8 (SBO 2.72,16–17), SC 51.10 (SBO 2:89,19–20), SC 52.6 (SBO 2:94,11), SC 53.1 (SBO 2:95,4), SC 75.5 (SBO 2:204,29).
176. SC 12.8 (SBO 1:65,17), SC 23.16 (SBO 1:149,16–20), SC 48.8 (SBO 2:72,16–17).
177. SC 33.6 (SBO 1:238,8–9), SC 47.4 (SBO 2:64,10).
178. SC 18.6 (SBO 1:107,16–17), SC 47.4 (SBO 2:64,10).
179. SC 10.9 (SBO 1:53,4), SC 22.3 (SBO 1:131,1).
180. SC 18.6 (SBO 1:108,5), Sent 3.121 (SBO 6b:229,18).

of a higher sensitisation. The soul becomes so involved in the spiritual order that there is a total lack of interest or concern in everything else — and this psychological attitude transposes itself onto the physical plane if it reaches completion. At heart, contemplation is a penetrating moment of perception which conveys something of the beauty and attractiveness of God which has the result of distracting the mind and the heart from absolutely everything else.[181]

Liberty of spirit and purity of heart are not ends in themselves, they are means to produce transparency of soul so that, on the one hand, the whole human being is irradiated with the glory of God and, on the other, it is totally taken up in recognising God's condescension and in praising him for it.[182] The soul is totally absorbed in God, it exists in a *stupor,* a state of wonder and amazement which nothing lesser can disturb.[183] When he is carried away by such wonder, the human being becomes one with the angels.[184]

The gift of contemplation is not something which is precipitated immediately and without effort. It is the by-product of a long history of co-operation with God.[185] A contemplative is 'a soul which not only lives for Christ but has already done so for a long time': *cui vivere Christus non tantum sit, sed et diu iam fuerit.*[186] Contemplation demands fervour and a zeal for progress.[187] It requires patience and the ability to wait since, 'it was through the odour of waiting that [Simeon] came to the

181. SC 22.3 (SBO 1:131,1).
182. Cf. SC 10.9 (SBO 1:53,2-5).
183. SC 23.11 (SBO 1:46,6-7).
184. SC 19.3 (SBO 1:110,16-20).
185. SC 27.11 (SBO 2:126,16-22).
186. SC 69.1 (SBO 2:202,11-12).
187. SC 49.7 (SBO 2:77,27-28).

taste of contemplation.'[188] If contemplative experience is a foretaste of the heavenly banquet, then the ability to await God's time with a quiet mind is also the 'odour' which anticipates the tasting. Preparedness to wait is the prelude of visitation. This is why Mary, who sat at the feet of Christ, is the model of contemplative expectation.[189]

In fidelity to his benedictine heritage, Bernard did not view contemplation as some phase of experience which could be achieved through education in appropriate skills or by the learning of techniques for the manipulation or dismantling of the processes of consciousness. It is, at root, the work of love. Such love begins as something conscious and even self-conscious, but as it grows it tends to become incarnate throughout the whole of a person's life, suffusing both disposition and behaviour with its warmth. Without love there is no contemplative experience, since no one can withdraw from self unless attracted to another. Contemplation cannot be produced directly, it is simply the fine point of a life lived in substantial and sustained conformity with the teaching of the Gospels.

Wisdom — Outshining of Eternal Light

The occasional intoxication of the contemplative experience[190] leaves a residue in the soul which acts as a leaven, secretly seasoning conduct and attitudes with a lingering sense of the divine. It is this which is at the very heart of Bernard's notion of wisdom; rather than one able to deliver answers, he conceives the sage as one with a taste for the spiritual, a sort of affinity with the

188. SC 67.6 (SBO 2:192,18–19).
189. SC 12.8 (SBO 1:65,17).
190. Cf. Div 87.4 (SBO 6a:331–332), Sent 2.166 (SBO 6b:55, 14–17).

divine, which enables him to perceive its presence amid a
welter of persuasive alternatives.

Sermon eighty-five is especially devoted to the pursuit of wisdom and to its growth.[191] Wisdom is presented
as a breath of eternal life which purifies the spiritual sensibilities of the human being and gives him the capacity
to become more interested in what is beyond sensation
and gratification.

Wisdom energetically overcomes malice in the
minds which it enters and eliminates the taste for
evil introduced by Eve and replaces it with a taste for
what is better. When wisdom enters, it makes a fool
of the fleshly sense. It purifies the understanding
and restores the palate of the heart.[192]

As was true with most writers in the latin tradition, the
connection between *sapientia* and *sapor* was never very
far from Bernard's mind. The idea of wisdom as a taste,
constantly recurs.

What taste is to the palate, wisdom is to the heart.
Do not, therefore, seek for wisdom in the eye of the
flesh, because flesh and blood do not reveal it, but
only the Spirit does that.[193]

It is through the Word who is wisdom that we are
gradually reformed according to wisdom.[194] Because he is
the outshining of eternal life and the figure of God's
substance,[195] it is his specific task to form the soul which he
visits in wisdom.[196] This is not an intellectual enterprise,

191. Cf. Bernard Piault, 'Le désir de la sagesse: Itinéraire de l'âme à
Dieu chez S. Bernard dans le sermon LXXXV sur le Cantique des cantiques', COCR 36 (1974) 24–44.

192. SC 85.8 (SBO 2:313,3–6).

193. SC 28.8 (SBO 1:197,14–16).

194. SC 85.7 (SBO 2:311,20–21).

195. SC 70.5 (SBO 2:210,11).

196. SC 69.2 (SBO 2:203,1–2): *erudire in sapientia.*

but a question of experience and initiation. 'The result of instruction is learned persons; it is experience which makes them wise.'[197] The Word gives to human beings the taste for what is divine; when they acquire this taste, then they are wise. *Sapor sapientem fecit:* 'It is taste which makes one wise'.[198] It is through wisdom that experience and activity are infused with eternal truth.[199] Therefore, although wisdom is the product of leisure, it is not idle. It is busy in reforming the human being and re-orienting his behaviour so as to lead him more directly to salvation.[200] Just as the Word permitted his light to be dimmed when he allowed it to be incarnate in flesh, so Wisdom adapts its brilliance to the benighted state of unredeemed humanity, inserting itself into the weakness of the human being so as to liberate him from what inhibits his growth, and thus to introduce him into the heavenly life.[201]

THE NEGATIVE PRINCIPLE

Part of the dynamic of desire is generated by the experience of the progressive realisation of its goal. The manifold ways in which union with God is achieved contribute toward building up a momentum which motivates and stimulates the soul in the continuance of its quest.

But spiritual growth is not, for Bernard, a matter of pure and unchallenged progress. It is a sustained struggle against weariness and discouragement, and a constant

197. SC 23.14 (SBO 1:147,24): *Instructio doctos reddit, affectio sapientes.*
198. SC 23.14 (SBO 1:148,7-8).
199. SC 50.8 (SBO 2:83,11-16).
200. SC 85.8 (SBO 2:312,17-18).
201. Cf. SC 28.2 (SBO 1:193,11).

effort to resist the allurement of alternative attractions. 'The languor of the soul is very great, and so is the difficulty of returning [to God].'[202] In growth under grace, the soul is not only aided by the anticipation of heavenly realities; its progress is also enhanced by its negative experiences. Oppression, opposition, indifference, discouragement, temptation, failure, and perceived decline may not seem like the stuff from which spiritual attainment emerges. But as the soul recognises its liabilities and grapples with the mystery of resistance to grace within itself, it comes to realise that without such compost growth is unlikely.

Bernard was under no illusion about the difficulty of even making a beginning. The first negative experience to be faced in responding to grace is the pain involved in reversing one's priorities in life. But development also brings it share of hardship, since it is a matter of constantly leaving behind what is familiar and reaching forth into the unknown. There is the difficutly involved in alternation itself and in the gentle acceptance that it is not, in this life, entirely possible to be uncompromised. Waiting on God, without turning to other gratifications and without losing courage and confidence, is not an easy task. The fact that human life is a prolonged warfare, beset with temptations and necessarily marked by failure and rejection, can be a source of great mental confusion.

Thus, in Bernard's view, there are many factors which make creative effort in the matter of human and spiritual growth hard and distasteful. This is not to say that he believed that things are profitable to the extent that they hurt. It is, rather, an affirmation that feeling is not always a clear guide in diagnosing states and discerning between

202. SC 84.3 (SBO 2:304,20).

choices. Where feeling alone is followed, many aspects of the human experience of seeking God will be denuded of meaning; confusion, insecurity and despair will be the result. 'Follow the judgement of faith, and not your own experience': *Iudicium fidei sequere, et non experimentum tuum.*[203]

> O how desirable is that weakness which is made up for by the power of Christ. Who will grant me not only to be weak, but to be totally destitute and to fail completely on my own resources, so that I may be sustained by the power of the Lord of hosts.[204]

Being converted and turning to the Lord in a new way of life is not, as Bernard recognised, a mere moment of enthusiasm and spiritual exaltation, but a dread-filled beginning of a life-long process of re-orientation. Bernard was suspicious of excessive fervour in the young,[205] recognising that often the attractiveness of grace is tempered by an unexpressed reluctance in the face of the demands it will inevitably make. The main components of this initial phase are, in Bernard's view, contrition or compunction, and the recognition and admission or confession of sin.[206] The fact that this is a stable conviction on Bernard's part is clear from the appearance of these items at the head of his many numerical sequences.[207] The presence of these factors should be sought more on

203. Quad 5.5 (SBO 4:364,20–21).

204. SC 25.7 (SBO 1:167,21–24).

205. SC 19.7 (SBO 1:112,71–113,18). Cf. Par 3.1 (SBO 6b:274).

206. QH 11.9 (SBO 4:445,7).

207. Cf. SC 10.4 (SBO 1:50,21), SC 12.1 (SBO 1:60,9–11), SC 16. 4 (SBO 1:91–92), SC 18.6 (SBO 1:108,4–6), p Epi 1.4 (SBO 4: 317,1–10), Asspt 4.3 (SBO 5:245–246), Div 40.3 (SBO 6a: 236–243), Div 87.1 (SBO 6a:330,1–7), Div 90.1–3 (SBO 6a:337–339), Div 118(SBO 6a:396,8–12), Sent 1.9 (SBO 6b:9,15–17 = Sent 2.169 (SBO 6b:56,1–4), Sent 1.34 (SBO 6b:18–19).

the effective rather than the affective level. However, there may not be a great sense of disgust or regret with regard to one's past or present life. There may be no tears and little dread. Sometimes this is because repression has taken place, sometimes it is merely because certain people operate habitually at a lower level of emotional drama than others. In some cases the experience is so uncategorised that persons do not really develop a vocabulary for expressing it until much later. The important thing is that change takes place in real life. *Effectively* there is the recognition that the old ways cannot continue, and steps are taken—however sluggishly—to counter the momentum of previous habit. The feeling which motivates such a positive re-alignment it to be understood as being, at least diffusely, what Bernard was talking about in these texts.

Although human beings constantly pray for grace, it is strange that, on its arrival, they often experience great resistance. The individual's first encounter with graces causes bitterness and confusion of soul.[208] From the very beginning, there is the dim, dread recognition that the soul will have to be corrected and change from its previous ways, even though they had appeared harmless enough. It is, according to Bernard, only by this unpleasant but necessary re-ordering of priorities that the soul begins to seek the Word.[209]

> So it is that the very beginnings of our conversion, as we are informed by common experience, involve, at first, an arousal of fear which causes those about to enter to experience a horror at the narrowness of the life and at the unaccustomed harshness of its discipline.[210]

208. SC 10.6 (SBO 1:51,21).
209. SC 85.2 (SBO 2:308,15–16). Cf. Piault, 'Le désir de la sagesse', p. 25.
210. SC 33.11 (SBO 1:241,21–23).

The soul's first tendency is to reject what it considers to be an imposition from outside itself. About to make a generous gesture, it is unwilling to be reminded of its own imperfections — its lack of application, its purity of intent marred by a need for praise, its hypocrisy and its indiscretion.[211] It refuses to be realistic. On the one hand it is too ambitious; on the other it is too easily depressed by its own liabilities and failures. This interplay of false fears and hopes causes it to draw back from self-understanding,[212] seeking to sink into the state of mindlessness it hitherto enjoyed. This is why the new convert needs, above all, to be formed in genuine humility — not only to secure more rapid progress, in the abstract, but to help him to develop a healthier attitude to life which will prevent his becoming depressed.

The soul making a beginning is called upon to demonstrate two special virtues. It must allow its previous experience to be questioned, renouncing the relative security of former familiar experiences and values. It needs to be prepared really to make a new beginning. Secondly, it must be willing to accept from God's hand whatever he sends, be it weal or woe. Right from the start it must submit to the painful process of pruning, whereby all that previously brought joy is cut off. At the same time it has no idea how long the purification will continue or how extensive its ravages will be.[213] There is a further problem. It is

211. SC 33.11–13 (SBO 1:241–243).
212. Sent 1.24 (SBO 6b:15,19–21).
213. SC 58.4 (SBO 2:129,11–12). Cf. Sent 1.10 (SBO 6b:10, 1–3). Bernard's teaching is worth comparing with the common monastic teaching on renunciation. The radical renunciation of property, family, and prospects is required at the very beginning of a monastic career, but the demands of self-spoliation will continue to assert themselves and the monk has to labour to build on the foundations he has so painfully laid. Thus Benedict's understanding of ascent through humility follows Cassian. Humility is the means by

not only beginners who make beginnings. All through life each person has to make up for what was lacking in the original act of conversion. It is permitted us in our weakness to change the direction of life substantially, without attending to all the implications of our action. Eventually, however, we have to attend to all of these. So it is that the beginnings of our life with God are prolonged indefinitely, and time and time again we have to re-commence. It is, as it were, like having a conversion on time-payment.

If it is true that, at the best of times, no more than glimmers of the divine light penetrate to the earthly sphere,[214] then it is especially to be expected that the early stages of spiritual and monastic development will be characterised by much darkness, in which sensible pleasures are no longer available and initiation into spiritual realities is, as yet, radically incomplete. There is a void between the end of the sensual and the beginning of the spiritual. The temptation follows that, if nothing seems to be forthcoming from God, one looks for some gratification from what one has previously renounced. But even this brings no great relief from the prevailing heaviness of heart.

> Many of you, I recall, have mentioned to me in private discussions, a similar heaviness and dryness of soul, and a weakness or dullness of mind which is not yet able to penetrate the deep and subtle mysteries of God. You have spoken of how little or

---

which renunciation (which is presupposed) is converted into perfect love. This is to say there is an interval between giving up one's goods and being totally possessed by God. The various phenomenological indications (or *indicia*, as Cassian says) that progress is being made are represented by the rungs of the ladder of humility.

214. SC 57.8 (SBO 2:124,14–16).

nothing of the sweetness of the Spirit is experienced. What is the state of such persons if not one of yearning for the kiss [of the bridegroom]? It is a fact that such ones are yearning and longing for the Spirit of wisdom and understanding—understanding so that they may comprehend, wisdom so that they may savour what they have understood.[215]

The *ennui* and dissatisfaction typical of the transition from a carnal life to spiritual endeavour is thus interpreted by Bernard as a form of desire. Not a pleasant, ardent outpouring of love, but a heavy deadness which is disconsolate at its distance from the goal and yet, mysteriously, unwilling to give itself to its former pursuits. This state of experienced deprivation Bernard interprets as an ache for the divine presence at the level of being. Instead of repressing an awareness of its condition, the soul needs to accept it, identify its true nature, and willingly embrace its movement so that the whole being becomes a single agonised call for the coming of God. 'When the Word leaves the soul, the enduring desire for him becomes one sustained cry until he come, "Return!".'[216] The worst possible thing to do is to blot out the sense of boredom by all sorts of novelties. In this way the solution is kept at a distance and the pain is unnecessarily prolonged.

To endure this negative state without being engulfed by unprofitable sadness is not easy.[217] What is most important is that the soul does not believe itself to be abandoned by grace in these circumstances and so find itself tempted to abandon the spiritual pursuit and return to a life which is more gratifying at a carnal level.[218] There is

215. SC 9.3 (SBO 1:43,28–44,4).
216. SC 74.2 (SBO 2:241,4–6).
217. SC 37.1 (SBO 2:14,20).
218. SC 35.1 (SBO 1:249,25–28).

scope here for the neglected virtue of endurance, based on confidence in God and in the knowledge coming from one's fellow-travellers that this is a normal and recurrent experience. And there is no obligation to enjoy it.

Bernard himself was prone to periods of disenchantment with the spiritual and describes the way in which the state was terminated.

> I am not ashamed to admit that, especially at the beginning of my monastic life, I often found that I was hard-hearted and cold in my search for the one whom my soul loves. I was not able to love him because I had not yet found him. My love was less than I would have wished it to be, and I sought him so that I might love him more — for I would not have sought him at all if I did not love him at least a little.
>
> So I sought him, in whom my weary and torpid spirit might find warmth and rest. Nowhere was there anyone who could help me, who could cause the cold winter which bound up my inner senses to yield. There was none who could bring back the gentle softness of a spiritual spring.
>
> I became more and more listless and filled with weariness, and my soul fell asleep from very boredom. I was sad and almost in despair, and I used to say to myself, 'Who can withstand the blast of his coldness?'[219]

Bernard then went on to narrate that this spell of depression was broken either by the edifying sight of some good person or through some mental inspiration. But he was convinced that it was due to God's action rather than to his own industry or merit that the sadness was dissolved and replaced with joy. He noted, however, that this period of gloom was of great utility in forming him to

219. SC 14.6 (SBO 1:79,19–80,2).

an appropriate humility and in increasing the degree of his dependence on God and of mistrust in his own skills.

Another text which speaks of such experiences as though they were well-known to Bernard's readers develops the theme of self-forgetfulness. Sadness comes from a pre-occupation with self, with more interest in receiving than in giving. To fight sadness one must be drawn out by confidence in Providence and by the willingness to wait placidly for the action of God.

> Therefore my advice to you, friends, is to turn aside from troubled and anxious reflection on your own progress, and escape to the easier paths of remembering the good things which God has done. In this way, instead of becoming upset by thinking about yourself, you will find relief by turning your attention to God.
>
> I want you to experience the truth of the Prophet's words, 'If you find your delight in the Lord, he will grant you your heart's desire'. Sorrow for sin is a necessary thing, but it should not prevail all the time. It is necessary, rather, that happier recollections of the divine bounty should counter-balance it, lest the heart should become hardened through too much sadness, and so perish through despair.[220]

The human being is always less than totally responsive to spiritual realities, especially in the earlier stages of development. There is always a tendency for him to lose his drive, to become too passive, powerless, unable to move or be moved, prone to an overwhelming spiritual sloth.[221] In such situations — and they are carefully to be

---

220. SC 11.12 (SBO 1:55,12–19). Cf. SC 32.4 (SBO 1:228,16–20), quoted in the previous chapter.

221. On this theme, see Siegfried Wenzel, *The Sin of Sloth: Acedia in Medieval Thought and Literature* (Chapel Hill: University of North Carolina Press, 1967).

distinguished from what we have been speaking about up to this point—a different stimulant is required. Whenever a soul finds itself tarrying at the junction, unable to go ahead and unwilling to decide between options—whether they are major or of minimal importance—Bernard saw the need for the gift of 'fear of the Lord'. If one is apathetic about reaching the goal one had accepted, it may be possible that this indifference needs to be acted upon by a salutary fear of the consequences of such immobility. Fear of the Lord is what starts one moving, it is what maintains one in motion when nothing else works, it is what keeps one faithful when the going is rough.

Central to the teaching of the monastic tradition on this theme is the text of Ps 110:10. 'To fear the Lord is the beginning of wisdom'. Fear of the Lord is a gift of the Holy Spirit which stimulates the soul to shake off all forgetfulness and to become active in putting into practice what it knows to be right. It is the opposite of a carefree, thoughtless existence where nothing is examined and anything allowed to happen. In the words of Benedict, it is flight from heedless living: *oblivionem omnino fugiat.*[222]

'The soul first begins to develop a taste for God when he strikes it with fear. It is not a question of his instructing it with knowledge.'[223] 'When you experience the conscience being scorched by the recollection of sins . . . then do not doubt that he himself is near, since fire goes before him and the Lord is near to those who are troubled in heart.'[224] Bernard continually notes that it is especially at times when the soul is not moved by an attraction for higher things that

222. RB 7.10. St Benedict discusses fear of the Lord in the context of humility, of which it is the first and fundamental indication. Cf. M. Casey, 'Mindfulness of God in the Monastic Tradition', CSt 17 (1982) 111–126.
223. SC 23.14 (SBO 1:148,5–6).
224. SC 57.6 (SBO 2:123,13–16).

fear has an important role to play. It intervenes to prevent material and carnal sources of gratification from exercising an unfair paramountcy in the absence of spiritual attraction. 'Fear is water which chills the heat of carnal desire.'[225] 'Fear is like an excellent arrow which pierces and kills carnal desires so the spirit may be safe.'[226]

> The fire which is God consumes, yet it does not wound; it burns gently and ravages to good effect. It is, certainly, a wasting coal, but its fiery power is directed toward vices; to the soul it acts as a soothing unction.[227]

The wound of fear is intended to produce compunction in the soul. 'You are well pierced if you are pierced by compunction. Many, when they feel this pain, amend their fault.'[228]

Fear of the Lord is closely connected, in Bernard's mind, with humility and vigilance and issues in a self-knowledge which is close to wisdom. It has the effect of rendering a person alert, diligent, and watchful of himself.[229] It is gained especially through contact with the Word of God in the Scriptures,[230] since before Christ can be experienced through sight he must be listened to in faith.[231] 'I wish that the Lord would open my ear, so that the word of truth might enter into my heart and purify my eye in preparation for that happy sight.'[232] Ultimately, fear of the Lord is based on the recognition of the holiness of God and of one's own unworthiness.

225. SC 54.12 (SBO 2:110,10–11).
226. SC 29.7 (SBO 1:208,8–9).
227. SC 57.7 (SBO 2:123,27–124,1).
228. SC 48.1 (SBO 2:67,21): *bene pungeris si compungeris.*
229. SC 48.1 (SBO 2:67,10–11), SC 54.9 (SBO 2:108,20–22).
230. SC 29.8 (SBO 1:208,12).
231. SC 28.6 (SBO 1:196,22–27).
232. SC 28.6 (SBO 1:196,12–13).

Fear looks to three things: to God's wisdom from which nothing is hidden; to God's power, to which all is possible; to God's justice which allows no sin to go unpunished. It is relative to these three qualities that that fear is born which purifies the hearts of human beings.[233]

Opposed to fear is a false sense of security, smugness, complacency. Even more so is that blatant brashness that acts as though God can be manipulated to acquiesce in petty acts of human autonomy. Bernard inveighed powerfully against such presumption, which he considered an affront to the majesty of God.

Consider how fearful and terrifying a thing it is to have despised the one who is Creator both of you and of all things, to have offended the Lord of majesty. All majesty is to be feared and all lordship is to be feared. How great, then, ought to be our fear of the Lord of majesty? If anyone offends the royal majesty he is, by the sentence of human laws, subject to capital punishment. What will be the outcome of one who despises the divine omnipotence? He is the One who touches the mountains and causes them to smoke. Does one valueless speck of dust, one slight breath which is easily dispersed and never seen again, does such a one dare to vex such fearful majesty? He only is the one to be feared who, after killing the body, has the power to send to hell.

I certainly fear hell. I fear the face of the One who is also the stern judge of the angelic powers. I tremble at his powerful wrath and at the anger of his countenance. I shake at the crash of a collapsing world, at the conflagration of the elements in a mighty storm, at the voice of the archangel and at the dread sentence. I tremble at the prospect of the infernal beast ready to devour, at hell's belly, where

233. Sent 3.119 (SBO 6b:217,28-30).

the demons prepare a feast. I shrink back from the gnawing teeth of the worm, from the river of fire, from the smoke, vapour and sulphur and from the blustering winds. I cringe at the prospect of being thrown out into exterior darkness.[234]

This thoroughly medieval evocation of hell reminds us that, as far as Bernard was concerned, the possibility of ultimate rejection and eternal punishment was a truth of faith not lightly to be set aside, and especially worth recalling when other inducements to fidelity lose their appeal. Fear of the Lord reminds us constantly of the outcome of our acts and omissions. By its operation we are enabled to discern what is eternally true and what is false. Fear consumes in us the attraction to what is base. It is intended to serve the advancement of what is good, not the undoing of whatever good has already been achieved.[235]

In the earlier section which dealt with the theme of alternation, we noted that Bernard often considered negative experience to have the effect of strengthening desire and increasing its intensity. The same holds for the fear which comes from God. It instills reverence in an otherwise greedy heart,[236] and throws light on the existence of pride and other vices which are in need of correction.[237] Through negative experience God ensures that the soul does not become complacent, satisfied with present tokens of love, instead of firmly fixing its eyes on the consummation which is ahead.[238]

Human life on earth is a sustained warfare, Bernard often quoted from the Book of Job.[239] The vocabulary he

234. SC 16.7 (SBO 1:93,16–94,1).
235. QH 6.2 (SBO 4:405,1–6).
236. SC 76.1 (SBO 2:255,5): *fruendi avida sed ignara mysterii.*
237. SC 54.10 (SBO 2:109,22–23).
238. Cf. Blanpain, 'Langage mystique', pp. 48–49.
239. For instance, SC 70.9 (SBO 2:213,17); cf. Job 7:1.

used for spiritual activity was drawn from that of military campaigning.[240] Trials and temptations cannot, therefore, be avoided in christian existence.[241] Bernard insisted on this because he realised that many are surprised on experiencing difficulty. They lose their nerve and so become a prey to even greater temptations, tedium, suspicion, impatience, gross sensuality, and eventually despair.[242] Everyone is invited to carry the cross of Christ, even those who appear outwardly as half-hearted.[243] Bernard was not trying to bring home to his readers a conviction of the universal misery of human existence. He was trying to remind them that pain cannot ultimately be avoided and that, therefore, rather than constantly attempting to minimise the pain of living, they should make some effort to spiritualise it, by associating it with the cross of Christ. Bernard sought to improve the subjective dispositions of his readers as they shoulder the burdens which life inevitably brings.

Negative experience is always possessed of a potential to advance spiritual growth; it can, accordingly, sometimes be experienced as meaningful, but it is *never* pleasant. Bernard does not offer a formula of instant transformation, but a lesson of hope and confidence in God, who brings good to the human race through many difficulties and reversals of fortune.

CONCLUDING REFLECTIONS

We have stated several times in the course of our discussion that Bernard's primary focus in his writing was practical or behavioural. For the most part, he wrote with

240. Cf. Stiegman, *Language of Asceticism*, pp. 104–107.
241. SC 64.1 (SBO 2:166,17).
242. Cf. SC 75.1 (SBO 2:247–248).
243. Sent 3.74 (SBO 6b:33,16–19).

a view, not to advancing theological speculation, but to ensuring that whatever promoted the expression of evangelical values in daily life was given due primacy. His work was, above all, orthopraxy.

On the practical level it is important, as Bernard knew, that individuals be helped to reconcile their own particular experiences and aspirations with commonly accepted theory. Too often persons assume too quickly that they are 'beyond the pale' and as a result either immure themselves in highly subjective assessments of what is involved in christian life or, alternatively, allow themselves to become depressed at their chronic irregularity. People operate best when they have a framework of meaning which relates closely to their experiences and which gives both clarity and force to their unformulated aspirations.

In this chapter we have been seeing how Bernard's view of desire for God not only embraces the more theoretical areas of anthropology and eschatology, but has much to say about the way such a reality is embodied in everyday life. The theme of alternation is particularly important in this respect, since it is often the variability of the spiritual process which defeats persons of good will who do not have the benefit of sound, practical instruction.

It is because desire for God is larger than the conscious processes of the human being that there is an element of unpredictability about it. It is dependent on being rather than on awareness, and so it often fails to conform to our personal ideals and expectations. It is shaped by what we are.

Desire for God is not controllable. It tends to have the most impact when there is considerable divergence between being and awareness. One who discovers within him a force of attraction to God which is not deducible from ordinary daily experience, is surprised and, perhaps, shaken. Thus desire is most obvious when it is weakest, because it constrasts with the prevailing apathy to spiritual realities. As this desire for God grows, however, and the person accepts it in consciousness and allows it to be somewhat incorporated into his pattern of existence, desire tends to become less noticeable, since being and consciousness are now (loosely) linked together. The stark constrast with the background has gone.

At this point something strange happens. Just when religion seems to have taken root, and especially when the *external* pattern of religious observance seems to have come together, the human being discovers that the progress made up to this point is not as final as it first appeared. Within himself, he discovers unconquered forces of ungodliness which threaten to drag him down to a level far lower than what obtained before his initial conversion. There is the humiliating experience of failure and the sense of having lost all the lightness and joy which previously characterised spiritual experience. As a result there is anxiety, a distrust of non-empirical realities, and a growing tendency to become absorbed in any alternative that offers itself.

This is a phase, sometimes lasting years, through which desire for God necessarily passes as it develops. Each individual has to struggle with the particular components of his crisis until he reaches a point at which some decision becomes feasible. The confusion and division tend to dissipate after the will has, contrary to its own comfort and in a sense of solidarity with the crucified Lord, decided to attach itself to the unseen power of divine love at the expense of more tangible gratifications. Unless one realises that divine life is always a collision of opposing forces, a *coincidentia oppositorum,* and thus rises to a knowedge of oneself as a sinner, yet saved, *simul peccator et iustus,* the attempt will be made to repress or rationalise one or other factor of experience. But development will cease until such time as

one learns to accept that there is duality in the experience
of christian discipleship.

It is in the acceptance of this paradox that the
human being permits to be formed in him a capability
for endurance which leaves him flexible under God's action. For Bernard, such an ability to withstand the
rigours of alternation was highly significant. It seemed to
him as the ultimate selflessness. It is true that divine life
and the heavenly reality are, under grace, daily growing
strong within us. But it is also true that we remain constantly the victims of our own malice, blindness, and
weakness. Our life is given its character by the manner in
which these opposing forces interact. Spiritual growth is
a matter of progressively being able to accept the *reality*
or life, irrespective of what *appearances* it has at any particular time. *Iudicium fidei sequere et non experimentum tuum.*

CONCLUSION

THIS STUDY of the thought of Bernard of Clairvaux on the subject of human desire for God is now complete. By its inner logic it has led us to most of the eighty-six *Sermons on the Song of Songs* and to a representative sampling of his other writings. It has introduced us to his major sources. It has touched upon most of the significant areas of his theological and pastoral concern. It offers us also some valuable insights into Bernard's own experience and into his personal priorites. It seems arguable, therefore, that the broad theme of desire for God, which is so well-entrenched at every phase of Bernard's work, is one of the cardinal points of his thought, and an appropriate channel of access in the task of understanding his theological and spiritual viewpoint.

Bernard's *Sermons on the Song of Songs* are a key to grasping the meaning of his life, spanning as they do the eighteen years of his most extensive activity and reflecting, in some way, the development of his thought during this turbulent period. Supported and completed by his other literary productions, this series of sermons has provided the main focus for our work.

What we have tried to do, in the first place, was to establish the organic connection between Bernard's teaching on desire for God and other features of his personal synthesis. This was done by drawing up the main components of the linguistic field surrounding this theme, the chains of expressions and images used by Bernard relative to desire for God. This provided sufficient evidence to demonstrate that, in Bernard's view, desire was operative in love for God, in seeking him, in spiritual growth and experience, and that, for the most part, a single series of images, phrases and word-sets prevailed throughout.

A review of Bernard's vocabulary of desire indicated something of the breadth of his concept. A first fact which emerged was the possibility of being able to state with certainty that desire for God could not be reduced to affective experience. As far as Bernard was concerned, there was more to it than a yearning for God in the context of his absence. On the contrary, Bernard understood that desire for God is a state of being, it operates primarily at a level more fundamental and more universal than that of experience.

Bernard's theological anthropology is a key to understanding how he could adopt such a position. He steadfastly taught that the human person is created with a capacity for union with God and with a tendency toward such union. This movement of the soul pre-exists experience. It is not the effect of conscious self-programming and personal choice. It is a consequence of being, as God has created it.

Bernard drew the inspiration and support for this position from the patristic doctrine of human creation to the image of God. Although there was some fluctuation of opinion about the details of the interpretation of Gen 1:26, by the twelfth century it had generally been agreed that the creation of the human being to God's image denoted a fundamental spiritaul capacity which raised humankind above the level of the brutes. This natural affinity with God remains intact throughout historical existence, even though it is tarnished by selfishness and sin. Christ's grace draws from this underlying capacity a burgeoning likeness to God which is expressed in the human person's gradual re-insertion into the *ordo* established by God in creation.

The *experience* of desire is, thus, a conscious reflection of this basic state of being. Movement toward God becomes a factor in conscious life to the extent that the human being is in contact with the truth of his own existence, and is reponsive to the concrete exigencies which confront him. For Bernard, finding oneself coincides with the desire for God: to discover one's identity is to affirm one's irreducible spirituality and to perceive oneself to be in motion beyond the known.

The movement, thus affirmed to be characteristic of human being, is impelled by both nature and grace and has as its object union with God. The soul thirsts to be united with God in his Word at the level of the Spirit. This union, which is at once so intimate and so complete, was described by Bernard in terms of the traditional image of spiritual marriage. Supporting this basic line of thought is his teaching on heaven, on the total, face-to-face encounter with God in the resurrection of the body.

Bernard's particular lesson about desire for God is not, however, to be reduced to an analysis of the ground of his movement and its goal. There are other questions to be asked. How does the human being recognise this desire when it is active in his life? How does it impinge on experience? How does it become a force in daily living, ordering responses and behaviour in fundamental harmony with itself? These are the points about which Bernard particularly sought information and guidance from the inspired text of the Song of Songs.

Desire for God, he concluded, follows the fundamental dialectic characteristic of all spiritual growth. It is subject to internal variation, being fuelled alternately by positive and negative elements. Thus, experience of desire is subject to change; movement toward God incarnates itself in the variety of components which each day provides. The same, fundamental, Godward tendency realistically exploits the situation as it is. Thus the experience of desire varies according to a range of factors. There is no single experience which can be isolated and guaranteed as a normative expression of authentic desire for God. In consequence, the response of the human being to desire is also characterised by flexibility. We noted that Bernard is one of the early proponents of a formal morality, with great emphasis on the role of conscience and on the need for purity of intention.

It follows that genuine spiritual experience is a healthy interplay between feelings of weakness and of strength. At some times it will seem as though the ultimate goal of human life is very close and is exerting a strong gravitational attraction. At other times, one will be more aware of being rooted in the earth, riddled with weakness and subject to sin. Both perceptions are, in Bernard's book, absolutely accurate. Since human response needs to build upon a flexible adaptability to perceived truth, there is an alternation in both experience and response according to what aspect of the truth is perceived as paramount at one particular moment. One who eschews rigidity thus leaves himself open to be moved, open to be changed thus liberated from the potential tyranny of habit, convention, and ideology, both within himself and in the social setting of which he forms a part.

Most of the elements of Bernard's teaching on desire for God were already in christian tradition, especially that of the monastic West. His synthesis of them and the brilliant verve with which he presented them to his own contemporaries are both characteristically Bernard's own. But it is worth noting that there are three points, especially, which were important to him which should be of interest to the seeker after truth in the last part of the twentieth century; for they are points which are little enough emphasised.

1. Reality and consciousness are not co-extensive, despite the conviction which has prevailed since the sixteenth century. There is more to human being than the contents of human consciousness—past and present. There is a zone of being which is beyond consciousness, which is pre-conscious. In spiritual growth what matters most comes from un-conscious sectors of human being, not what hap-pens at the level of awareness. When the human be-ing is sensitive to the movements of his being, he is open to a transformation of consciousness from within himself. If God dwells in and acts upon the human heart, then it is at this primary level that he is to be sought and, by his grace, found.

2. Spiritual experience does not cease to conduct the human being to his goal when it ceases to be pleasurable. The existence of evil in human life, due to the incompleteness of development and to the effects of sin, means that experience will not mirror reality if it is always positive. Apperception of the consequences of life without God is some-times a more powerful incentive toward growth than

more positive and pleasurable inducements.
Negative experience does not signify that spiritaul
progress has stopped. It is, rather, a renewed
challenge to greater detachment from immediate
satisfaction and to greater fervour in hoping for
what is unseen.

3. The goal of all spiritual endeavour is beyond human
calculation. It is important that one who is
dedicated to spiritual life grow in his acceptance of
the transcendence of God and the mystery of his
ways. Acceptance of union with One so above
human knowing is already a willingness to walk the
ways of unknowing, to live in the shadow of faith. It
involves a certain scoffing at the vanity of human expectation and a preparedness to accept, as from the
hand of God, whatever life sends.

It seems that these three elements of Bernard's
spiritual synthesis are those which most effectively complement contemporary insights and are worthy points of
dialogue. But Bernard has more to offer. Beyond the
content of his teaching, it seems that something can be
gleaned also from Bernard's manner of approaching his
subject, from his style of theologising.

1. The possibility of exploiting the tradition of the
Church in pursuance of answers to contemporary
questions is demonstrated by Bernard. He had a
confidence in 'theology' as a source of guidance to
people in concrete situations. The Word of God was
accepted as a practicable norm for human
behaviour, without there being any loss to common
sense or integrity.

2. On the other hand, the approach to the Scriptures
which we find in Bernard was habitually ordered to
practice. The same is true of his quarrying in tradition. He was not afraid to unite scriptural and profane language and imagery creatively. When he

spoke, he did not limit himself to the text, but drew from his own experience and, as it were, from the hearts of those whom he was addressing. His basic concern was not scientific, but the practical up-building of the lives of all.

3. Bernard did not hesitate to employ art in his pro-clamation of the Word. He used his talent to write lyric prose which, whilst charming the sensibilities, is able to instruct and give direction to life. His works breathe an air of beauty, order, and tranquili-ty, which are flattering to his message.

4. Bernard's writing bears the imprint of his personality and communicates something of the holiness and wholeness which were his. He was not perfect—many pages of his works reveal the scars of sin. He was, however, a good man who had the talent to place whatever gifts of grace he had received at the diposal of others. He always wrote what he was and, increasingly, as his life reached its climax, he was what grace had made him.

This essay in monastic theology is intended as a beginning rather than as an end, as a sort of thematic in-troduction to the *Sermons on the Song of Songs*. No doubt, as bernardine scholarship proceeds, many of its conclusions will seem rudimentary. Even its limited survey of the theme of desire for God must, however, lead to the conviction that in Bernard's teaching on this subject we have a coherent theological whole which is not without utility some eight centuries later.

Adimplevit laetitia;
sed desiderii non erit finis;
ac per hoc nec quaerendi.

1. ABBREVIATIONS OF THE WORKS OF ST BERNARD AND OTHER CISTERCIAN AUTHORS CITED

The Works of Bernard of Clairvaux

Adv	Sermo in adventu Domini
And	Sermo in natali sancti Andreae
Apo	Apologia ad Guillelmum abbatem
Asc	Sermo in ascensione Domini
Asspt	Sermo in assumptione B. V. M.
Csi	De consideratione livri v
Ded	Sermo in dedicatione ecclesiae
Dil	Liber de diligendo Deo
Div	Sermones de diversis
Gra	Liber de gratia et libero arbitrio
IV HM	Sermo in feria iv hebdomadae sanctae
V HM	Sermo in cena Domini
Hum	Liber de gradibus humilitatis et superbiae
Humb	Sermo in obitu Domni Humberti
In cel adv	In celebratione adventus (= De triplici inferno)
Mart	Sermo in festivitate sancti Martini episcopi
Nat	Sermo in nativitate Domini
Nat BVM	Sermo in nativitate B. V. M.
I Nov	Sermo in dominica I novembris
O Pasc	Sermo in octava Paschae
OS	Sermo in festivitate Omnium Sanctorum
Palm	Sermo in ramis palmarum
Par	Parabolae
Pasc	Sermo in die Paschae
p Epi	Sermo in dominica I post octavam Epiphaniae
Pent	Sermo in die sancto pentecostes
Pre	Liber de praecepto et dispensatione
PP	Sermo in festo SS. apostolorum Petri et Pauli

QH	Sermo super psalum Qui habitat
Quad	Sermo in quadragesima
SC	Sermo super cantica canticorum
Sent	Sententiae
Sept	Sermo in septuagesima
Tpl	Liber ad milites templi (+ De laude novae militiae)
Vict	Sermo in natali sancti Victoris
V Nat	Sermo in vigilia nativitatis domini

The Works of Aelred of Rievaulx

Inst incl	De institutione inclusarum
Orat past	Oratio pastoralis
Spec car	Speculum charitatis

2. PRIMARY SOURCES

For all bernardine texts I have used the critical edition in nine tomes, edited by Jean Leclercq, Henri Rochais and C. H. Talbot, under the title *Sancti Bernardi Opera*. This has been published by Editiones Cistercienses, Rome between 1957–1977. I have abbreviated this SBO. The abbreviations of individual works is that which has become standard in the last twenty years. Each reference gives the work, followed by the citation of section and sub-section; then the reference to the volume, page and line(s) of SBO is given.

For Pseudo-Bernardine texts and for the *Vita Prima* and the other lives, I have used the edition of Jean Mabillon, *Sancti Bernardi abbatis Clarae-Vallensis Opera Omnia*, Paris: Gaume, 1839. (Abbreviation: *Opera Omnia.*)

For patristic texts I have used Migne (Abbreviation: PG, PL), or, where available, a critical edition from

Sources Chrétiennes (Abbreviation: SChr) or Corpus Christianorum (Abbreviation: CChr). In each case I have given the work and sectional reference, followed by the series, volume and page or column reference. Other critical texts are cited in full. With two exceptions all texts have been translated afresh. I have consulted available translations and have profited from them, but in order to facilitate harmonious cross-reference I have re-translated everything.

3. BIBLIOGRAPHIES

At present there are three complementary bibliographies, supplemented by listings in monastic periodicals and by the *Bulletin of Monastic Spirituality* published in *Cistercian Studies* and in *Collectanea Cisterciersia*.

Bouton, Jean de la Croix, *Bibliographie Bernardine: 1891–1957*. Paris: Lethielleux, 1958.

Janauschek, L., *Bibliographia Bernardina*, Vienna: A. Hoelder, 1891.

Manning, Eugène, *Bibliographie Bernardine: 1957–1970*, Documentation Cistercienne. Rochefort, 1972.

4. MONASTIC-PATRISTIC SERIALS

Following is a list of the serials most often quoted in these pages, together with the abbreviation used.

ABR   *American Benedictine Review*
ASOC   *Analecta Sacri Ordinis Cisterciensis* subsequently, *Analecta Cisterciensia*

CF	Cistercian Fathers Series
CChr	Corpus Christianorum: Series Latina
Cist	*Cistercium*
CN	*Cîteaux in de Nederlanden* subsequently, *Cîteaux: Commentarii Cistercienses*
COCR	*Collectanea Ordinis Cisterciensium Reformatorum* subsequently, *Collectanea Cisterciensia*
CS	Cistercian Studies Series.
CSt	*Cistercian Studies*
DR	*Downside Review*
DSp	*Dictionnaire de spiritualité, ascétique et mystique, doctrine et histoire.*
GuL	*Geist und Leben*
MedSt	*Mediaeval Studies*
MonSt	*Monastic Studies*
PG	Migne: *Patrologia Graeca*
PL	Migne: *Patrologia Latina*
RAM	*Revue d'ascétique et de mystique* subsequently, *Revue d'histoire de spiritualité*
RBS	*Regulae Benedicti Studia: Annuarium Internationale*
RechSR	*Recherches de science religieuse*
RMAL	*Revue du moyen âge latin*
RSR	*Revue des sciences religieuses*
RTAM	*Recherches de théologie ancienne et mediévale*
SBO	Sancti Bernardi Opera
SChr	Sources Chrétiennes
StA	Studia Anselmiana
StMe	*Studi Medievali*
StMon	*Studia Monastica*
ThLL	*Thesaurus Linguae Latinae*
TJ	*Tjurunga: An Australasian Benedictine Revue*

5. COLLECTIVE WORKS

Comparatively few full-length books have been written about Bernard of Clairvaux; most of the material used in researching this present work has come from collections of papers read at various gatherings, mainly since 1953. Following is a list of those used, in the order of the abbreviations given them thoughout this work.

Analecta

Analecta Nos 1–7, Ed. J. Leclercq, (StA 20, 31, 37, 41, 43, 50, 53). Rome: Herder, 1948–1965.

Canonization Studies

Saint Bernard of Clairvaux: Studies Commemorating the Eighth Centenary of his Canonization (CS28), ed. M. Basil Pennington. Kalamazoo: Cistercian Publications, 1977.

Chimaera

The Chimaera of his Age: Studies on Bernard of Clairvaux (CS63), edd. E. Rozanne Elder and John R. Sommerfeldt. Kalamazoo: Cistercian Publications, 1980.

Commission d'histoire

Saint Bernard de Clairvaux, ed. Commission d'histoire de l'Ordre de Cîteaux. Paris: Alsatia, 1953.

Die Chimaere

Die Chimaere seines Jahrhunderts: Vier Vortraege ueber Bernhard von Clairvaux, ed. J. Spoerl. Würzburg: Werkbund-Verlag, 1953.

History 1

Studies in Medieval Cistercian History presented to Jeremiah F. O'Sullivan (CS 13). Spencer: Cistercian Publications, 1971.

History 2

Studies in Medieval Cistercian History II (CS 24), ed. John R. Sommerfeldt, Kalamazoo: Cistercian Publications, 1976.

Homme d'Église

Saint Bernard: Homme d'Église, (Cahiers de la Pierre-qui-Vire, 38–39). Paris: Desclée de Brouwer, 1953.

Ideals

Cistercian Ideals and Reality (CS 60), ed. John R. Sommerfeldt, Kalamazoo: Cistercian Publications, 1978.

Influence

The Influence of St Bernard: Anglican Essays, ed. Benedicta Ward. Oxford: SLG Press, 1976.

Leclercq Studies

Bernard of Clairvaux: Studies presented to Dom Jean Leclercq (CS 23), Washington: Cistercian Publications, 1973.

Mélanges

Mélanges Saint Bernard. Dijon: Association des amis de saint Bernard, 1954.

One Yet Two

One Yet Two: Monastic Tradition East and West (CS 29), ed. M. Basil Pennington, Kalamazoo: Cistercian Publications, 1976.

Sint Bernardus

Sint Bernardus van Clairvaux: Gedenkboek. Rotterdam: Uitgeverij de Forel, 1953.

Son Temps

Saint Bernard et son temps (2 vols). Dijon: Académie des sciences, arts et belles-lettres, 1928–1929.

Studi

Studi su San Bernardo di Chiaravalle nell'ottavo centenario della canonizzazione (Bibliotheca Cisterciensis 6). Rome: Editiones Cistercienses, 1975.

Théologien

Saint Bernard Théologien, (ASOC 9 [1953], fasc 3–4), ed. J. Leclercq. Rome: Editiones Cistercienses, 1953.

6. THE WORKS OF JEAN LECLERCQ

A selection from the writings of Jean Leclercq which has been found most useful in developing the present theme is given below in chronological order. Works often quoted and abbreviated in the body of the text are followed by the usual abbreviation in italics.

(With J.-P. Bonnes), *Un Maître de la vie spirituelle: Jean de Fécamp,* Paris: Vrin, 1946. (= Fécamp)
   'Le Commentaire de Gilbert de Stanford sur le Cantique des Cantiques, *Analecta 1:* pp. 205–230.
   'Origène au XIIe siècle', *Irénikon* 24 (1951) 425–439.
   'S. Bernard et la théologie monastique du XIIe siècle', *Théologien,* pp. 7–23.
   Études sur S. Bernard et le texte de ses écrits, ASOC 9 (1953) fasc 1–2. (= Études)
   Études sur le vocabulaire monasticque du moyen âge (StA 48). Rome: Herder, 1961. (= *Vocabulaire*)
   Recueil d'études sur saint Bernard et ses écrits I. Rome: Ed. di storia e letteratura, 1962. (= *Recueil 1*)

Aux sources de la spiritualité occidentale: Étapes et constants. Paris: Cerf, 1964. (= *Sources*)

Témoins de la spiritualité occidentale. Paris: Cerf, 1965. (= *Témoins*)

Chances de la spiritualité occidentale. Paris: Cerf, 1966. (= *Chances*)

Recueil d'études sur saint Bernard et ses écrits II. Rome: Ed. di storia e letteratura, 1966. (= *Recueil 2*)

Essais sur l'ésthetique de S. Bernard, *StMe* 9 (1968) 688-728.

Recueil d'études sur saint Bernard et ses écrits III. Rome: Ed. di storia e letteratura, 1969. (= *Recueil 3*)

'St Bernard and the Rule of Benedict,' in *Rule and Life: An Interdisciplinary Symposium* (CS 12), ed. M. Basil Pennington. Spencer: Cistercian Publications, 1971, pp. 151-167.

'Were the Sermons on the Song of Songs Delivered in Chapter?', Introduction to CF 7, *Bernard of Clairvaux On The Song of Songs,* vol 2. Kalamazoo: Cistercian Publications, 1976.

Nouveau visage de Bernard de Clairvaux: Approaches psychohistoriques. Paris: Cerf, 1976. (= *Nouveau visage*)

The Love of Learning and the Desire for God: A Study of Monastic Culture. London: SPCK, 2nd edn 1978. (= *Love of Learning*)

Aspects of Monasticism (CS 7). Kalamazoo: Cistercian Publications, 1978. (= *Aspects*)

Contemplative Life (CS 19). Kalamazoo: Cistercian Publications, 1978. (= *Contemplative*)

Monks and Love in Twelfth Century France: Psycho-Historical Essays. Oxford: University Press, 1979. (= *Monks and Love*)

7. GENERAL INDICATIONS

Following is a small number of articles and books dealing with the theme. Only those items which have been of particular help have been included.

Altermatt, Alberich, 'Christus pro nobis: Die Christologie Bernhards von Clairvaux in den "Sermones per annum"', ASOC 33 (1977) 3–176.

Ballano, Agustín, 'La peregrinación en San Bernardo', Cist 22 (1970) 101–116, 196–205.

Blanpain, Jacques, 'Langage mystique, expression du désir dans les Sermons sur le Cantique des Cantiques de Bernard de Clairvaux', COCR 36 (1974) 45–68, 225–247; 37 (1975) 145–166.

Bodard, Claude, 'Christus-Spiritus: incarnation et résurrection dans la théologie de saint Bernard', Sint Bernardus, pp. 89–104. 'La Bible, expression d'une expérience religieuse chez S. Bernard', Théologien, pp. 24–45.

Bredero, Adriaan H., 'Études sur la "Vita Prima" de S. Bernard', ASOC 17 (1961) 3–72, 215–260; 18 (1962) 3–59.

Brown, Peter, Augustine of Hippo: A Biography. London: Faber and Faber, 1967.

Casey, Michael, The Advent Sermons of Bernard of Clairvaux, Australian Benedictine Studies Series. Belgrave, 1979.

—, 'Benedict the Observer' in Goad and Nail, Studies in Medieval Cistercian History, 10. Kalamazoo: 1985, pp. 1–20.

—, 'Intentio Cordis (RB 52.4)', RBS 6/7 (1980), pp. 105–120.

—, 'In Pursuit of Ecstasy: Reflections on Bernard of

Clairvaux's De Diligendo Deo', *Monastic Studies* 16 (1985, pp. 139–156.

—, 'Saint Benedict's Approach to Prayer', CSt 15 (1980) 327–343.

—, 'Spiritual Desire in the Gospel Homilies of Saint Gregory the Great', CSt 16 (1981), 297–314.

—, 'Mindfulness of God in the Monastic Tradition', CSt (1982) 111–126.

—, 'Nature and Grace in St Bernard of Clairvaux', *Tjurunga* 23 (1982) 39–49.

—, 'The Benedictine Promises', Tjurunga 24 (1983) 17–34.

—, 'The Prayer of Psalmody', CSt 18 (1983) 106–120.

Constable, Giles, *Religious Life and Thought (11th–12th centuries)*. London: Variorum Reprints, 1979.

Delfgaauw, Pacificus, 'La nature et les degrés de l'amour chez saint Bernard', *Théologien*, pp. 234–252.

Dimier, Anselme, 'Les amusements póetiques de S. Bernard', COCR (1950) 52–55.

—, *Saint Bernard: Pêcheur de Dieu*. Paris: Letouzey & Ané, 1953.

—, 'Sur le pas de S. Bernard', CN 25 (1974) 223–248.

Farkasfalvy, Denis, 'The Role of the Bible in St. Bernard's Spirituality', ASOC 25 (1969) 3–13.

—, 'St. Bernard's Spirituality and the Benedictine Rule in the *Steps of Humility*', ASOC 36 (1980) 248–262

Gilson, Étienne, *The Mystical Theology of Saint Bernard* (trans A. H. C. Downes). London: Sheed and Ward, 1940.

—, ' "Regio Dissimilitudinis" de Platon à S. Bernard de Clairvaux', MedSt 9 (1947) 108–130.

Hiss, Wilhelm, *Die Anthropologie Bernhards von Clairvauxe*. Berlin: Walter de Gruyter, 1964.

Javelet, Robert, 'Psychologie des auteurs spirituels du

XIIe siècle', Rech SR 33 (1959) 18–64, 97–164, 209–268.

—, 'Intelligence et amour chez les auteurs spirituels du XIIe siécle', RAM 37 (1961) 271–290, 429–450.

—, *Image et ressemblance au douzieme siécle: de S. Anselme à Alain de Lille* (2 vols). Paris: Letouzey & Ané, 1967.

Mikkers, Edmundus, 'De kerk als bruid in de hoogliedcommetaar van Sint Bernardus', *Sint Bernardus,* pp. 195–214.

McGinn, Bernard, 'St Bernard and Eschatology', *Leclercq Studies,* pp. 161–186.

—, 'Resurrection and Ascension in the Christology of the Early Cistercians', CN 30 (1979) 5–22.

Ohly, Friedrich, *Hohelied-Studien: Grundzüge einer Geschichte der Hoheliedsauslegung des Abendlandes bis um 1200.* Wiesbaden: Franz Steiner Verlag, 1958.

Olivera, Bernardo, 'Bases de la teologia mistica de san Bernardo', Cist 23 (1971) 187–210.

Pascoe, Louis B., *Saint Bernard of Clairvaux: The Doctrine of the* Imago *and its relationship to Cistercian Monasticism,* Unpublished M.A. thesis, Fordham University, New York, 1960.

Piault, Bernard, 'Le désir de la sagesse: Itinéraire de l'âme à Dieu chez S. Bernard dans le sermon LXXXV sur le Cantique des Cantiques', COCR 36 (1974) 24–44.

Standaert, Maur, 'Le principe de l'ordination dans la théologie spirituelle de S. Bernard', COCR 8 (1946) 176–216.

—, 'La doctrine de l'image chez S. Bernard', ETL 23 (1947) 70–129.

Stiegman, Emero J. Jr., *The Language of Asceticism in St Bernard of Clairvaux's 'Sermons super Cantica Canticorum',* unpublished Ph. D. thesis, Fordham University, 1973.

—, 'The Literary Genre of Bernard of Clairvaux's *Sermones Super Cantica canticorum*', *Simplicity and Ordinariness: Studies in Medieval Cistercian History IV* (CS 61), ed. J. Sommerfeldt, Kalamazoo: Cistercian Publications, 1980, pp. 68–93.

Thomas, Robert, *Fichier S. Bernard* (2 vols). Chambarand: privately circulated, 1958.

Vernet, André, *La Bibliothèque de l'abbaye de Clairvaux du XIIe au XVIIIe siècle*. Paris: Editions du C.N.R.S., 1979.

Scriptural citations have been made according to the Vulgate enumeration.

SCRIPTURAL INDEX

BERNARDINE INDEX

Pasc	4.2	203n		Quad	5.5	300n
Pent	1.6	101n		Quad	6.1	73n
Pent	3.3	206n		Quad	6.1	229n
PP	1.3	36n		Quad	9.2	113n
PP	1.3	53n		SC	1.1–2	254n
PP	2.6	72n		SC	1.2	45n
Pre	49	286n		SC	1.8	68n
Pre	54	288n		SC	1.9	174n
Pre	59	212n		SC	1.11	73n
Pre	59	214n		SC	1.11	76n
Pre	60	214n		SC	2	55
QH	1.1	227n		SC	2.1	76n
QH	2.1	224n		SC	3	56
QH	2.3	116n		SC	3	254
QH	3.3	225n		SC	3.1	228n
QH	3.4	227n		SC	3.4	255n
QH	4.1	226n		SC	3.5	93n
QH	6.2	229n		SC	3.5	206n
QH	6.2	310n		SC	3.5	249n
QH	7.1	229n		SC	3.5	255n
QH	7.2	218n		SC	4	56
QH	8.2	235n		SC	4.1	255n
QH	8.3	72n		SC	5	56
		218n		SC	5	138f
QH	8.6	235n		SC	5	139n
QH	8.11	201n		SC	5	255
QH	9.2	118n		SC	5.4	255n
QH	9.9	80n		SC	5.5	255n
QH	10.1	224n		SC	5.5	289n
QH	10.3	235n		SC	5.7	32
QH	10.5	237n		SC	6	55
QH	11.9	300n		SC	5	56
Quad	1.4	113n		SC	6	57
Quad	2.3	103n		SC	6	255
Quad	3.1f	113n		SC	6.6	256n

Sept	1.3	220n	V Nat	2.3	86n
Sept	1.3	221n	V Nat	2.3	179n
Sept	1.3	226n	V Nat	2.3	179n
Sept	2.3	218n	V Nat	2.3	240n
Tpl	3	286n	V Nat	3.6	118n
Tpl	12	204n	V Nat	4.8	224n
V HM	4	104n	V Nat	5.7	66n
V Nat	2.1	231n	Vict	1.5	125n
V Nat	2.3	66n			

INDEX OF PERSONS

355

TOPICAL INDEX

CISTERCIAN PUBLICATIONS INC.

Kalamazoo, Michigan

TITLES LISTING

THE CISTERCIAN FATHERS SERIES

Texts and Studies
in the
Monastic Tradition

* Temporarily out of print   † *Forthcoming*

THE CISTERCIAN STUDIES SERIES

MONASTIC TEXTS

CHRISTIAN SPIRITUALITY

MONASTIC STUDIES

CISTERCIAN STUDIES

* Temporarily out of print   † *Forthcoming*

* Temporarily out of print   *† Forthcoming*

Eight Chapters on Perfection and Angel's Song
(Walter Hilton)

Creative Suffering (Iulia de Beausobre)

Bringing Forth Christ. Five Feasts of the Child
Jesus (St Bonaventure)

Gentleness in St John of the Cross

Distributed in North America only for Fairacres Press.

DISTRIBUTED BOOKS

St Benedict: Man with An Idea (Melbourne Studies)

The Spirit of Simplicity

Benedict's Disciples (David Hugh Farmer)

The Emperor's Monk: A Contemporary Life of
Benedict of Aniane

A Guide to Cistercian Scholarship (2nd ed.)

*North American customers may order
through booksellers or directly
from the publisher:*

Cistercian Publications
WMU Station
Kalamazoo, Michigan 49008
(616) 383-4985

*Cistercian Publications are available in
Britain, Europe and the Common-
wealth through A. R. Mowbray &
Co Ltd   St Thomas House   Oxford
OX1 1SJ.
For a sterling price list, please consult
Mowbray's General Catalogue.*

*Cistercian monks and nuns have been
living lives of prayer & praise, meditation &
manual labor since the twelfth century.
They are part of an unbroken tradition
which extends back to the fourth century
and which continues today in the Catholic
church, the Orthodox churches, the
Anglican communion, and, most recently,
in the Protestant churches.*

*Share their way of life and their search for
God by reading Cistercian Publications.*

*A complete catalogue of texts-in-
translation and studies on early,
medieval, and modern Christian
monasticism is available at no cost
from Cistercian Publications.*